Cambridge Essentials

Mathematics

Julie Bolter
Simon Bullock
Susan Timperley

Series editors: Graham Newman
Peter Sherran

Extension 9

CAMBRIDGE
UNIVERSITY PRESS

CAMBRIDGE UNIVERSITY PRESS
Cambridge, New York, Melbourne, Madrid, Cape Town, Singapore,
São Paulo, Delhi, Dubai, Tokyo

Cambridge University Press
The Edinburgh Building, Cambridge CB2 8RU, UK

www.cambridge.org
Information on this title: www.cambridge.org/9780521723848

© Cambridge University Press 2010

First published 2010

Book printed in the United Kingdom at the University Press, Cambridge

A catalogue record for this publication is available from the British Library

ISBN 978-0-521-72384-8 Paperback with CD-ROM for Windows and Mac

Contents

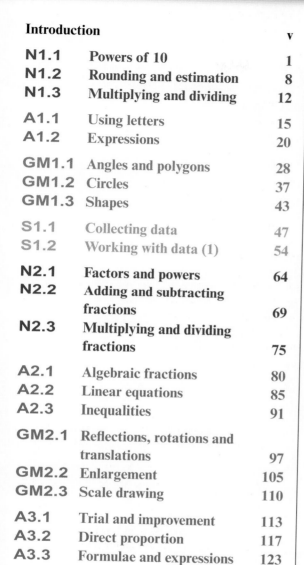

Introduction

Take advantage of the pupil CD

Cambridge Essentials Mathematics comes with a pupil CD in the back. This contains the entire book as an interactive PDF file, which you can read on your computer using free Adobe Reader software from Adobe (www.adobe.com/products/acrobat/readstep2.html). As well as the material you can see in the book, the PDF file gives you extras when you click on the buttons you will see on most pages; see the inside front cover for a brief explanation of these.

To use the CD, simply insert it into the CD or DVD drive of your computer. You will be prompted to install the contents of the CD to your hard drive. Installing will make it easier to use the PDF file, because the installer creates an icon on your desktop that launches the PDF directly. However, it will run just as well straight from the CD.

If you want to install the contents of the disc onto your hard disc yourself, this is easily done. Just open the disc contents in your file manager (for Apple Macs, double click on the CD icon on your desktop; for Windows, open My Computer and double click on your CD drive icon), select all the files and folders and copy them wherever you want.

Take advantage of the teacher CD

The *Teacher Material* CD-ROM for *Cambridge Essentials Mathematics* contains enhanced interactive PDFs. As well as all the features of the pupil PDF, teachers also have access to e-learning materials and links to the *Essentials Mathematics* Planner – a new website with a full lesson planning tool, including worksheets, homeworks, assessment materials and guidance. The e-learning materials are also fully integrated into the Planner, letting you see the animations in context and alongside all the other materials.

Powers of 10

- Working with positive and negative powers of 10
- Multiplying and dividing by powers of 10
- Writing numbers in standard form

Keywords

You should know

explanation 1a   explanation 1b

1 Find the value of each of these numbers.

   a 10^3 **b** 10^6 **c** 10^0 **d** 10^8

   e 10^{10} **f** 10^{-1} **g** 10^{-2} **h** 10^{-4}

2 Write these numbers as powers of 10.

   a one thousand   **b** 10 000   **c** one million   **d** 100 000

   e 1   **f** one tenth   **g** 0.001   **h** one millionth

3 Write these quantities using powers of 10.

   a The length of the Earth's orbit around the Sun is about 1 000 000 000 km.

   b The distance between two nearby stars is about 10 000 000 000 000 km.

   c In a hydrogen bomb explosion about 0.001 kg of mass converts into energy.

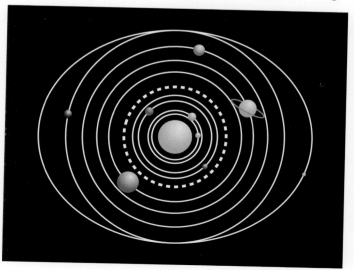

4 Write each number as a multiple of a power of 10.

> One billion = one thousand million

   a 800   **b** five hundred thousand

   c 90 000 000   **d** 6 billion   **e** 0.4

   f 0.0005   **g** 0.000 000 03

5 Write each expression as a number.

   a 5×10^3 **b** 4.2×10^4 **c** 1.7×10^1

   d 0.9×10^4 **e** 6×10^0 **f** 5×10^{-2}

   g 41×10^{-3} **h** 0.31×10^{-1}

6 These prefixes are associated with given powers of 10.

Power	Prefix	Power	Prefix
10^9	giga	10^{-2}	centi
10^6	mega	10^{-6}	micro
10^3	kilo	10^{-9}	nano

> 1 megabyte = 1×10^6 bytes
> = $1 \times 1 000 000$ bytes

   a Write 2 megabytes in bytes.   **b** Write 8 kilowatts in watts.

   c Write 6 nanoseconds in seconds.   **d** Write 4 micrometres in metres.

   e Write 12 centilitres in litres.   **f** Write 0.3 gigahertz in hertz.

> explanation 2a   explanation 2b   explanation 2c

7 Work these out without using a calculator.

   a 29×1000 **b** $215 \times 10 000$ **c** 23.6×1000

   d $0.894 \times 100 000$ **e** 2.8×0.1 **f** 15.706×0.01

   g 450.8×0.001 **h** 0.64×0.0001 **i** $0.98 \times 0.000 01$

8 Work these out without using a calculator.

   a $68 \div 1000$ **b** $5.2 \div 100$ **c** $78.8 \div 10 000$

   d $0.432 \div 1000$ **e** $4.6 \div 0.01$ **f** $26.3 \div 0.001$

   g $12.5 \div 0.0001$ **h** $0.37 \div 0.01$ **i** $0.024 \div 0.0001$

9 Find the value of the missing number that would make each statement true.

a $6.3 \times \square = 630$

b $\square \times 1000 = 440$

c $0.081 \times \square = 810$

d $\square \times 0.1 = 120$

e $730 \div \square = 7300$

f $\square \div 0.01 = 0.45$

g $0.6 \div \square = 0.006$

h $\square \div 1000 = 0.14$

i $4.76 \times \square = 4760$

j $\square \div 0.001 = 5600$

k $\square \times 0.1 = 0.0701$

l $11.7 \div \square = 1170$

10 a Cartons of maths textbooks weigh 17.15 kg each.

Each carton contains 10 books.
What is the weight of each book?

b A container holds 100 000 cartons.
What is the total weight of these cartons?

11 For commercial use, metered water is priced at 0.01 pence per litre.

Four shops receive these bills for the water they used.

How many litres of water has each used?

a   £39.50   b   £62.15   c   £152.33   d   £201.03

12 a David used this method to work out 0.3×10^2 and $45 \div 10^{-2}$.

$$0.3 \times 10^2 = 0.3 \times 100 = \square \qquad 45 \div 10^{-2} = 45 \div \frac{1}{100} = 45 \times 100 = \square$$

Copy and complete David's working.

b Use David's method to find answers to these.

i 0.5×10^2 ii 0.36×10^3 iii $34 \div 10^2$ iv $218.4 \div 10^3$

v 61×10^{-1} vi 302×10^{-3} vii $73 \div 10^{-2}$ viii $12.71 \div 10^{-3}$

explanation 3a   explanation 3b

13 Work these out without using a calculator.

a 500×0.3

b $80\,000 \times 0.4$

c $0.09 \times 50\,000$

d 0.3×0.07

e 0.0008^2

f 0.6×0.000045

g 0.0023×0.07

h $0.000\,11 \times 0.0012$

i $0.006 \times 0.003 \times 0.2$

14 Work these out without using a calculator.

a $400 \div 0.8$

b $540 \div 0.9$

c $720 \div 0.08$

d $3600 \div 0.06$

e $4.2 \div 0.7$

f $0.64 \div 0.8$

g $0.0063 \div 0.003$

h $0.049 \div 0.0007$

i $12.1 \div 0.011$

j $0.0125 \div 0.0025$

k $0.00096 \div 0.0012$

l $0.0072 \div 0.03 \div 0.4$

15 Find the missing number in each calculation.

a $400 \times \square = 40$

b $700 \times \square = 0.7$

c $4.5 \div \square = 450$

d $\square \div 0.001 = 360$

e $800 \times \square = 400$

f $48 \times \square = 2.4$

g $2.6 \div \square = 130$

h $\square \div 0.02 = 32$

16 These tables give the approximate numbers of kilojoules (kJ) in some raw fruits.

	kJ per gram
Apples	1.9
Bananas	3.6

	kJ per 100 g
Pears	280
Oranges	180

Find the number of kilojoules in these.

a   600 g of apples

b   900 g of bananas

c   70 g of pears

d   60 g of oranges

For parts **c** and **d** find the mass as a decimal fraction of 100 g.

17 Write two possible questions using multiplication or division by decimals (as in questions **7** to **16**) which would give you each answer.

a   280

b   6.3

c   0.22

d   7500

e   0.0081

explanation 4a   explanation 4b   explanation 4c

18 Which of these are written in standard form?

a 7.3×10^4

b 63.8×10^2

c 0.76×10^3

d 6.01×10^{-3}

e 7.6^{-3}

f 7.4×10^1

g 45.8×10^{-4}

h 1.067×10^{-23}

19 Find the missing index number for these conversions from ordinary numbers to standard form. The first one has been done for you.

    a $45.6 = 4.56 \times 10^1$

    b $654.2 = 6.542 \times 10^{\square}$ **c** $65 = 6.5 \times 10^{\square}$

    d $4362 = 4.362 \times 10^{\square}$ **e** $34.6 = 3.46 \times 10^{\square}$

    f $116.7 = 1.167 \times 10^{\square}$ **g** $6092 = 6.092 \times 10^{\square}$

    h $760\,203 = 7.602\,03 \times 10^{\square}$ **i** $44.81 = 4.481 \times 10^{\square}$

20 Write these numbers in standard form.

a 72	**b** 623	**c** 6382	**d** 5460	**e** 45.3
f 2000	**g** 70.3	**h** 602	**i** 430	**j** 620.5
k 30.67	**l** 45.65	**m** 412.3	**n** 273.62	**o** 1976.3

21 Write each expression as a number.

    a 3.4×10^2 **b** 8.2×10^4 **c** 7.92×10^3 **d** 2.91×10^5

    e 9.47×10^1 **f** 3.2×10^9 **g** 3.6×10^0 **h** 8.05×10^2

    i 2.84×10^3 **j** 9.006×10^2 **k** 1.212×10^6 **l** 1.009×10^4

    m 6.98×10^5 **n** 3.06×10^3 **o** 9.99×10^4

22 a Copy and complete this table converting ordinary numbers to standard form.

Ordinary number	Standard form
5600	5.6×10^3
560	
56	
5.6	5.6×10^0
0.56	
0.056	5.6×10^{-2}
0.0056	

  b What do you notice about the powers of 10 in the standard form, as the ordinary numbers get smaller?

  c Copy and complete this statement: *When converting ordinary numbers less than 1 into standard form, the index number is always a _____ number.*

23 Match the ordinary numbers in Box A with their equivalent standard form in box B.

Box A

0.51	0.0004
0.705	
0.093	0.0093
0.051	
0.007 05	0.000 093
0.004	

Box B

5.1×10^{-2}	7.05×10^{-1}
	4.0×10^{-3}
9.3×10^{-2}	7.05×10^{-3}
	9.3×10^{-3}
5.1×10^{-1}	4.0×10^{-4}
	9.3×10^{-5}

24 Write these numbers in standard form.

a   0.56   b   0.832   c   0.0072   d   0.043   e   0.6205

f   0.0006   g   0.0026   h   0.004 55   i   0.0632   j   0.467

k   0.000 87   l   0.004 28   m   0.009   n   0.0205   o   0.0051

25 Write each expression as a number.

a 7.04×10^{-3} b 5.9×10^{-1} c 5.0×10^{-4} d 4.02×10^{-4}

e 6.19×10^{-3} f 8.0×10^{-6} g 8.05×10^{-2} h 1.604×10^{-7}

i 5.9×10^{-4} j 9.006×10^{-3} k 4.8×10^{-5} l 3.002×10^{-4}

26 Ruth completed these tables by filling in the blue shaded boxes.

Some of her answers are incorrect.

Find the wrong answers and correct them.

	Ordinary number	Standard form
a	354.7	3.547×10^2
b	0.00598	5.98×10^{-3}
c	0.483	4.83×10^2
d	407 000	4.07×10^4

	Ordinary number	Standard form
e	0.00001008	1.008×10^5
f	0.0068	6.8×10^{-3}
g	862	8.62×10^{-2}
h	2006.4	2.0064×10^2

27 The diameter of an atom is about 0.000 000 000 1 mm.

Write this measurement in standard form.

28 Write these facts about Saturn in standard form.

a	Average distance from the Sun	1 426 700 000 km
b	Diameter	120 540 km
c	Orbital period	29.4 years
d	Orbital velocity	79 390 km/h

29 Write these facts about light as ordinary numbers.

a   The speed of light is about 2.99×10^5 km/s.

b   In a year, light travels about 9.46×10^{12} km (one light-year).

c   The wavelength of visible light is about 5.0×10^{-5} cm.

d   Some of the most distant objects are 1.5×10^{10} light-years from Earth.

30 Find the corresponding ordinary number or standard form number for the population figures in this table.

Country	Population (ordinary number)	Population (standard form)
China	1 330 000 000	a
South Africa	b	4.43×10^7
United Kingdom	60 000 000	c
USA	300 000 000	d
Indonesia	e	2.375×10^8
India	f	1.15×10^9

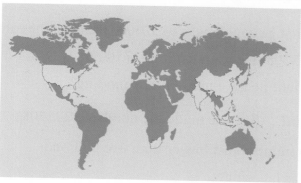

Rounding and estimation

- Rounding numbers appropriately for the question
- Writing numbers to a given number of significant figures
- Using rounding to make estimates

Keywords

You should know

explanation 1a | explanation 1b

1 Round each number to the degree of accuracy given.

a 342 (nearest 10)
b 5387 (nearest 100)
c 4098 (nearest 10)
d 86495 (nearest 1000)
e 5000 (nearest 10000)
f 398999 (nearest 10)

2 Copy and complete this table of world population data.

Always work with the original population numbers.

Country	Rounded to nearest 1000	Rounded to nearest 100 000	Rounded to nearest 1 000 000
Australia 21 007 310			
Canada 33 212 696			
France 64 057 792			
India 1 147 995 904			
World 6 706 993 152			

3 Glenn had these number cards.

3 5 7 0 2 8

a What is the closest number that he could make to 570000 using all the cards?

b Glenn made the number 275 308. He rounded it to 275 000.

What degree of accuracy might he have used in his rounding?

c Glenn was given another card: 5 . He made the number 5 275 308.

He said that he had made a number just bigger than five million.

What degree of accuracy was he using?

4 Round these decimals to the nearest whole number.

a   34.8   b   103.2   c   134.62   d   1005.56

e   4419.652   f   4805.993   g   2989.57   h   369 999.56

5 When Vicky checked her online bank statement she had these totals in her different accounts.

Cheque £132.56   Savings £1084.37   Visa statement £245.86

Round each amount to the nearest pound sterling (£).

6 The cost of a twin pack of tennis balls is £6, rounded to the nearest pound.

a   What is the smallest amount of money that the twin pack could cost?

b   What is the largest amount?

explanation 2a   explanation 2b   explanation 2c

7 Round each number to the degree of accuracy given.

a   24.35 (1 d.p.)   b   609.604 (2 d.p.)   c   90.899 (2 d.p.)

d   207.806 (1 d.p.)   e   0.0877 (3 d.p.)   f   9.035 63 (4 d.p.)

g   455.987 (1 d.p.)   h   340.4704 (3 d.p.)   i   1.000 654 (4 d.p.)

j   3.333 33... (3 d.p.)   k   67.6767 (2 d.p.)   l   0.999 (1 d.p.)

8 Use a calculator to work these out.

Round each answer to the number of decimal places given.

a   82 ÷ 11 (1 d.p.)   b   2.7 ÷ 31 (2 d.p.)

c   1.8 × 2.6 × 1.3 (1 d.p.)   d   84.3 × 3.67 (1 d.p.)

e   0.23 × 4.6 ÷ 0.4 (1 d.p.)   f   52.7 ÷ 2.6 (2 d.p.)

9 The value of the number pi (π) to 10 d.p. is 3.141 592 653 5.

Round this number to these numbers of decimal places.

a   1 d.p.   b   2 d.p.   c   3 d.p.   d   4 d.p.   e   5 d.p.

10 Calculate the area of each shape. Round each answer to two decimal places.

a

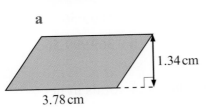

3.78 cm
1.34 cm

b

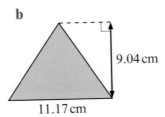

11.17 cm
9.04 cm

c $A = \pi r^2$
$r = 2.6\,\mathrm{cm}$

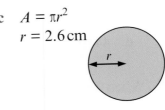

r

11 At the National Swimming Competition, Sally was recorded as swimming 100 m in 58.7 seconds, rounded to one decimal place.

What are her fastest and slowest possible times to get this result?

explanation 3a   explanation 3b   explanation 3c

12 How many significant figures does each of these numbers have?

a   628   b   0.0042   c   90.43   d   0.000 504

e   4.00   f   23.0302   g   34 066.04   h   1.000 000 03

13 Round these numbers to **i** one significant figure, **ii** two significant figures.

a   0.234   b   0.3615   c   0.4368   d   0.0288   e   0.005 62

f   0.020 54 g   0.604   h   0.000 455 5 i   563   j   3607

k   2005   l   5564   m   44 355   n   10 543   o   48 704

14 Round these numbers to three significant figures.

a   36.15   b   204.99   c   3.562   d   550.606   e   203.9

f   10.6505   g   56.037   h   40.943   i   45.606   j   67.988

15 Round these numbers to the degree of accuracy given.

a   0.210 23 (3 s.f.)   b   0.004 003 02 (4 s.f.)   c   450.43 (3 s.f.)

d   35.0055 (3 s.f.)   e   0.077 77 (2 s.f.)   f   0.000 007 0 (2 s.f.)

16 The mass of a car and trailer is 1370.056 kg.

Round this mass to these numbers of significant figures.

a   1 s.f.   b   2 s.f.   c   3 s.f.   d   4 s.f.   e   5 s.f.

17 Use your calculator to find the answers to these.

Round each answer to two significant figures.

a $19 \div 6$ b $4 \div 71$ c 2600×88 d $3 \div 21$

e $0.0055 \div 0.18$ f $\frac{2}{3}$ of 140   g 1.25^2 h $2.34 \times 1.6 \div 8.4$

explanation 4

18 Estimate the answers to these calculations. Do not use a calculator.

a 684×24 b $12\,403 \div 579$ c 54.8×18.6

d $923.03 \div 29.4$ e $(23.2 + 43.8) \times 4.8$ f $52.1 \div (3.2 + 1.92)$

19 Estimate answers to these calculations. Do not use a calculator.

Show your working.

a $\dfrac{147 + 54}{38 + 59}$ b $\dfrac{62 \times 19}{9 \times 32}$ c $\dfrac{18.9 + 11.42}{52.6 - 39.9}$ d $\dfrac{29.05 \times 37.4}{101.2 \div 4.6}$

20 Twelve customers spent these amounts at a local corner shop.

£12.45   £16.83   £21.52   £9.03   £14.67   £6.78

£7.86   £24.79   £32.81   £11.23   £3.77   £18.30

a   Estimate the average amount spent per customer.

b   On average, the shop has 863 customers each week.

About how much is spent in the shop each week?

21 The population density (population/km²) of a region is found using this formula.

$$\frac{\text{Population}}{\text{Area of region (km}^2\text{)}}$$

Estimate the population density of the places listed in the table.

Country	Population	Area in km²
Austria	8 205 533	83 870
Germany	82 369 552	357 021
UK	60 943 912	244 820

22 The surface area of a sphere is found using the formula $A = 4\pi r^2$.

$\pi = 3.1416$ (4 d.p.)

Estimate the surface area of a sphere with each radius.

a 2.92 cm   b 9.43 cm   c 21.05 m   d 113.2 mm

Multiplying and dividing

- Recognising and using reciprocals
- Understanding the effects of multiplying and dividing positive numbers by numbers between 0 and 1

Keywords

You should know

explanation 1

1 Rewrite each statement using an appropriate inverse operation.

  a $37 \times 8 = 296$ **b** $58 \times 12 = 696$ **c** $567 \div 63 = 9$ **d** $2754 \div 18 = 153$

2 Rewrite each statement using an inverse operation and solve it.

  a $\square \times 30 = 870$ **b** $\square \div 37 = 20$ **c** $12 \times \square = 180$ **d** $\square \div 50 = 24$

3 Write an equation for this question, then use an inverse operation to solve it.

Michelle had a pile of building blocks to share equally among 25 children.

Each child received 200 building blocks.

How many building blocks did Michelle start with?

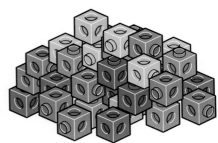

explanation 2a   explanation 2b

4 Find the reciprocals of these.

  a $\dfrac{1}{6}$ **b** $\dfrac{3}{4}$ **c** $\dfrac{8}{7}$ **d** $\dfrac{12}{7}$ **e** 11

  f $\dfrac{6}{13}$ **g** $\dfrac{7}{10}$ **h** $\dfrac{1}{2}$ **i** 25 **j** $\dfrac{50}{63}$

5 a To find the reciprocal of 0.6 Jamie first rewrote 0.6 as $\dfrac{6}{10}$.

  His answer was $\dfrac{10}{6}$. Is this correct?

  b Use Jamie's method to find the reciprocals of these numbers.

  i 0.2   **ii** 0.9   **iii** 0.24   **iv** 0.56   **v** 0.884   **vi** 0.345

6 Copy and complete these statements.

    a Multiplying by $\frac{1}{7}$ is the same as dividing by $\square$.

    b Multiplying by $\square$ is the same as dividing by 12.

    c Dividing by $\frac{1}{3}$ is the same as multiplying by $\square$.

    d Dividing by $\square$ is the same as multiplying by 15.

7 **a** Which of these is the correct statement for 'How many quarters are in 7?'?

       A $7 \times \frac{1}{4}$ **B** $7 \div \frac{1}{4}$ **C** $\frac{1}{4} \div 7$ **D** $\frac{1}{4} \times 7$

    b What is the answer?

8 Find the answers to these.

    a $12 \div \frac{1}{6}$ **b** $15 \div \frac{1}{5}$ **c** $13 \div \frac{1}{8}$ **d** $36 \div \frac{1}{3}$ **e** $50 \div \frac{1}{7}$

9 Copy and complete these statements.

    a $35 \times \frac{1}{7} = \square$ therefore $\square \div \frac{1}{7} = 35$

    b $96 \times \frac{1}{12} = \square$ therefore $\square \div \frac{1}{12} = 96$

    c $125 \times \frac{1}{25} = \square$ therefore $\square \div \frac{1}{25} = 125$

10 Rewrite these statements as multiplications using a fraction.

    a $120 \div 24 = 5$ **b** $207 \div 9 = 23$ **c** $210 \div 15 = 14$ **d** $308 \div 11 = 28$

11 Copy and complete these sentences.

    Give an example for each of them.

    a Multiplication by a fraction is equivalent to division by its _____ .

    b Division by a fraction is equivalent to multiplication by its _____ .

explanation 3

12 Which of these calculations will have an answer *greater* than 0.65?

    a 0.65×1.2 **b** $0.65 \div 1.2$ **c** 0.65×0.4 **d** $0.65 \div 0.005$

    e 0.65×0.06 **f** $0.65 \div 2.5$ **g** 0.65×3.4 **h** $0.65 \div 0.99$

13 Which of these calculations will have an answer *less* than 150?

    a 150×0.4 **b** $150 \div 2.1$ **c** 150×8.6 **d** $150 \div 0.5$

    e 150×1.4 **f** 150×0.07 **g** $150 \div 13.2$ **h** $150 \div 0.003$

14 Which calculations in each set have an answer *less* than 2.06?

    a   **A** 2.06×3.1 **B** 2.06×0.31 **C** $2.06 \div 0.31$

    b   **A** $2.06 \div 0.64$ **B** $2.06 \div 6.4$ **C** 2.06×0.64

    c   **A** 2.06×0.206 **B** 2.06×2.06 **C** $2.06 \div 2.06$

    d   **A** $2.06 \div 0.99$ **B** 2.06×9.9 **C** $2.06 \div 9.9$

15 Weston did this calculation.

How can you tell, without doing the calculation, that it is wrong?

$$5.02 \times 0.6 = 30.12$$

16 When a positive number n is multiplied by 0.4, the answer is less than n.

    a   What is the inverse of multiplying by 0.4?

    b   If a positive number p is divided by 0.4, is the answer more or less than p?

17 Copy and complete these sentences.

Give an example for each of them.

    a   When a positive number m is multiplied by a number between 0 and 1, the answer will be _____ than m.

    b   When a positive number r is divided by a number between 0 and 1, the answer will be _____ than r.

Using letters

- Distinguishing between equations, formulae and functions
- Identifying and using an identity
- Using negative indices
- Using the index laws in algebra and with standard form

Keywords

You should know

explanation 1a | explanation 1b | explanation 1c | explanation 1d

1 Solve these equations.

a $3x - 7 = 17$

b $\frac{x}{4} + 5 = 23$

c $3(2x - 5) = 24$

d $6x + 5 = 8x - 5$

e $4(2x - 7) = 8 - x$

f $\frac{2x - 3}{5} = 7$

2

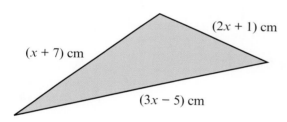

$(2x + 1)$ cm

$(x + 7)$ cm

$(3x - 5)$ cm

The triangle has a perimeter of 27 cm.

Form an equation and solve it to find the value of x and the length of each side of the triangle.

3 Jane is x years old and her brother Tom is two years older than her, while her sister Hannah is three times her age. The sum of their ages is 57.

a Write expressions in terms of x for Tom's age and Hannah's age.

b Write an equation for the sum of their ages.

c Solve your equation to find Jane's age.

explanation 2a   explanation 2b   explanation 2c   explanation 2d

4 State whether each of the following is a formula, equation or function.
Some parts may have more than one answer.

a $5x - 3 = 17$ **b** $\dfrac{c}{6} - 5 = \dfrac{3}{5}$ **c** $y = 5x - 7$

d $A = \pi r^2$ where A is the area and r is the radius of the circle.

e $p = 2l + 2w$ where p is the perimeter, l is the length and w is the width.

f $y = 3x^3 + 5$ **g** $5(x + 2) = 3x - 7$ **h** $3x + 2y = 18$

5 Copy and complete the table of values for these functions without using a calculator.

a $y = 6x - 1$ **b** $y = 7 - 2x$ **c** $2y + 3x = 12$

x	−1	−3		5		
y			0		11	−5

6 The volume of a cone is given by the formula $V = \dfrac{1}{3}\pi r^2 h$.

Find the volume of these cones.

a $r = 4\,\text{cm}$, $h = 6\,\text{cm}$

b $r = 7\,\text{cm}$, $h = 12\,\text{cm}$

c $r = 1.2\,\text{cm}$, $h = 3.5\,\text{cm}$

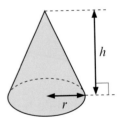

7 The perimeter P of a right-angled triangle is given by the formula
$P = a + b + \sqrt{a^2 + b^2}$.

Find the perimeter of each of these triangles.

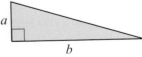

a $a = 3\,\text{cm}$, $b = 4\,\text{cm}$

b $a = 12.5\,\text{cm}$, $b = 30\,\text{cm}$

c $a = 6.1\,\text{cm}$, $b = 3.2\,\text{cm}$

8 Copy and complete these identities. Check by substituting some values of x.

   a $4(x + 7) \equiv 4x + \Box$

   b $7(2x + 5) \equiv \Box x + \Box$

   c $2(\Box - 7) \equiv 6x - \Box$

   d $9x - 12 \equiv 3(\Box - 4)$

   e $5(2x - 3) \equiv \Box - \Box$

   f $15x + 25 \equiv 5(\Box + \Box)$

9 Which of these expressions are identically equal to $r \div \frac{s}{t}$?

   A $\frac{r \div s}{t}$ **B** $r \times \frac{t}{s}$ **C** $\frac{r}{1} \div \frac{s}{t}$ **D** $\frac{t}{rs}$ **E** $\frac{rt}{s}$

10 Which of these expressions are identically equal to $7 + 3(x + 2)$?

   A $7 + 3x + 2$ **B** $10x + 20$ **C** $7 + 3x + 6$

   D $9 + 3x$ **E** $3x + 13$

> explanation 3a   explanation 3b   explanation 3c

11 Write these using indices.

   a $d \times d \times d \times d \times e \times e$

   b $g \times h \times h \times g \times h \times g \times h \times g \times h \times g$

   c $4 \times p \times p \times p \times q \times q \times r$

   d $4 \times y \times y \times 5 \times z \times z \times z \times z$

   e $6 \times a \times a \times 4 \times b \times b \times c \times c \times c$

   f $4 \times m \times 4 \times n \times n \times n \times 2 \times p \times p \times p \times p$

12 Find the value of each of these without using a calculator.

   a 2^3 **b** 4^3 **c** 3^4 **d** 2^5 **e** 10^8 **f** $(-2)^2$

   g $(-3)^3$ **h** $2^3 \times 5^2$ **i** $10^2 \div 5^2$ **j** $(-5)^2 + 3^4$ **k** $27 - 5^3$

13 Simplify these, leaving your answer as a power.

   a $6^5 \times 6^2$ **b** $5^{12} \div 5^4$ **c** $(3^4)^6$ **d** $\dfrac{7^5 \times 7^2}{7^3}$

   e $a^2 \times a^7$ **f** $(b^5)^3 \div b^6$ **g** $\dfrac{x \times x^3}{x^{-2}}$ **h** $(g^{10})^{-2} \times g^{20}$

14 Copy and complete these statements.

a $\quad 4^{-1} = \dfrac{1}{4^1} = \dfrac{1}{\Box}$

b $\quad 5^{-2} = \dfrac{1}{\Box} = \dfrac{1}{\Box}$

c $\quad 10^{-1} = \dfrac{1}{\Box} = \dfrac{1}{\Box}$

d $\quad 10^{-2} = \dfrac{\Box}{\Box} = \dfrac{\Box}{\Box}$

15 Match each index statement in the top row to its value from the bottom row.

$$4^{-2} \qquad 10^{-3} \qquad (-4)^2 \qquad 5^{-3} \qquad (-10)^3 \qquad -(4)^2 \qquad 5^3 \qquad (-5)^3$$

$$125 \qquad -16 \qquad -125 \qquad \frac{1}{16} \qquad -1000 \qquad 16 \qquad \frac{1}{125} \qquad \frac{1}{1000}$$

16 Find the value of each expression without using a calculator.

a $\quad 2^{-3}$ 　　　 b $\quad 4^{-2}$ 　　　 c $\quad 3^{-2}$ 　　　 d $\quad 2^{-4}$ 　　　 e $\quad 10^{-5}$

f $\quad (-2)^{-2}$ 　 g $\quad (-3)^{-3}$ 　 h $\quad 2^{-6}$ 　　　 i $\quad (-6)^{-3}$ 　 j $\quad 10^{-4}$

17 How many values can you find for x and y to make this statement true?

$x^y = 64$

18 Simplify these, leaving your answer as a power.
Write each answer in two different ways.

a $\quad 5^2 \div 5^3$

b $\quad 6^2 \div 6^5$

c $\quad a^2 \div a^7$

d $\quad \dfrac{3^5 \times 3^2}{3^{10}}$

e $\quad \dfrac{y^{-1} \times y^3}{y^5}$

f $\quad (p^{10})^2 \div p^{30}$

19 Use the index laws to simplify these expressions.

a $\quad 3a \times 5a^2$

b $\quad 2c^3 \times 2c^2$

c $\quad 4n^2 \times n^{-2}$

d $\quad m^2 \times 3m$

e $\quad 4b^3 \times 3b^2$

f $\quad 4p^2 \div 2p^3$

g $\quad 8x^2 \div 2x^{-1}$

h $\quad 4xy^2 \times 3x^3y^2$

20 Use the index laws to simplify these expressions.

a $4n^4p \div 2n^2p$ b $4t^8r^3 \times 3t^4$ c $3g^2 \times 2g^3 \times 2g$ d $10b^8 \div 5b^8$

e $\dfrac{9a^2}{3a}$ f $\dfrac{10n^6p^8}{2n^5p^3}$ g $c^4 \times 3c^2 \times 2c^5 \times c^3$ h $\dfrac{(3b^2 \times 4b^4)}{6b^3}$

i $(2x^7)^3$ j $(10y^3)^4$ k $(6a^2)^2$ l $(2m^3)^{-3}$

21 Write an expression for the area of each shape.
Use the index laws to simplify them.

a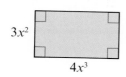

$3x^2$

$4x^3$

b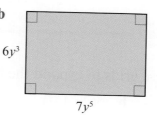

$6y^3$

$7y^5$

c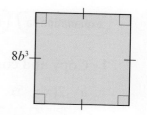

$8b^3$

22 Write and simplify an expression for the red length of each shape.

a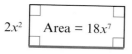

$2x^2$ Area = $18x^7$

b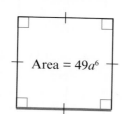

Area = $49a^6$

23 Work these out. Give your answers in standard form.

a $(3 \times 10^2) \times (2 \times 10^5)$ b $(3.2 \times 10^{-3}) \times (3 \times 10^2)$

c $(4 \times 10^6) \times (6 \times 10^4)$ d $(3.2 \times 10^6) \times (3 \times 10^5)$

e $(7 \times 10^{-2}) \times (3 \times 10^4)$ f $(6 \times 10^{-4}) \times (2.5 \times 10^{-3})$

g $(6 \times 10^6) \div (2 \times 10^2)$ h $(8.4 \times 10^{-3}) \div (4 \times 10^5)$

i $(9.6 \times 10^3) \div (2 \times 10^{-5})$ j $(3 \times 10^7) \div (6 \times 10^5)$

k $(2 \times 10^6) \div (8 \times 10^5)$ l $(4.8 \times 10^{-5}) \div (2 \times 10^{-2})$

m $(6 \times 10^6)^2$ n $(5 \times 10^3)^3$

o $(2 \times 10^{-2})^4$ p $(2 \times 10^4)^{-2}$

Expressions

- Expanding single brackets in more complicated algebraic expressions
- Factorising expressions by taking out common factors
- Expanding pairs of brackets
- Factorising quadratic expressions
- Solving quadratic equations by factorising

Keywords

You should know

explanation 1a   explanation 1b

1 Copy and complete these grids to expand the brackets.

a $2(x + 5)$

×	x	$+5$
2		

b $5(2x + 7)$

×	$2x$	$+7$
5		

c $3(4x - 5)$

×	$4x$	-5
3		

d $6(5 - x)$

×	5	$-x$
6		

e $-2(3x + 9)$

×	$3x$	$+9$
-2		

f $-3(4 - 2x)$

×	4	$-2x$
-3		

2 Expand the brackets. You may use any method.

a $3(x + 5)$ **b** $6(a - 4)$ **c** $2(3x + 7)$ **d** $5(3a + 2b)$

e $-2(3x + 7)$ **f** $-4(6 + x)$ **g** $-5(3 - x)$ **h** $-6(2x - 3)$

3 Expand the brackets.

a $a(a + 2)$ **b** $2x(3x - 5)$ **c** $-3x(x + 7)$ **d** $-6(5a - 2b)$

e $3x(2x + 5y)$ **f** $4xy(3y + 5x^2)$ **g** $-6a(3a - 2)$ **h** $3xyz(z + 2xy)$

explanation 2a   explanation 2b

4 Write equivalent expressions, with brackets and without brackets, for the perimeters of these regular polygons.

a

$(2x - 3)$

b

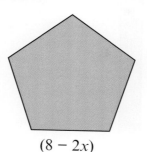

$(8 - 2x)$

c

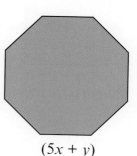

$(5x + y)$

5 Write equivalent expressions, with brackets and without brackets, for the perimeters of these rectangles.

a

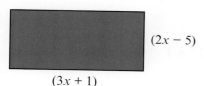

$(2x - 5)$

$(3x + 1)$

b

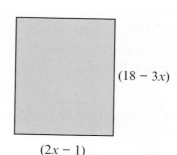

$(18 - 3x)$

$(2x - 1)$

6 Expand the brackets and simplify each expression.

a $3(2x + 1) + 2(x - 3)$

b $4(a + 3) + 5(3a - 1)$

c $5(d - 4) + 4(3 + d)$

d $6(3p - 3) + 3(-2p - 2)$

e $3(y - 2) - 2(y + 3)$

f $5(2m - 3) + 3(2 - m)$

7 Expand the brackets and simplify each expression.

a $5m(m + 2n) - m(3m - n)$

b $4a(6b - 3a) - 2a(4a - 2b)$

c $2x(5 - x) + 3x(4x + 1)$

d $7y(2y - 5) - 4y(5 - 2y)$

e $-5m(2m - 3n) - 5n(3m - 2n)$

f $-4y(7x + y) - 5x(3y - 2x)$

8 The square and the rectangle have equal perimeters.

Write an equation using brackets and solve it to find the value of x.

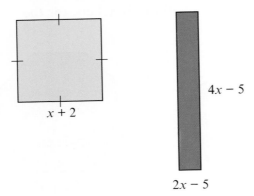

$x + 2$

$4x - 5$

$2x - 5$

9 Tom has a garden pond with a path around it. The length and width of the path and pond are shown on the diagram. The path has width 0.5 m. Find a simplified expression for the perimeter of the pond.

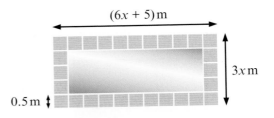

$(6x + 5)$ m

$3x$ m

0.5 m

explanation 3a   explanation 3b

10 Copy and complete these partly factorised expressions.

a $8x + 12 = 4(\square + \square)$

b $9a + 15b = \square(3a + \square)$

c $4x + 6y + 8z = 2(\square + \square + \square)$

d $3x^2 + 9xy = \square(\square + 3y)$

11 Factorise fully these expressions.

a $5x + 10$

b $14a + 21$

c $10 - 2x$

d $21s + 28t$

e $6x + 9y + 12z$

f $18s - 15t$

g $20x + 25st$

h $56r - 63s$

i $24f + 16g$

j $26x + 28y$

k $3x + 6y + 9z$

12 Factorise fully these expressions.

a $x^2 + 2x$

b $5y + y^2$

c $15x - 7x^2$

d $pqr + 2r$

e $7st - 8s$

f $4gy + 5py$

g $4x^2 + x^3$

h $2p^3 - 3p$

i $x + xy - x^2$

j $3x^2 + x^3 - x^2z$

k $wxy - wd + 5w$

13 Factorise fully these expressions.

a $3y^2 + 3y$ b $2m^2 - 4m$ c $8y^2 - 2y$ d $4b^2 + 8b^3$

e $10m^2 - 5m^3$ f $12n^2 + 14n$ g $8f - 24f^2$ h $3x^2 + 6xy$

i $12ab - 48ab^2$ j $2p^2 - 2p + 4pq$ k $4a^2b - 4ab + 8ab^2$

l $15p^2q + 25pq - 5q^2p$

14 The area of a rectangle is $12x^2 + 16x$.

One possible expression for the length × the width of the rectangle is $x(12x + 16)$.

Write two more possible expressions for the length × width of the rectangle.

explanation 4a   explanation 4b

For questions **15**, **16**, **18** and **19**, use either of the methods given in Explanation 4.

15 Multiply out these brackets and give each answer in its simplest form.

a $(x + 3)(x + 5)$ b $(x + 5)(x + 7)$ c $(x + 8)(x + 1)$

d $(x + 1)(x - 6)$ e $(x - 4)(x + 5)$ f $(x - 2)(x - 9)$

g $(x - 3)(x - 4)$ h $(x - 4)(x + 3)$ i $(x - 7)(2x - 3)$

16 Expand the brackets and simplify the result.

$(x + 1)^2 = (x + 1)(x + 1)$

a $(x + 3)^2$ b $(x + 1)^2$ c $(x + 2)^2$

d $(x + 6)^2$ e $(x + 9)^2$ f $(x - 7)^2$

g $(a - 2)^2$ h $(p - 10)^2$ i $(n - 12)^2$

17 What do you notice about the results for question **16**?

Write down the identities for $(a + b)^2$ and $(a - b)^2$.

18 Find the area of each rectangle and give each answer in its simplest form.

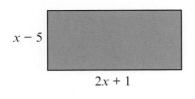

$x - 5$

$2x + 1$

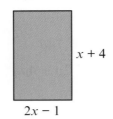

$x + 4$

$2x - 1$

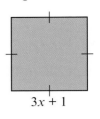

$3x + 1$

19 Expand and simplify these.

a $(x + 3)(x - 3)$ b $(x - 5)(x + 5)$ c $(x + 10)(x - 10)$

20 What do you notice about the results for question **19**?

Write the expanded form of $(a + b)(a - b)$.

explanation 5a   explanation 5b

21 Use the difference of two squares to factorise these.

a $x^2 - 64$ b $x^2 - 144$ c $a^2 - 100$ d $p^2 - 81$

22 Which of these expressions can be factorised using the difference of two squares?

A $x^2 + 4x$ B $x^2 - 16x$ C $x^2 - 36$ D $x^2 + 36$

E $36x^2 - 49$ F $x^2 - 49x$ G $x^2 + 49$

23 Which of the expressions in question **22** cannot be factorised by either using the difference of two squares or by taking out a common factor?

24 Factorise the expression for the area of each rectangle, using one of the methods from question **23**. Use your answer to find expressions for the lengths of the sides of these rectangles.

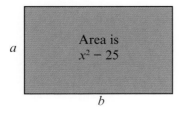

a

Area is
$x^2 - 25$

b

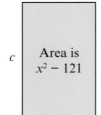

c

Area is
$x^2 - 121$

d

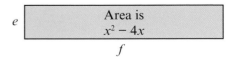

e

Area is
$x^2 - 4x$

f

explanation 6a   explanation 6b   explanation 6c

25 Copy and complete these factorisations.

a $x^2 + 8x + 7 = (x + 7)(\square + \square)$ b $x^2 + 5x + 6 = (x + \square)(x + \square)$

c $x^2 + 6x + 9 = (\square + \square)(\square + \square)$ d $x^2 + 10x + 16 = (\square + \square)(\square + \square)$

e $x^2 + 7x + 10 = (\square + \square)(\square + \square)$ f $x^2 + 16x + 28 = (\square + \square)(\square + \square)$

26 Factorise these.

a $x^2 + 4x + 3$ b $x^2 + 6x + 5$ c $x^2 + 8x + 12$

d $x^2 + 10x + 21$ e $x^2 + 9x + 20$ f $x^2 - 4x + 3$

g $x^2 - 13x + 42$ h $x^2 - 8x + 12$ i $x^2 - 20x + 100$

j $x^2 - 17x + 70$ k $x^2 + 15x + 56$ l $x^2 - 7x + 12$

explanation 7a   explanation 7b

27 Factorise these.

a $x^2 - 2x - 3$ b $x^2 + 4x - 5$ c $x^2 - 5x - 6$

d $x^2 - 2x - 8$ e $x^2 + 3x - 10$ f $x^2 + 2x - 15$

g $x^2 - 5x - 24$ h $x^2 + 5x - 36$ i $x^2 - 2x - 99$

j $x^2 + 5x - 14$ k $x^2 - 20x - 300$ l $x^2 + 28x - 60$

28 Factorise these.

a $3x^2 - 9x$ b $x^2 + 5x - 14$ c $x^2 - 15x - 34$

d $x^2 - 121$ e $x^2 + 6x - 40$ f $x^2 - 12x + 27$

g $16x^2 + 4x$ h $36 - x^2$ i $x^2 - 9x - 220$

j $x^2 + 12x + 36$ k $x^2 - 15x$ l $400 - x^2$

explanation 8a | explanation 8b | explanation 8c

29 Solve these quadratic equations by factorising.

a $x^2 - 15x + 56 = 0$

b $a^2 + 5a = 0$

c $b^2 - 1 = 0$

d $d^2 - 5d - 150 = 0$

e $15x^2 - 20x = 0$

f $f^2 - 400 = 0$

g $x^2 + 20x + 96 = 0$

h $x^2 + 9x - 36 = 0$

i $x^2 + 6x + 9 = 0$

30 Solve these quadratic equations by factorising.
You will need to rearrange them first.

a $x^2 + 3x = 40$

b $x^2 = 18 - 7x$

c $14x - 24 = x^2$

d $x^2 = 5x$

e $x^2 - 6x = -9$

f $-2x = -x^2 + 8$

31 The area of this rectangle is $24 \, \text{cm}^2$.

$(x + 7) \, \text{cm}$

$(x + 5) \, \text{cm}$

a Show that $x^2 + 12x + 11 = 0$.

b Solve the equation $x^2 + 12x + 11 = 0$.

c Which of your solutions is not sensible for this problem?

d Write the length and width of the rectangle.

32 Stephen is x years old and Anna is two years older than Stephen.
The product of their ages is 80.

a Show that $x^2 + 2x - 80 = 0$.

b Solve the quadratic equation $x^2 + 2x - 80 = 0$.

c How old is Stephen?

33 The area of the right-angled triangle is 27 cm².

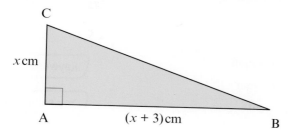

a Show that $x^2 + 3x - 54 = 0$.

b Solve the quadratic equation $x^2 + 3x - 54 = 0$ and find the length of AB.

34 Two positive numbers differ by 3 and their product is 180.
The smaller of the two numbers is x.

a Show that $x^2 + 3x - 180 = 0$.

b Solve this quadratic equation to find the two numbers.

35

x cm

$(x + 7)$ cm

$(x + 8)$ cm

a Pythagoras' theorem states that for any right-angled triangle the square
of the length of the longest side is equal to the sum of the squares of the
other two sides.

Use Pythagoras' theorem to show that $x^2 - 2x - 15 = 0$ for this
right-angled triangle.

b Solve the quadratic equation to find the side lengths of the triangle.

Angles and polygons

- Finding the sum of the exterior angles of a polygon
- Finding the sum of the interior angles of a polygon
- Finding the angle between a radius and tangent
- Proving statements in geometry

Keywords

You should know

explanation 1a   explanation 1b   explanation 1c   explanation 1d

1 In each diagram, find the size of x. Give reasons for your answers.

a

37°, x

b

51°, x

c

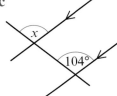
x, 104°

d

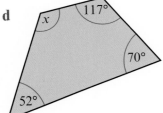
x, 117°, 70°, 52°

e

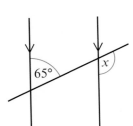
65°, x

f

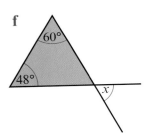
60°, 48°, x

2 Find the size of each angle marked by a letter.
Give reasons for your answers.

a

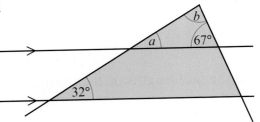
b, a, 67°, 32°

b

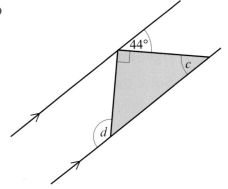
44°, c, d

3 In each diagram, find the size of x.

a

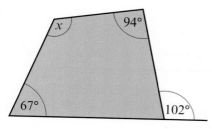

b

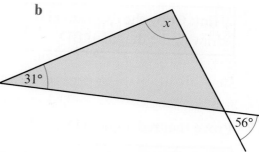

c

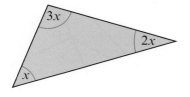

d

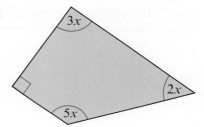

explanation 2

4 Prove that angle TPQ = $2x$.

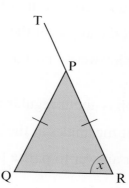

5 Prove that angle DCA = angle CAB + angle ABC.

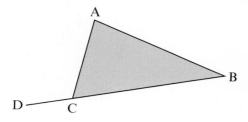

Note
Your answer proves that, in general:
The exterior angle of a triangle
equals the sum of the two interior
opposite angles.

6 Prove that angle ADC = angle ABC.

Hint: Copy the diagram and
draw in the diagonal BD.

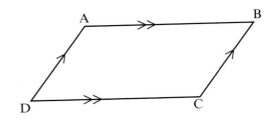

7 Prove that red angle ADC = 2 × angle ABC.

Hint: Copy the diagram and label
angle ABD as x and angle DBC as y.

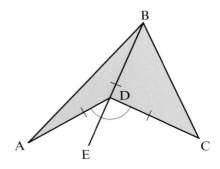

explanation 3a   explanation 3b

8 This question is about regular hexagons.

　a Work out the angles at the centre of a regular hexagon.

　b Use your answer to part **a** to draw a regular hexagon.

9 This question is about regular nonagons.

　a Work out the angles at the centre of a regular nonagon.

　b Use your answer to part **a** to draw a regular nonagon.

10 The diagram shows a regular pentagon, with centre O.

　a Work out the size of angle AOB.

　b Work out the size of angle OAB.

　c Work out the size of angle EAB.

　d EAB is an interior angle of the polygon.
　　Work out the sum of all the interior angles
　　in the pentagon.

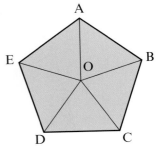

11 Work out the sum of all the interior angles in a regular octagon.
　Use a similar method to that in question **10**.

explanation 4a   explanation 4b

12 In each diagram, find the size of x.

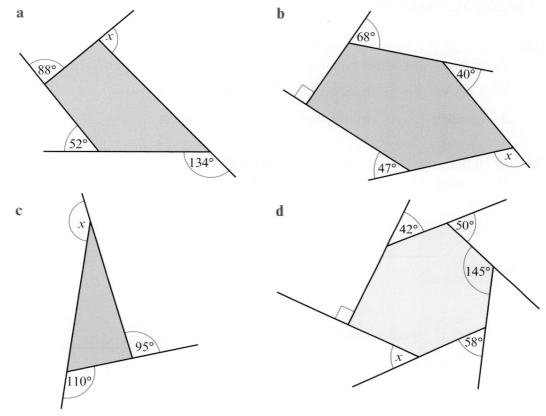

a

b

c

d

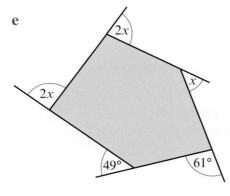

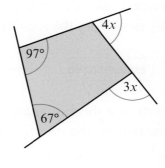

e

f

13 The exterior angles of a pentagon are $2x$, $2x$, $3x$, $4x$ and $4x$.

    a Find the value of x.

    b What is the size of each of the pentagon's exterior angles?

14 The exterior angles of a hexagon are x, $2x$, $3x$, $3x$, $4x$ and $5x$.
What is the size of each of the hexagon's exterior angles?

> explanation 5a　　explanation 5b

15 Below are the numbers of sides of regular polygons.
What is the size of an exterior angle in each regular polygon?

   a　5 sides　　　　**b**　8 sides　　　　**c**　10 sides

   d　15 sides　　　　**e**　16 sides　　　　**f**　30 sides

16 Each diagram shows part of a regular polygon.
How many sides does each regular polygon have?

   a

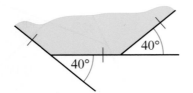

   b

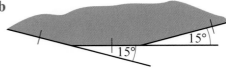

   c　**d**

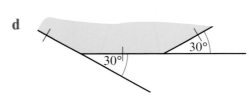

17 Each exterior angle of a regular polygon is 20°.
How many sides does the regular polygon have?

> explanation 6a　　explanation 6b

18 Below are the numbers of sides of regular polygons.
What is the sum of the interior angles in each regular polygon?

   a　5 sides　　　　**b**　8 sides　　　　**c**　12 sides

19 Below are the numbers of sides of regular polygons.
What is the size of an interior angle in each regular polygon?

   a　6 sides　　　　**b**　9 sides　　　　**c**　20 sides

20 In each of the following questions, find the size of the angle marked x.

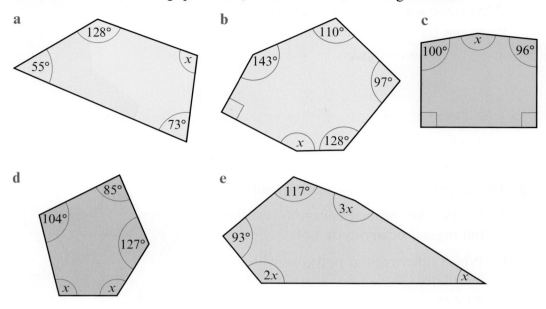

a

b

c

d

e

21 Eloise says: 'The sum of the interior angles of a decagon is double the sum of the interior angles in a pentagon.'

Is Eloise correct? Give an explanation for your answer.

22 Each diagram shows part of a regular polygon.
In each case, work out the number of sides of the regular polygon.

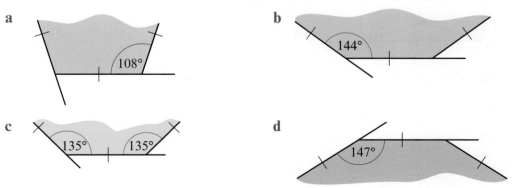

a

b

c

d

23 Sahil says: 'I have drawn an accurate regular polygon. All the interior angles add up to 1000°.'

Could Sahil have drawn this regular polygon? Explain your answer.

24 The diagram shows a regular hexagon and
a regular pentagon.
Work out the size of the angle marked x.

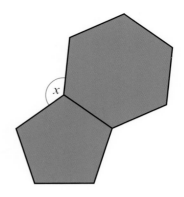

25 The diagram shows a tessellation using hexagons.

a Explain why regular hexagons tessellate
but regular octagons do not.

b Which other regular polygons will
tessellate? Give an explanation for your
answers.

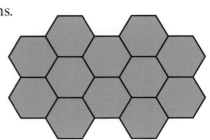

(explanation 7a) (explanation 7b) (explanation 7c)

26 Find the sizes of the angles a to f. Give reasons for your answers.

a

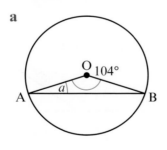

b

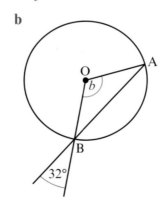

c

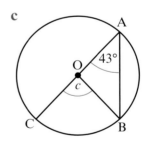

d

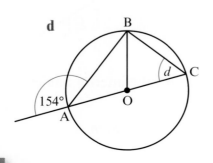

e

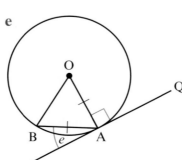

f

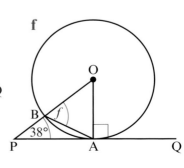

27 In each diagram, PT is a tangent to the circle.

Find the sizes of the angles *a*, *b*, *c*, *d* and *e*. Give reasons for your answers.

a

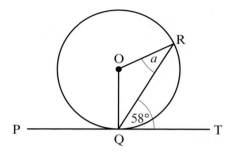

b

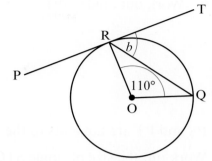

c

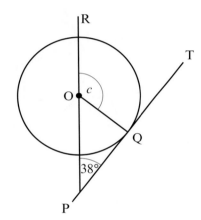

d

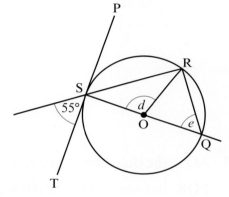

28 In these diagrams, PS and PT are both tangents to the circle.

Find the sizes of the angles marked *a* and *b*. Give reasons for your answers.

a

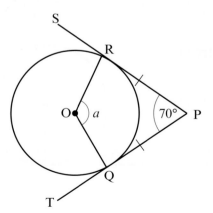

b

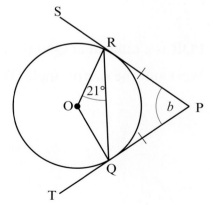

29 PS is a tangent to the circle.

    a Work out angle OPS.

    b Work out angle OPT.

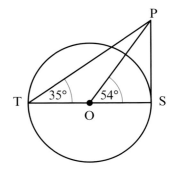

30 PS and PT are tangents to the circle centre O.

Work out the size of angle STO.

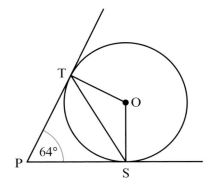

31 AQ is the diameter of a circle, centre O.

PQR is a tangent to the circle at Q.

Work out the size of angle PQB.

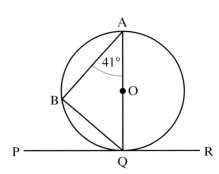

32 PQR is a tangent at Q to the circle, centre O.

Work out the size of angle OTQ.

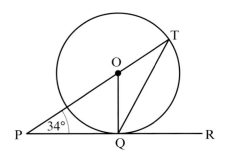

Circles

- Naming the different parts of a circle
- Finding the circumference and area of a circle
- Finding the length of an arc
- Finding the area of a sector

Keywords

You should know

explanation 1a   explanation 1b   explanation 1c   explanation 1d

1 Find the circumference of circles with these diameters or radii.

    a diameter 9 cm   **b** diameter 6.9 cm   **c** radius 8 mm

    d diameter 24 m   **e** radius 4.3 m   **f** radius 9.15 m

2 What is the circumference of a circle of diameter 6.4 cm?

3 What is the circumference of a circle of radius 2.1 m?

4 Find the circumference of each circle.

  a

8 cm

  b

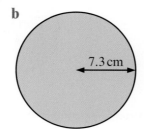

7.3 cm

  c

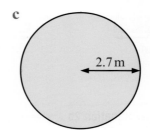

2.7 m

  d

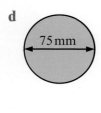

75 mm

5 A circular tablecloth has a radius of 45 cm. What is the distance around the edge of the tablecloth? Give your answer correct to the nearest centimetre.

6 A 2p coin has a diameter of 26 mm. Jack rolls a 2p coin along the floor. The coin makes 20 complete revolutions. How far does the coin travel? Give your answer in metres.

7 Gail pushes her bike. The wheels make 150 complete revolutions. Each wheel has a radius of 28 cm. How far does the bike travel? Give your answer in metres.

8 Kylie has a circular rug of radius 1.7 m. She wants to put some edging around the whole of the edge of the rug.

   a How much edging will she need?

   b The edging costs 84p per metre and can only be bought in whole numbers of metres. How much will the edging cost?

9 Rob wants to measure the length of his field. He has a trundle wheel which has a radius of 20 cm. Rob walks the length of his field pushing the trundle wheel. The wheel makes 128 complete revolutions.

What is the length of the field? Give your answer correct to the nearest metre.

10 Jan's bicycle has wheels of diameter 66 cm. Mark's bicycle has wheels of diameter 74 cm. They each cycle so that the wheels complete 100 revolutions.

How much further than Jan does Mark travel? Give your answer in metres correct to the nearest centimetre.

11 Work out the perimeter of each shape.

   a
   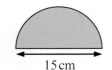
   15 cm

   b

   5.5 cm

   c
   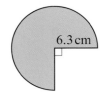
   6.3 cm

explanation 2a   explanation 2b

12 Find the area of circles with these radii or diameters.

   a radius 12 cm   **b** radius 7.8 m   **c** diameter 6.2 cm

   d radius 15.3 m   **e** diameter 45 cm   **f** diameter 6.7 m

13 Work out the area of a circle of diameter 12 cm.

14 Work out the area of a circle of radius 3.5 cm.

15 Find the area of each circle.

a
2.1 m

b
15.7 cm

c
3 mm

d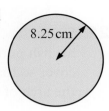
8.25 cm

16 A circular pond has a diameter of 6 m. Work out the surface area of the pond.

17 A circular tablecloth has a radius of 45 cm. Work out the area of the tablecloth.

18 In each design, the red circle has a radius of 7.5 cm.

    i What is the area of the blue part?

    ii What is the area of the red part?

a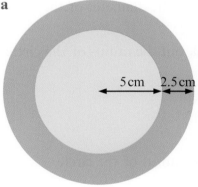
5 cm 2.5 cm

b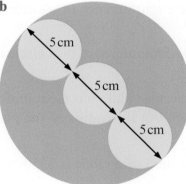
5 cm
5 cm
5 cm

19 The diameter of this dartboard is 47 cm.

Work out the area of the dartboard.

20 The diameter of a 2p coin is 26 mm. Work out the area of one side of the coin.

21 Simon has a square sheet of plastic of side length 5 m. He cuts out a cover for his fish pond, which is in the shape of a circle of radius 2.1 m. He cuts out the cover so that there is a 10 cm overlap all the way round the pond. Work out the area of the plastic that will be left over.

22 Work out the area of each shape.

a
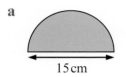
15 cm

b

5.5 cm

c
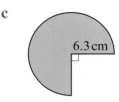
6.3 cm

| explanation 3a | explanation 3b |

23 The circumference of a circle is 60 m. Work out the diameter of the circle.

24 The circumference of a circle is 123 cm. Work out the radius of the circle.

25 A circular plate has a circumference of 93.7 cm.
Work out the radius of the plate.

26 The area of a circle is 8350 cm². Work out the radius of the circle.

27 The area of a circle is 1.88 m². Work out the diameter of the circle.

28 Jane pushes a bicycle for 200 m.

The wheels of the bicycle complete 120 revolutions.

Work out the radius of the wheels of the bicycle.

29 A tabletop is in the shape of a circle. The area of the top of the table is 3.46 m². Jim has a tablecloth that is 200 cm in diameter. Will the tablecloth fit the table? Give an explanation for your answer.

30 The large circle has an area of 129 cm².

What is the area of the shaded region?

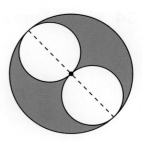

explanation 4a | explanation 4b | explanation 4c

31 Look at each sector.

    i What is the area of the sector?

    ii What is the length of the arc?

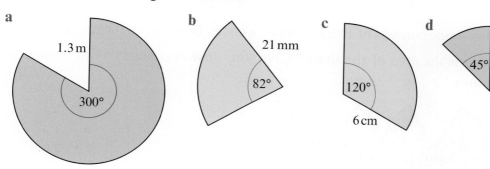

a 1.3 m 300°

b 21 mm 82°

c 120° 6 cm

d 45° 3.4 cm

32 Work out the perimeter of each shape.

a 9 cm 60°

b 40° 4.2 cm

c 100° 7.3 cm

33 A company designs a pattern to use as its logo.
It is in the shape of a circle of diameter 4.5 cm.
Work out the area of the circle that is shaded.

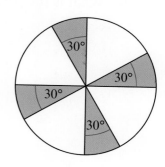

41

34 Find the area of the shaded segment.

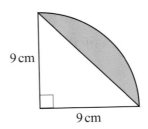

9 cm

9 cm

35 Harriet makes an earring out of wire. The earring is in the shape of a sector of a circle of radius 3.5 cm. Work out the length of wire used in the earring.

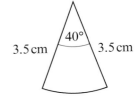

40°

3.5 cm   3.5 cm

36 This shape consists of two sectors of a circle. Both circles have a radius of 18 cm.

What is the area of the shape? Give your answer correct to two significant figures.

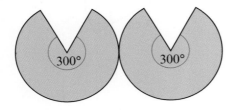

300°   300°

37 The diagram shows a rectangle with a 45° sector of a circle, centre A.

   a What is the area of the shape?

   b What is the perimeter of the shape?

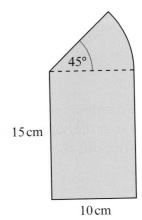

45°

15 cm

10 cm

Shapes

- Finding the perimeter of compound 2–D shapes
- Finding the area of compound 2–D shapes

Keywords

You should know

explanation 1a   explanation 1b

1 Find the perimeter of each of these shapes.

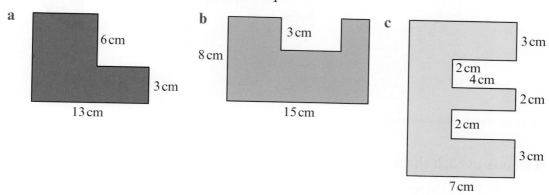

a
6 cm
3 cm
13 cm

b
3 cm
8 cm
15 cm

c
3 cm
2 cm
4 cm
2 cm
2 cm
3 cm
7 cm

2 James has seven tiles. Each tile is a square that has sides of length 1 cm.

The tiles must be laid edge to edge. Here is an example.

a How can James arrange the seven tiles so that the resulting shape has the greatest possible perimeter?

b How can James arrange the seven tiles so that the resulting shape has the smallest possible perimeter?

3 Find the perimeter of each shape.

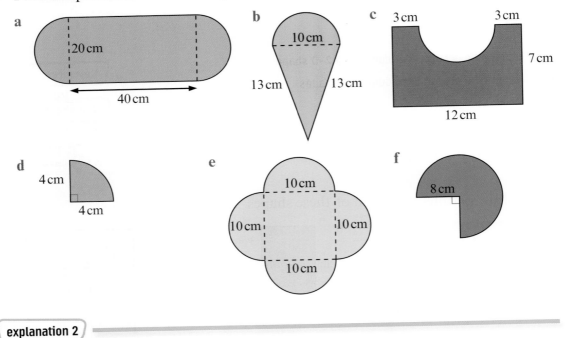

a
20 cm
40 cm

b
10 cm
13 cm   13 cm

c
3 cm   3 cm
7 cm
12 cm

d
4 cm
4 cm

e
10 cm
10 cm   10 cm
10 cm

f
8 cm

explanation 2

4 Look at each shape.

    i Find its perimeter.   **ii** Find its area.

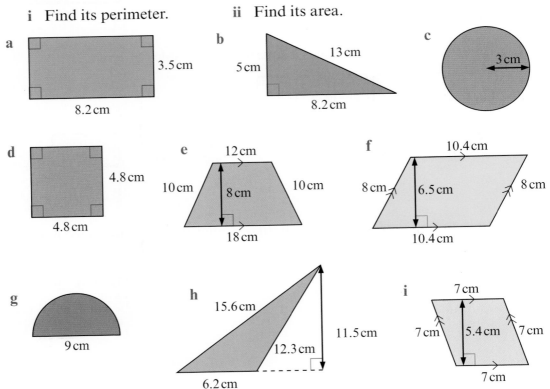

a
3.5 cm
8.2 cm

b
13 cm
5 cm
8.2 cm

c
3 cm

d
4.8 cm
4.8 cm

e
12 cm
10 cm   8 cm   10 cm
18 cm

f
10.4 cm
8 cm   6.5 cm   8 cm
10.4 cm

g
9 cm

h
15.6 cm
11.5 cm
12.3 cm
6.2 cm

i
7 cm
7 cm   5.4 cm   7 cm
7 cm

explanation 3

5 Find the area of each of these shapes.

a
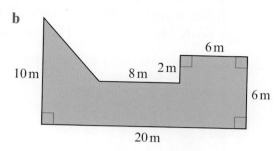

b

c
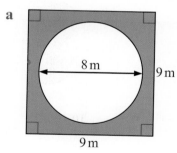

d
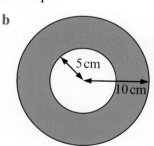

6 Find the area of the shaded part of each shape.

a
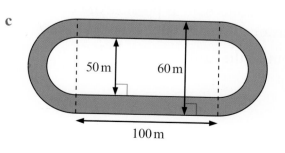

b

c
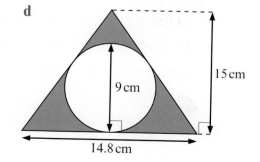

d

45

explanation 4a   explanation 4b

7 Angela has a rug that is in the shape of a rectangle with a semi-circle at either end. She wants to put some tape all the way around the edge of the rug. The tape costs 78p per metre. The shop will only sell the tape in multiples of 0.5 m.

What is the total cost of the tape?

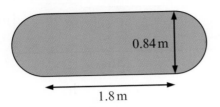

0.84 m

1.8 m

8 A farmer wants to sell his field. He wants more than £24 per square metre.

Ms Howarth offers him a total of £90 000 for the field.

Should the farmer accept this offer?
Give an explanation for your answer.

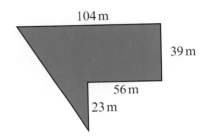

104 m

39 m

56 m

23 m

9 Sunil is painting a wall in his house.

He wants to buy enough paint to cover the wall but not the door.

A small tin of paint will cover $13\,\text{m}^2$.

Will there be enough paint in a small tin?
Give an explanation for your answer.

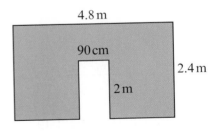

4.8 m

90 cm

2.4 m

2 m

10 Mike wants to cut as many circles of radius 6 cm as possible out of a rectangular piece of card that measures 36 cm by 60 cm.

  a How many circles can he cut out of the card?

  b How much card will be wasted?

Collecting data

- Identifying possible sources of bias and minimising them
- Organising data into grouped frequency tables

Keywords

You should know

explanation 1a   explanation 1b   explanation 1c

1 Decide whether you would collect primary or secondary data for these investigations.

    a The predicted population in the UK over the next 50 years.

    b The hours of sport done each week by pupils in the UK.

    c The style of jeans preferred by pupils in your class.

    d The number of goals scored by Manchester United last season.

    e The number of left-handed pupils in your school.

    f The number of taxis waiting at your nearest railway station at 6 p.m. on a weekday.

2 Write whether the data in each set is discrete or continuous and explain how you decided.

    a Year 9 examination results.

    b The times taken by pupils in your class to run 100 m in a race.

    c The heights of sunflowers in a field.

    d The weights of books in the school bags of pupils in your class.

    e Birthdays of pupils in your class.

    f Distances jumped by the long jump team on sports day.

    g The time taken by your classmates to get to school.

    h The age of each pupil in your class on their last birthday.

3 Say whether the following data is qualitative or quantitative.
If the data is quantitative, state whether it is discrete or continuous
and explain how you decided.

  a The heights of pupils in your year.

  b Favourite sports personalities.

  c The foot lengths of pupils in your year.

  d The shoe sizes of pupils in your year.

  e The colours of the cars in the school car park.

  f Different forms of renewable energy.

  g The names of pupils in your year.

explanation 2a   explanation 2b   explanation 2c   explanation 2d

4 Write whether each of these methods of collecting data might give biased data
and if so why.

  a You want to investigate the favourite computer games of pupils in your
     school. You select a sample of 15 girls and 5 boys in your year.

  b You want to investigate the amount of sleep pupils in your school get.
     You ask pupils in the first two years.

  c You want to investigate the music preferred by young people. You ask young
     people in the High Street between 9 a.m. and 10 a.m. on Saturday morning.

  d The government wants to find pupils' opinions of the range of sport offered
     in schools. It asks pupils from all the schools in Birmingham.

  e A local political party want to know the voting intentions of the adults
     in a town of 50 000 people. It asks 70 people using the shopping mall one
     Monday morning.

5 A television talent show invites people to vote for their favourite singer.
Do you think unbiased results would be obtained from each of these
methods of data collection? Explain your answer for each part.

  a Viewers must phone to vote for their favourite singer.

  b Viewers must text to vote for their favourite singer.

  c Viewers must vote online for their favourite singer.

  d Viewers can choose their own method of voting
     for their favourite singer.

6 Jo wants to test the hypothesis that, in her school, most pupils' favourite type of food is Chinese. Explain how she could select a representative sample of pupils.

7 You plan to survey the pupils in your class to find out about how they spend their free time.

    a Write suitable questions to find the following information, trial them on a small number of respondents and refine them if necessary.

       i Favourite leisure activity

      ii Hours of sport played each week

     iii Hours spent on the internet each week

    b Write two more questions you could include in the survey.

8 This data collection question could be improved.
Write a better version with response boxes for the answers.

> What kind of cool music do you like: Indie, rock, hard rock or metal?

---

explanation 3

---

9 These are the results for 26 pupils in a mathematics examination.

    a Copy the grouped frequency table so the teacher can allocate end-of-term grades. Use it to group the marks.

70	57	55	56	69	66	65	74	78	60	86	67	68
76	91	90	87	88	70	63	70	79	85	68	72	66

    b Which class interval has the greatest number of pupils?

Mark in examination	Tally	Frequency
50–59		
60–69		
70–79		
80–89		
90–99		

10 These are the heights to the nearest centimetre of 24 boys.

133   150   142   139   143   129   158   144   159   135   134   146

150   168   188   136   172   153   142   172   155   138   176   158

a   Copy and complete the grouped frequency table.

Height, h (cm)	Tally	Frequency
$120 \leq h < 130$		
$130 \leq h < 140$		
$140 \leq h < 150$		
$150 \leq h < 160$		
$160 \leq h < 170$		
$170 \leq h < 180$		
$180 \leq h < 190$		

b   Which class interval has the greatest frequency?

11 These were the total numbers of goals scored by the 20 teams in the Premier League in one season.

80   65   71   48   74   20   41   46   66   50

36   36   38   67   55   42   45   34   43   45

a   Put the information into a grouped frequency table choosing suitable class intervals.

These were the total numbers of goals scored by the 20 teams in the Premier League in the previous season.

83   29   47   63   45   38   57   43   32   34

35   52   44   57   52   29   38   37   52   64

b   Put the information into a grouped frequency table using the same class intervals as in part **a**.

c   Which class interval has the greatest frequency for each of your grouped frequency tables?

12 Annie is collecting data for a science project.
She measures the lengths of 30 leaves.
These are the lengths of the leaves measured
in centimetres correct to the nearest millimetre.

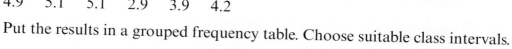

4.3	2.6	3.7	3.2	5.4	3.9
4.2	4.3	5.2	2.8	3.2	3.1
5.3	2.4	2.7	5.3	3.0	3.4
5.3	2.1	2.5	4.7	4.5	3.2
4.9	5.1	5.1	2.9	3.9	4.2

Put the results in a grouped frequency table. Choose suitable class intervals.

13 The data below shows the times, correct to the nearest 0.01 second,
taken to run 100 m by 24 world-class athletes.

9.81	9.85	10.01	10.06	10.12	9.90	9.92	10.06
10.04	9.83	9.78	10.07	9.97	10.13	9.94	9.95
10.10	10.02	10.02	9.87	10.02	10.08	9.95	9.91

Put the results in a grouped frequency table with suitable class intervals.

explanation 4

14 Chris surveyed everyone in her year group.
She displayed her findings in a two-way table.

	Right-handed	Left-handed	Total
Girls	52	7	
Boys	68	17	
Total			

a   How many pupils did she survey?

b   What question do you think she asked?

c   How many boys are there in the year group?

d   How many left-handed pupils are there in the year group?

e   Chris picks a pupil at random.
What is the probability that the pupil will be a left-handed boy?

15 Pupils had to choose between art and music.
This table shows the choices of 52 pupils.
Some of the table has been filled in.

	Art	Music	Total
Boys	5		
Girls	20	7	
Total			

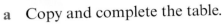

a   Copy and complete the table.

b   What does the figure in pink represent?

c   What does the figure in the blue space represent?

d   What percentage of these pupils chose art?
Give your answer correct to one decimal place.

16 This table shows the type of accommodation 100 people stayed in for their
summer holiday. Some of the table has been filled in.

	Hotel	Camping	Other	Total
July		11	5	20
August	15		8	
September		14		32
Total	28			100

a   What does the figure in orange represent?

b   What does the figure in blue represent?

c   Copy and complete the table.

d   What percentage of people did not stay in a hotel?

17

	Can swim	Cannot swim	Total
Boys			
Girls			
Total			

40 pupils were asked if they can swim or not.

28 of the pupils were girls.

8 boys cannot swim.

23 girls can swim.

Use this information to complete the two-way table.

18 Sahil asked 60 English-speaking adults if they could also speak another language.

6 of the women could speak another language.

28 of the adults were men.

51 adults could not speak another language.

a Design a two-way table to show this information.

b Put the given information into your two-way table.

c Complete your two-way table.

19 Mandy asked 80 pupils in her year if they preferred biology, chemistry or physics.

36 of the pupils were girls.

15 of the boys preferred chemistry.

45 pupils preferred biology.

12 pupils preferred physics.

19 boys preferred biology.

a Design a two-way table to show this information.

b Put the given information into your two-way table.

c Complete your two-way table.

Working with data (1)

- Determining whether two sets of data are correlated
- Drawing a line graph to see how data changes over time
- Understanding which average to use for data
- Representing data in a stem and leaf diagram

Keywords

You should know

explanation 1a | explanation 1b | explanation 1c | explanation 1d | explanation 1e

1 **a** Which of these graphs shows positive correlation? Explain how you know.

   b Which of these graphs shows negative correlation? Explain how you know.

   c Which of these graphs shows no correlation? Explain how you know.

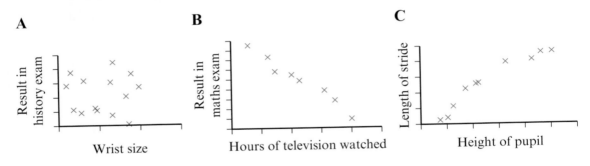

A — Result in history exam / Wrist size

B — Result in maths exam / Hours of television watched

C — Length of stride / Height of pupil

2 What type of correlation would you expect with these data sets?

   a Height of a person and speed at which they can run.

   b Age of a second-hand car and its value.

   c Colour of eyes and distance walked to school.

   d Height and weight of pupils in a school.

   e Shoe size and the length of feet.

   f Time taken to walk to school and the walking speed.

3 Here are the maths and art test scores for 12 pupils.

Maths	75	23	51	67	65	72	18	48	50	34	78	61
Art	27	72	43	31	36	22	65	45	61	75	29	30

a Plot this data as a scatter graph and draw a line of best fit.

b Describe the correlation between the maths and art test scores.

c Use your graph to find the likely maths score of a pupil who scores 50 in their art exam.

4 Ricky wants to buy a secondhand car.
He finds the following prices on the internet for the make and model that he likes.

Age (months)	42	36	36	24	24	18	18	12	12
Price (£)	10000	10300	10400	11400	11300	11700	11800	12000	12200

a Plot this data as a scatter graph and draw a line of best fit.

b What does the scatter graph show about the relationship between the age of the car and its price?

c The local garage is selling a 36-month-old car for £11800.
Plot this point on the scatter graph.
Is it likely to be the same make and model? Explain your answer.

5 This table gives details of the age and the diameter (in years) of the trunk (in inches) of some grapefruit trees in an orchard.

Age	8	7	10	6	7	8	5	9	10	5	6	6
Diameter	6.5	5.7	7.1	5.5	6.2	6.2	4.2	6.6	7.0	4.6	5.0	5.2

a Plot this data as a scatter graph and draw a line of best fit.

b What does the scatter graph show about the relationship between the age of a grapefruit tree and the diameter of its trunk?

c A different tree is 6 years old and the diameter of its trunk is 7.5 inches.
Use the graph to explain why it is likely to be a different variety of tree.

d Another grapefruit tree in this orchard is $7\frac{1}{2}$ years old.
Estimate the diameter of its trunk.

6 If one shape is an enlargement of another, the two shapes are *similar* to each other. The table gives the width and length of some similar rectangles.

Width of rectangle (cm)	4	8	6	11	5	2	10	7
Length of rectangle (cm)	6	12	9	16.5	7.5	3	15	10.5

    a Plot this data as a scatter graph.

    b What does the scatter graph show about the relationship between the width and length of similar rectangles?

    c Draw a line of best fit.

    d Another rectangle has a width of 5 cm and a length of 10 cm.
Plot this point on the scatter graph.
Use the graph to determine whether this rectangle is similar to the others.

7 This scatter graph shows the class results in a mock examination and in the actual paper, five months later.

    a Describe the correlation between the results in the two examinations.

    b In which paper did most pupils do better? Explain your reasoning.

Mock and actual examination results

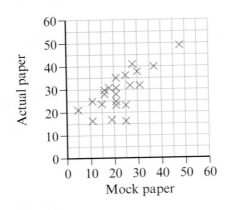

explanation 2

8 These are the monthly sales figures in thousands of pounds from a company.

Jan	Feb	Mar	Apr	May	Jun	Jul	Aug	Sep	Oct	Nov	Dec
54	62	56	59	67	61	58	55	54	50	52	66

a   Draw a line graph to display the data, plotting the months on the horizontal axis and the sales figures on the vertical axis.

b   The company ran an advertising campaign from March to May.

   Do you think the advertising campaign was successful? Explain your answer.

9 The table shows the actual population in the UK and in Italy from 1950 to 2000 and the forecasted population up to the year 2050.

a   Plot the data as two line graphs on the same axes.

b   What are the predicted populations in the UK and Italy in 2015?

c   Calculate the difference between the populations of the two countries for each year shown in the table.

d   In which year will there be the greatest difference in the populations of the two countries?

Year	Population (millions) UK	Population (millions) Italy
1950	50	47
1960	52	50
1970	56	54
1980	56	56
1990	57	57
2000	60	58
2010	61	58
2020	63	57
2030	64	55
2040	64	53
2050	64	50

10 These are the average monthly temperatures in degrees Celsius at London Heathrow and in Moscow. Plot them both as line graphs on the same axes.

	Jan	Feb	Mar	Apr	May	Jun	Jul	Aug	Sep	Oct	Nov	Dec
Heathrow	4	4	6	8	12	15	17	16	14	10	7	5
Moscow	−10	−9	−4	4	12	16	18	16	10	4	−2	−8

    a What is the minimum temperature in Moscow?

    b What is the range of temperatures in Moscow?

    c In which month is there the greatest difference between the temperature at London Heathrow and the temperature in Moscow?

(explanation 3a)   (explanation 3b)   (explanation 3c)

11 Jordan wrote down the number of texts he received each hour one Saturday.

    0 1 6 2 8 5 3 5 6 3 1 1 1 2 4

    Find the range, mean, median and mode of the number of texts he received.

12 Hayley counted the number of emails she received each day over a two-week period.

    9 10 12 9 8 11 6 0 7 12 10 8 12 6

    Find the range, mean (to 1 d.p.), median and mode of the number of emails she received.

13 These are the results in an end-of-term test.

    54 34 22 29 25 20 26 28 19 16 32 31 31 41 25

    a Find the range, mean, median and mode of the marks.

    b An extra mark was added and the mean changed to 28.5.

       What was the new mark?

14 These are the average monthly temperatures in degrees Celsius in the Russian city of Vladivostok.

    −14, −11, −3, 4, 9, 13, 18, 20, 16, 8, −2, −12

    Find the range and mean (to 1 d.p.) of the monthly temperatures.

15 The mean of six numbers is 17. Five numbers are 34, 12, 22, 10 and 15.
What is the sixth number?

16 Five numbers have a mean, mode, median and range of 4.
What are the numbers?

17 Eight pupils each took five examinations in June.
For each pair, write down a set of five possible marks for each pupil.
Which pupil do you think did better?
Is there more than one possible answer?

   a Emily had a range of 80% and Taylor had a range of 20%.

   b Ryan had a mean of 56% and Cally had a mean of 50%.

   c Kofi had a median of 56% and Jessica had a median of 60%.

   d Josh had a mode of 50% and Chelsey had a mode of 84%.

18 The mean score of a group of five cricketers was 34 runs.
When a sixth cricketer joined the group their mean score went down to 32.
Work out the score of the sixth cricketer.

19 Four pupils worked out that their mean score in a test was 67%.
When Anna joined the other four pupils, their mean score went up to 73%.
What was Anna's score in the test?

20 There are five players in each quiz team.
The mean number of points scored per team member in team A was 24.8.
The mean number of points scored per team member in team B was 18.6.
How many more points did team A score than team B?

21 Which of the three averages, mean, median or mode, would be used to find the following?

  a Average age in years and months in a class.

  b Average age in years in Uganda.

  c Average shoe size in a class.

  d Average number of children per woman in the UK.

  e Favourite flavour of ice cream in the school.

  f Average salary in a manufacturing company where the manager has a salary of £5 000 000 per year.

  g Average weight of a baby at birth.

  h Most common colour of car in the staff car park.

22 Max went to four different birthday parties last year. He worked out statistics for the ages of the people attending each party.
What age was each party to celebrate?
Explain how you know.

Part **a** has been completed for you.

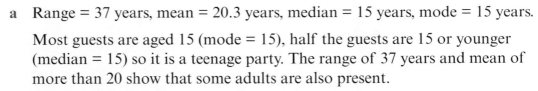

  a Range = 37 years, mean = 20.3 years, median = 15 years, mode = 15 years.

     Most guests are aged 15 (mode = 15), half the guests are 15 or younger (median = 15) so it is a teenage party. The range of 37 years and mean of more than 20 show that some adults are also present.

  b Range = 62 years, mean = 46.7 years, median = 49 years, mode = 50 years.

  c Range = 40 years, mean = 12.2 years, median = 7 years, mode = 6 years.

  d Range = 74 years, mean = 70.3 years, median = 79.5 years, mode = 80 years.

23 Cameron says that the average person has less than two legs. Penny disagrees and says that the average person has two legs. How did they calculate their answers? Which average is more appropriate to use?

24 Students with the top 50% of the marks in an exam pass; the others fail. Which average should the exam board use to set the pass mark?
Explain your answer.

25 A local Scout group consists of 4 adult leaders and 15 scouts who are between the ages of 11 and 14.

    a Write down possible ages for the members of the group.

    b Calculate the mean, median, mode and range of the ages of the members.

    c Which averages represent the age of the group most fairly? Explain your answer.

26 In 2007, the median age in Uganda was 14.9 years and the median age in Japan was 43.5 years.

    a Describe one difference between the populations of Uganda and Japan.

    b Why do you think the median age is low in many African countries?

    c The UK had a median age of 39.6 years in 2007. What problems do you think a high median age may cause the UK in the future?

explanation 4a   explanation 4b

27 Jade surveyed some of her friends to find out how many texts they each received in a week.
She used the results of her survey to draw a stem and leaf diagram.

0	9
1	3 7 8 9 9
2	0 1 4 4 5 8
3	3 4 4 4 4 7 8 9
4	2 5 7

Key
1|3 means 13 texts.

    a How many friends did Jade survey?

    b How many people received 19 texts?

    c What is the modal number of texts?

    d Work out the range.

    e Work out the median number of texts.

28 Roy found the weight of 25 apples. Their weights, correct to the nearest gram, are shown in this stem and leaf diagram.

```
17 | 3 4 6 7
18 | 0 0 0 3 4 5 6 6 7 8 8
19 | 2 3 4 4 6 7 9
20 | 0 1 2
```

Key
17|3 means 173 grams.

a   What is the modal weight of the apples?

b   Find the range of the weights.

c   Work out the median weight.

Roy finds and measures two more apples.
Their weights are 178 g and 201 g.

d   If he adds these results into his stem and leaf diagram will the mode and median be affected? Give an explanation for your answers.

29 In a biology experiment Aaisha measured the length of 20 woodlice.
The measurements, correct to the nearest mm, are given below.

7	18	23	12	29	15	8	9	11	21
19	23	12	7	23	27	28	17	18	27

a   Draw a stem and leaf diagram for these lengths.

b   What is the modal length?

c   Find the range of the lengths.

d   Work out the median length.

30 Annie is collecting data for a science project. She measures the lengths of 30 leaves in centimetres, correct to the nearest millimetre. These are her results.

4.3	2.6	3.7	3.2	5.4	3.9	4.2	4.3	5.2	2.8
3.2	3.1	5.3	2.4	2.7	5.3	3.0	3.4	5.3	2.1
2.5	4.7	4.5	3.2	4.9	5.1	5.1	2.9	3.9	4.2

a   Draw a stem and leaf diagram for these lengths.

b   What is the modal length?

c   Find the range of the lengths.

d   Work out the median length.

31 Anil and Brandon recorded the number of texts they received each day for 21 days. This information is shown in the back-to-back stem and leaf diagram.

					Anil					**Brandon**					
		8	5	4	3	3	2	**0**	7	8	9				
9	7	6	4	2	1	0	0	**1**	1	5	6	6	6	7	8
		6	5	3	2	2	1	**2**	2	4	7	8	9	9	
							7	**3**	0	1	2	1	3		

Key
2|1 means 21 texts.

a Work out the range and median number of texts for each boy.

b Write a short paragraph comparing the numbers of texts that the boys received.

32 Ceri measured the heights of 20 boys and 20 girls correct to the nearest centimetre. Here are her results.

Girls

158	156	152	160	163	159	147	160	162	149
151	167	154	158	148	157	163	165	154	168

Boys

165	172	170	166	175	178	182	167	167	170
177	175	173	169	182	176	174	180	178	181

a Draw a back-to-back stem and leaf diagram to display the data.

b What does the shape of the diagram suggest?

c Find the range and median heights for the boys and for the girls.

d Write a short paragraph comparing the heights of the girls and the heights of the boys.

Factors and powers

- Writing a number as a product of primes
- Writing fractions and square and cube roots using index notation
- Calculating approximate values for square roots and cube roots
- Simplifying expressions that involve surds

Keywords

You should know

explanation 1a   explanation 1b

1 Which of the numbers in the box is *not* a factor of the given number?

a 120

| 24 | 12 |
| 4 | 48 |

b 252

| 9 | 53 |
| 21 | 126 |

2 Which of the numbers in the box is *not* a multiple of the given number?

a 12

| 24 | 84 |
| 158 | 228 |

b 15

| 45 | 90 |
| 180 | 365 |

3 Find the first number greater than 25 that is a multiple of 6 *and* a factor of 96.

4 For each list, write down the numbers that are *not* prime numbers.

a 1, 3, 7, 17, 27, 31, 33, 47, 51, 67   **b** 11, 28, 43, 53, 77, 83, 93, 101, 153, 179

5 Why is 2 the only even number that is a prime number?

6 Find values for these without using a calculator.

a 4^3 **b** -6^2 **c** $(-6)^2$ **d** 5^3

e $(-3)^4$ **f** 5×2^2 **g** $-2^3 \times 3^2$ **h** $(-7)^2 \times 2$

explanation 2a   explanation 2b   explanation 2c

7 Colin started to find 72 as the product of prime factors using a table.

2	72
2	36
2	18

   a Copy and complete the table.

   b Write 72 as a product of prime factors using index notation.

8 Use a factor tree or a table to express each number as a product of primes. Write the product of prime factors using index notation.

   a 84   **b** 252   **c** 450   **d** 3168

9 Find the HCF of each pair of numbers.

   a 32 and 144   **b** 45 and 210   **c** 28 and 350   **d** 84 and 252

10 Find the LCM of each pair of numbers.

   a 12 and 18   **b** 30 and 75   **c** 15 and 24   **d** 84 and 252

11 Two numbers have a HCF of 8 and a LCM of 480.

   What might they be? Find all possible answers.

12 Suzie used a Venn diagram to find the HCF of two algebraic expressions, $4xyz$ and $2ax$.

   HCF $= 2x$

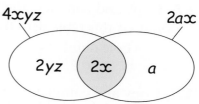

   Use Venn diagrams to find the HCFs of these expressions.

   a $2xy$ and $6y$ **b** $4ab$ and $8bc$

   c $5abc$ and $10b^2$ **d** $12xy^2z$ and $4x^2y$

explanation 3

13 Use index laws to multiply these expressions. Leave your answers in index form.

   a $4^4 \times 4^5$ **b** $6^2 \times 6^4$ **c** $3^5 \times 3^7$ **d** $5^5 \times 5^6$

   e $8^3 \times 8^6$ **f** $3^3 \times 3^0$ **g** $3^5 \times 5^2 \times 3^2$ **h** $3^2 \times 4^3 \times 3^2 \times 4^4$

14 Use index laws to divide these expressions. Leave your answers in index form.

a $4^8 \div 4^5$ b $7^7 \div 7^4$ c $9^5 \div 9^2$ d $5^5 \div 5^3$

e $\dfrac{3^3}{3^0}$ f $\dfrac{3^9}{3^2}$ g $2^9 \div 2^2 \div 2^5$ h $3^{12} \div 3^2 \div 3^4$

15 Use index laws to simplify these.

Leave your answers in index form.

a $2^5 \times 2^4 \div 2^3$ b $5^4 \div 5^3 \times 5^6$ c $10^7 \times 10^8 \div 10^6$

d $5^6 \times 3^4 \div 5^4$ e $7^5 \times 6^5 \times 7^2 \div 6^4$ f $\dfrac{3^7 \div 4^5 \times 4^6}{3^3}$

16 To simplify $(3^2)^3$ Jaydeep wrote $3^2 \times 3^2 \times 3^2 = 3^6$.

a Simplify these powers in a similar way.

i $(4^3)^2$ ii $(5^3)^3$ iii $(4^3)^4$ iv $(3^4)^2$

b What relationship do you notice between the powers in the question and the answer?

c Copy and complete this law. $(a^n)^m = a^{m\,\square\,n}$

explanation 4a   explanation 4b   explanation 4c

17 Copy and complete the bottom row of this table with fractions or whole numbers.

5^{-3}	5^{-2}	5^{-1}	5^0	5^1	5^2	5^3
						125

18 Copy and complete these.

a $\dfrac{1}{6^2} = 6^{\square}$ b $4^{-5} = \dfrac{1}{4^{\square}}$ c $\dfrac{1}{25} = \dfrac{1}{5^{\square}} = 5^{\square}$ d $\dfrac{1}{81} = 9^{\square}$

19 Without using a calculator write these without powers.

a 2^{-3} b 3^{-2} c 5^{-1} d 4^{-2} e 6^{-2} f 5^{-3}

20 Write these fractions using negative powers.

a $\dfrac{1}{2^2}$ b $\dfrac{1}{4^5}$ c $\dfrac{1}{6^3}$ d $\dfrac{1}{4^4}$

e $\dfrac{1}{4}$ f $\dfrac{1}{36}$ g $\dfrac{1}{27}$ h $\dfrac{1}{16}$

For parts **e** to **h** first write the denominator as a power of another number.

21 Copy and complete these.

    a $\sqrt{36} = 36^{\square}$ **b** $\sqrt{28} = 28^{\square}$ **c** $\sqrt{100} = 100^{\square}$

    d $\sqrt[3]{64} = 64^{\square}$ **e** $\sqrt[3]{125} = 125^{\square}$

22 Without using a calculator find these.

    a $4^{\frac{1}{2}}$ **b** $16^{\frac{1}{2}}$ **c** $9^{\frac{1}{2}}$ **d** $100^{\frac{1}{2}}$ **e** $49^{\frac{1}{2}}$

    f $81^{\frac{1}{2}}$ **g** $144^{\frac{1}{2}}$ **h** $8^{\frac{1}{3}}$ **i** $27^{\frac{1}{3}}$ **j** $125^{\frac{1}{3}}$

> explanation 5a   explanation 5b

23 Find these positive and negative roots.

    a $\pm\sqrt{25}$ **b** $\pm\sqrt{121}$ **c** $\pm\sqrt{144}$ **d** $\pm\sqrt{400}$ **e** $\pm\sqrt{10\,000}$

24 Find the answers to these. Use a calculator if necessary.

    a $\sqrt[3]{27}$ **b** $\sqrt[3]{-27}$ **c** $\sqrt[3]{-125}$ **d** $\sqrt[3]{64}$ **e** $\sqrt[3]{-216}$

25 Which of these are true?

    A $\sqrt{9} + \sqrt{25} = \sqrt{9 + 25}$ **B** $\sqrt{25} - \sqrt{9} = \sqrt{25 - 9}$

    C $\sqrt{9} \times \sqrt{25} = \sqrt{9 \times 25}$ **D** $\sqrt{9} \div \sqrt{4} = \sqrt{9 \div 4}$

26 The square root of some numbers can be can be found by factorising.

    Find these square roots by factorising.

    a $\sqrt{400}$ **b** $\sqrt{256}$ **c** $\sqrt{324}$ **d** $\sqrt{441}$ **e** $\sqrt{484}$

$$\begin{aligned} \sqrt{225} &= \sqrt{9 \times 25} \\ &= \sqrt{9} \times \sqrt{25} \\ &= 3 \times 5 \\ &= 15 \end{aligned}$$

27 **a** Copy and complete these statements about $\sqrt{42}$.

        i 42 lies between the consecutive square numbers $\square$ and $\square$.

        ii This can be written as $\square < 42 < \square$.

        iii So $6 < \sqrt{42} < \square$.

    b Find an approximate value for $\sqrt{42}$ to two decimal places.

        Write your answer in the form $a < \sqrt{42} < b$.

        Do not use the $\sqrt{}$ key on your calculator.

28 Find approximations for these to two decimal places.

    a $\sqrt{8}$ **b** $\sqrt{32}$ **c** $\sqrt{90}$ **d** $\sqrt{24}$

> explanation 6a   explanation 6b

29 Which of these are surds? Use a calculator if necessary.

    a $\sqrt{4}$ **b** $\sqrt{7}$ **c** $\sqrt{17}$ **d** $\sqrt{25}$

    e $\sqrt{58}$ **f** $\sqrt{144}$ **g** $\sqrt{20.25}$ **h** $\sqrt{5.68}$

    i $\sqrt{4.84}$ **j** $\sqrt{70.56}$ **k** $\sqrt{110.25}$ **l** $\sqrt{218.12}$

30 Find an exact answer or simplified surd form for each of these.

    a $\sqrt{7} \times \sqrt{7}$ **b** $\sqrt{3} \times \sqrt{3} \times \sqrt{3}$ **c** $\sqrt{9} \times \sqrt{9}$

    d $\sqrt{13} \times \sqrt{13} \times \sqrt{13}$ **e** $\sqrt{8} \times \sqrt{8}$ **f** $\sqrt{20} \times \sqrt{20}$

    g $\sqrt{4} \times \sqrt{4} \times \sqrt{4} \times \sqrt{4}$ **h** $\sqrt{4} \times \sqrt{4} \times \sqrt{4} \times \sqrt{4} \times \sqrt{4}$ **i** $\sqrt{3} \times \sqrt{3} \times \sqrt{3}$

31 What is the exact area of each square?

    a   **b**    **c**

$\sqrt{1}$ cm $\sqrt{27}$ cm $\sqrt{2}$ cm

32 What is the length of one side of a square with these areas?

    Where appropriate leave answers in surd form.

    a $81\,\text{cm}^2$ **b** $28\,\text{cm}^2$ **c** $50\,\text{m}^2$ **d** $56.25\,\text{mm}^2$

33 Find an exact answer for these. Do not use a calculator.

    a $\sqrt{4} \times \sqrt{9}$ **b** $\sqrt{32} \times \sqrt{2}$ **c** $\sqrt{2} \times \sqrt{50}$

    d $\sqrt{3} \times \sqrt{27}$ **e** $\sqrt{8} \times \sqrt{18}$ **f** $\sqrt{10} \times \sqrt{2} \times \sqrt{5}$

    g $\sqrt{5} \times \sqrt{10} \times \sqrt{8}$ **h** $\sqrt{5} \times \sqrt{45}$ **i** $\sqrt{5} \times \sqrt{10} \times \sqrt{18}$

    j $\sqrt{5} \times \sqrt{10} \times \sqrt{50}$ **k** $\sqrt{8} \times \sqrt{10} \times \sqrt{20}$ **l** $\sqrt{5} \times \sqrt{125}$

Adding and subtracting fractions

- Adding and subtracting fractions using efficient methods
- Understanding that a recurring decimal is an exact fraction
- Converting a recurring decimal to a fraction

Keywords

You should know

explanation 1a   explanation 1b

1 Work these out.

a $\dfrac{3}{5} + \dfrac{4}{5}$

b $\dfrac{7}{12} + \dfrac{5}{12}$

c $\dfrac{15}{21} - \dfrac{8}{21}$

d $\dfrac{17}{20} + \dfrac{7}{20} - \dfrac{13}{20}$

2 Work these out.

a $\dfrac{3}{8} + \dfrac{1}{4}$

b $\dfrac{5}{7} - \dfrac{3}{14}$

c $\dfrac{11}{12} - \dfrac{1}{6}$

d $\dfrac{3}{5} + \dfrac{7}{10}$

e $\dfrac{5}{6} - \dfrac{1}{3}$

f $\dfrac{11}{18} + \dfrac{1}{9}$

g $\dfrac{17}{20} - \dfrac{2}{5}$

h $\dfrac{3}{5} + \dfrac{7}{25}$

i $\dfrac{29}{30} - \dfrac{5}{6} + \dfrac{1}{5}$

j $\dfrac{11}{24} + \dfrac{3}{8} - \dfrac{1}{4}$

k $\dfrac{2}{9} + \dfrac{1}{6} - \dfrac{1}{18}$

l $\dfrac{7}{20} + \dfrac{4}{5} - \dfrac{7}{10}$

3 Find the answers to these.

a $\dfrac{1}{4} + \dfrac{2}{3}$

b $\dfrac{5}{6} - \dfrac{1}{5}$

c $\dfrac{1}{10} + \dfrac{3}{4}$

d $\dfrac{6}{7} - \dfrac{2}{3}$

e $\dfrac{3}{8} + \dfrac{2}{5}$

f $\dfrac{4}{5} + \dfrac{3}{7}$

g $\dfrac{7}{9} - \dfrac{4}{7}$

h $\dfrac{3}{11} + \dfrac{6}{7}$

i $\dfrac{9}{10} - \dfrac{1}{5} - \dfrac{1}{2}$

j $\dfrac{8}{9} + \dfrac{2}{3} - \dfrac{11}{18}$

k $\dfrac{1}{8} + \dfrac{5}{6} - \dfrac{2}{3}$

l $\dfrac{6}{7} - \dfrac{1}{2} + \dfrac{1}{3}$

4 Jack's football team won $\dfrac{2}{5}$ of their games and drew $\dfrac{1}{4}$ of them.
How many did they lose?

5 These are unit fraction cards.

$\frac{1}{2}$ $\frac{1}{3}$ $\frac{1}{4}$ $\frac{1}{5}$

a Which two cards make this true?   ☐ + ☐ = $\frac{7}{12}$

b Which two cards make this true?   ☐ − ☐ = $\frac{1}{6}$

c Which three cards make this true?   ☐ + ☐ − ☐ = $\frac{7}{12}$

d Which three cards make the biggest answer for this?

☐ + ☐ − ☐ = ☐

Write out the calculation and answer.

6 In a bag of coloured counters $\frac{3}{16}$ are red, $\frac{1}{4}$ green and $\frac{5}{12}$ are yellow.

The rest are blue.

What fraction are blue?

7 $1 = \frac{1}{3} + \frac{4}{6}$

1 is written as the sum of two fractions.

Each of the digits in the fractions is different.

Find four other ways of writing 1 using two fractions and four different digits.

8 Write two questions that would give the answer $\frac{5}{12}$ for each calculation.

a adding two fractions   **b** subtracting two fractions

explanation 2a   explanation 2b

9 Work these out.

a $1\frac{1}{2} + 3\frac{1}{4}$

b $2\frac{3}{5} + 1\frac{1}{10}$

c $3\frac{5}{6} - 1\frac{2}{3}$

d $2\frac{3}{10} + 1\frac{1}{5}$

e $4\frac{1}{2} - 2\frac{1}{6}$

f $5\frac{7}{12} - 3\frac{1}{2}$

g $7\frac{17}{20} + 1\frac{3}{10}$

h $5\frac{3}{8} + 7\frac{1}{2}$

i $4\frac{1}{6} - 1\frac{2}{3}$

j $5\frac{7}{9} + 2\frac{2}{3}$

k $3\frac{5}{12} - 1\frac{5}{6}$

l $3\frac{1}{4} + 6\frac{11}{12}$

10 Find the answers to these.

a $2\frac{3}{4} - 1\frac{2}{5}$

b $3\frac{2}{5} + 1\frac{1}{2}$

c $3\frac{2}{3} - 1\frac{1}{4}$

d $4\frac{4}{7} - 2\frac{3}{4}$

e $5\frac{3}{8} + 2\frac{3}{5}$

f $2\frac{1}{6} - 1\frac{3}{4}$

g $4\frac{3}{10} + 3\frac{3}{8}$

h $4\frac{5}{6} - 2\frac{8}{9}$

i $1\frac{3}{5} + 2\frac{1}{2} + \frac{7}{10}$

j $4\frac{5}{6} - \frac{11}{12} + 1\frac{1}{3}$

k $5\frac{11}{20} + 2\frac{2}{5} - 1\frac{3}{4} + 4\frac{3}{10}$

11 Zoe did $3\frac{1}{2}$ hours homework on Saturday and $2\frac{3}{5}$ hours on Sunday.

How long did she spend doing homework over the weekend?

12 Jason and Simon were preparing advertising brochures for posting.
Jason used $5\frac{5}{12}$ boxes of brochures and Simon used $4\frac{2}{3}$ boxes.

How many more boxes did Jason use?

13 Find the perimeter of each shape.

a

$2\frac{1}{5}$ inches $2\frac{1}{5}$ inches

$1\frac{7}{8}$ inches

b

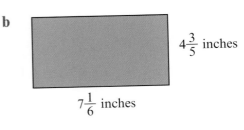

$4\frac{3}{5}$ inches

$7\frac{1}{6}$ inches

c

$5\frac{1}{6}$ feet

$7\frac{7}{8}$ feet

$2\frac{3}{4}$ feet

3 feet

14 Find the next term in each sequence.

a $\frac{3}{4}, 1\frac{5}{8}, 2\frac{1}{2}, 3\frac{3}{8}, \ldots$

b $2\frac{2}{3}, 4\frac{5}{6}, 7, 9\frac{1}{6}, \ldots$

15 What number is exactly halfway between $1\frac{2}{3}$ and $2\frac{1}{12}$?

16 Copy and complete this magic square.

$1\frac{1}{3}$		$4\frac{1}{3}$
	$3\frac{7}{12}$	
		$5\frac{5}{6}$

The numbers in each row, column and diagonal of a magic square have the same total.

17 Write two questions that would give the answer $5\frac{3}{8}$ for each calculation.

a adding two mixed numbers

b subtracting two mixed numbers

18 When I printed a text document it covered $12\frac{3}{4}$ pages of A4 paper.

When I changed the font size the document covered only $10\frac{4}{5}$ pages.

How much less space does the document now take?

19 Sally had 12 empty jam jars.

She filled $9\frac{5}{6}$ of the jars with strawberry jam.

$3\frac{1}{4}$ jars of jam were eaten.

What fraction of the jars are now empty?

---

explanation 3a   explanation 3b   explanation 3c

20 James said that $\frac{3}{20}$ could be written as a terminating decimal because the prime factors of 20 are 2 and 5.

a   Is James correct? Explain.

b   Why will a fraction convert to a terminating decimal if its denominator only has prime factors of 2 and 5?

21 Without using your calculator, state which of these fractions are terminating decimals.

How do you know?

a $\frac{3}{8}$ b $\frac{13}{16}$ c $\frac{6}{9}$ d $\frac{7}{20}$ e $\frac{13}{15}$

f $\frac{11}{25}$ g $\frac{19}{100}$ h $\frac{7}{12}$ i $\frac{213}{500}$ j $\frac{21}{30}$

22 Write these fractions as decimals. Use your calculator where necessary.

a $\frac{7}{20}$ b $\frac{1}{8}$ c $\frac{5}{7}$ d $\frac{2}{3}$ e $\frac{12}{25}$

f $\frac{21}{50}$ g $\frac{23}{36}$ h $\frac{18}{30}$ i $\frac{22}{30}$ j $\frac{13}{18}$

23 Write each decimal as a fraction in its lowest terms.

a   0.4   b   0.375   c   0.38   d   0.275

e   0.3333...   f   0.6666...   g   0.2222...   h   0.9999...

24 Copy and complete these workings to find the fraction equal to each decimal.

a $0.\dot{6}\dot{7}$ Let $x = 0.676\,767...$ and $100x = 67.676\,767...$

$$100x = 67.676\,767...$$
$$-\quad x = 0.676\,767...$$
$$\overline{}$$
$$99x = \underline{}$$
$$x = \underline{}$$

b $0.4\dot{5}\dot{6}$ Let $10x = 4.565\,656...$ and $1000x = 456.565\,656...$

$$1000x = 456.5656...$$
$$-\quad 10x = 4.5656...$$
$$\overline{}$$
$$990x = \underline{}$$
$$x = \underline{}$$

c $0.30\dot{4}\dot{5}$ Let $100x = 30.454545...$ and $10\,000x = 3045.454\,545...$

$$10\,000x = 3045.454\,545...$$
$$-\quad 100x = 30.454\,545...$$
$$\overline{}$$
$$9900x = \underline{}$$
$$x = \underline{}$$

d In part **a** values of x and $100x$ are used, in part **b** $10x$ and $1000x$ and in part **c** $100x$ and $10\,000x$. Explain why these numbers were chosen.

25 What multiples of x would you use to convert these recurring decimals into fractions?

Do not work out the fractions.

a $0.5\dot{8}$ **b** $0.6\dot{4}\dot{3}$ **c** $0.8\dot{4}0\dot{5}$

26 Convert these recurring decimals into fractions.

a $0.\dot{3}\dot{4}$ **b** $0.\dot{8}\dot{1}$ **c** $0.7\dot{2}\dot{3}$

d $0.5\dot{1}\dot{9}$ **e** $0.2\dot{4}\dot{3}\dot{7}$ **f** $0.\dot{2}13\dot{4}$

Multiplying and dividing fractions

- Multiplying fractions by fractions
- Dividing fractions by fractions using the inverse
- Finding fractions of quantities

Keywords

You should know

explanation 1a   explanation 1b

1 Work these out.

a $\dfrac{2}{3} \times \dfrac{4}{5}$

b $\dfrac{2}{7} \times \dfrac{3}{8}$

c $\dfrac{12}{25} \times \dfrac{10}{11}$

d $\dfrac{9}{15} \times \dfrac{5}{6}$

e $\dfrac{8}{11} \times \dfrac{33}{40}$

f $\dfrac{9}{10} \times \dfrac{15}{36}$

g $\dfrac{32}{45} \times \dfrac{18}{25}$

h $\dfrac{6}{7} \times \dfrac{21}{30} \times \dfrac{2}{3}$

2 Kevin think that three eighths of one fifth is the same as three fifths of one eighth. Is he correct?

3 Three quarters of Sarah's friends have brown hair.

Two fifths of those with brown hair also have blue eyes.

a What fraction of Sarah's friends have brown hair and blue eyes?

b What is the smallest number of friends that Sarah could have?

4 Find three different pairs of fractions that multiply to give $\dfrac{5}{12}$.

5 Work these out.

a $1\dfrac{3}{4} \times \dfrac{5}{8}$

b $2\dfrac{2}{3} \times 1\dfrac{1}{5}$

c $2\dfrac{3}{5} \times 2\dfrac{1}{3}$

d $3\dfrac{1}{3} \times 1\dfrac{3}{7}$

e $4\dfrac{1}{6} \times 3\dfrac{4}{5}$

f $5 \times 6\dfrac{7}{8}$

g $5\dfrac{11}{12} \times 24$

h $2\dfrac{5}{6} \times 4\dfrac{2}{7}$

i $5\dfrac{3}{8} \times 3\dfrac{1}{5}$

j $3\dfrac{7}{10} \times 3\dfrac{2}{6}$

k $1\dfrac{1}{4} \times 2\dfrac{1}{3} \times 3\dfrac{1}{2}$

l $2\dfrac{1}{5} \times 3\dfrac{3}{4} \times 1\dfrac{3}{22}$

6 Work these out. Remember to use BIDMAS.

a $\left(1\dfrac{3}{7}\right)^2$

b $\left(1\dfrac{3}{4}\right)^3$

c $\dfrac{1}{4}\left(2 - \dfrac{1}{3}\right)$

d $\dfrac{2}{3}\left(\dfrac{2}{3} + 1\dfrac{1}{6}\right)$

7 Calculate the areas of these photo frames.

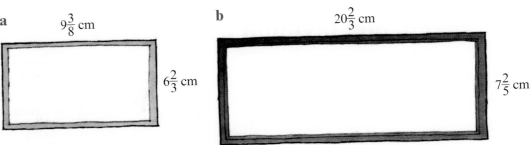

a $9\frac{3}{8}$ cm

$6\frac{2}{3}$ cm

b $20\frac{2}{3}$ cm

$7\frac{2}{5}$ cm

8 Jenny walks at $4\frac{1}{3}$ km/h and Kim jogs at $7\frac{1}{5}$ km/h.

They leave at the same time from the same place and go for a walk or jog.

a   How far apart will they be after $\frac{3}{4}$ hour if they both travelled in the same direction?

b   How far apart will they be after $\frac{3}{4}$ hour if they travelled in opposite directions?

explanation 2a   explanation 2b   explanation 2c

9 Work these out.

a $18 \div \frac{1}{3}$

b $\frac{3}{4} \div 8$

c $72 \div \frac{5}{6}$

d $\frac{7}{12} \div 21$

e $\frac{7}{15} \div \frac{5}{6}$

f $\frac{9}{25} \div \frac{15}{21}$

g $\frac{9}{22} \div \frac{4}{11}$

h $\frac{7}{8} \div \frac{6}{7}$

i $\frac{14}{15} \div \frac{21}{40}$

j $\frac{25}{32} \div \frac{5}{48}$

k $\frac{56}{81} \div \frac{14}{54}$

l $\frac{85}{132} \div \frac{25}{48}$

10 A ferry completes a crossing of an inlet in $\frac{2}{3}$ hour.

What is the largest number of crossings the ferry could make in 15 hours?

11 Indira had $\frac{17}{20}$ kg of apples.

She divided the apples into bags weighing $\frac{3}{10}$ kg.

How many bags of apples did she get?

12   Find three different pairs of fractions that give the answer $\frac{3}{5}$ when one is divided by the other.

13   Work these out.

   a $2\frac{1}{2} \div \frac{3}{4}$
   b $2\frac{2}{3} \div \frac{4}{5}$
   c $5\frac{5}{12} \div \frac{10}{21}$
   d $1\frac{7}{8} \div 1\frac{1}{4}$

   e $6\frac{4}{9} \div 2\frac{2}{3}$
   f $3\frac{1}{7} \div 1\frac{2}{9}$
   g $2\frac{1}{2} \div 4\frac{3}{5}$
   h $3\frac{4}{5} \div 3\frac{1}{3}$

   i $7\frac{3}{5} \div 1\frac{2}{10}$
   j $5\frac{7}{8} \div 1\frac{1}{4}$
   k $6\frac{5}{12} \div 1\frac{1}{10}$
   l $3\frac{4}{7} \div 3\frac{3}{14}$

14   The area of a rectangular paved patio is $4\frac{4}{5}$ square metres.

   It is $2\frac{2}{3}$ metres long.

   How wide is the patio?

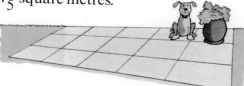

15   It takes $2\frac{3}{4}$ metres of fabric to make a dress.

   How many dresses can be made from $12\frac{7}{8}$ metres of fabric?

16   Work these out.

   a $\frac{3}{4} \times \frac{7}{10} \div \frac{1}{5}$
   b $\frac{6}{15} \div \frac{3}{10} \times \frac{12}{25}$
   c $1\frac{3}{4} \times 2\frac{1}{2} \div \frac{5}{6}$
   d $1\frac{2}{3} \times \frac{9}{10} \div 2\frac{1}{6}$

17   Which is larger, $\frac{4}{7} \times 1\frac{1}{6}$ or $3\frac{3}{4} \div 4\frac{3}{8}$?

18   A photocopier can enlarge printed material by a factor of $1\frac{9}{20}$.

   A picture measuring $12\frac{1}{2}$ inches by $10\frac{4}{5}$ inches is enlarged.

   What is the length of each side of the enlarged picture?

19 What is the largest and smallest answer that you can make using two of the numbers from the box?

You can either multiply or divide the numbers.

$$\frac{3}{5} \qquad 1\frac{3}{4}$$
$$\frac{1}{10} \qquad 3\frac{5}{6}$$
$$\frac{1}{8} \qquad 2\frac{2}{3}$$

explanation 3a   explanation 3b

20 Find these amounts.

a $\frac{4}{5}$ of 35

b $\frac{3}{8}$ of 64

c $\frac{7}{11}$ of 110

d $\frac{3}{5}$ of 750

e $\frac{11}{15}$ of 45

f $\frac{9}{20}$ of 8000

g $\frac{11}{25}$ of 150 m

h $\frac{14}{60}$ of 1200 g

i $\frac{19}{40}$ of £280

j $\frac{35}{36}$ of 144 ml

k $\frac{39}{44}$ of 220 litres

l $\frac{23}{27}$ of £108

21 Suriya earned £360 last week. She saves $\frac{2}{9}$ of her salary every week.

How much did she save last week?

22 A day on Jupiter is about $\frac{3}{8}$ of a day on Earth.

Approximately how many hours are there in a Jupiter day?

23 This recipe for lemon pepper chicken serves 24 people.

1 kg = 1000 g
1 litre = 1000 ml

Lemon Pepper Chicken

3 kg chicken

1.68 kg green pepper

144 g butter

3.6 litres chicken stock

1.2 kg chopped onion

12 lemons

240 g flour

6 handfuls of fresh herbs

a   How much of each ingredient will you need for 16 people?

b   How much of each ingredient will you need for 5 people?

24 A school had 1080 pupils.

$\frac{5}{12}$ were European and $\frac{2}{9}$ were of African descent.

How many pupils were neither European nor of African descent?

25 A test took 180 minutes.

Joe took $\frac{1}{6}$ of the time to answer the multiple-choice section,

$\frac{1}{4}$ for the problem-solving section, $\frac{3}{8}$ for the essay and

the rest for the short answers.

How long did Joe spend on each section?

26 Millie worked a total of 35 hours last week. She did not work on Tuesday.

One quarter of her hours were worked on Monday, $\frac{1}{6}$ on Wednesday and $\frac{5}{12}$ at the weekend.

How many hours and minutes in total did Millie work on the other days of the week?

27 Bob cut $\frac{1}{8}$ off the end of a 50 m length of rope.

a How long was this piece of rope in metres?

b How long was the piece of rope in centimetres?

28 Three friends all left London at the same time.

	Liverpool	Norwich	Portsmouth
London to	280 km	160 km	100 km

After one hour,

Jimmy had travelled $\frac{3}{8}$ of the way to Norwich,

Carla had travelled $\frac{2}{7}$ of the way to Liverpool,

Lewis travelled $\frac{3}{5}$ of the way to Portsmouth.

Who had travelled the furthest?

Algebra A2.1

Algebraic fractions

- Finding and identifying equivalent algebraic fractions
- Adding and subtracting algebraic fractions

Keywords

You should know

explanation 1a   explanation 1b

1 Find three number fractions that are equivalent to each of these fractions.

    a $\dfrac{1}{3}$ **b** $\dfrac{2}{5}$ **c** $\dfrac{4}{5}$ **d** $\dfrac{7}{8}$ **e** $\dfrac{9}{10}$

2 In each group of fractions, find the odd one out.

    a $\dfrac{1}{2}, \dfrac{9}{16}, \dfrac{19}{38}, \dfrac{7}{14}, \dfrac{56}{112}$ **b** $\dfrac{3}{5}, \dfrac{9}{15}, \dfrac{42}{75}, \dfrac{21}{35}, \dfrac{180}{300}$ **c** $\dfrac{4}{7}, \dfrac{46}{84}, \dfrac{36}{63}, \dfrac{12}{21}, \dfrac{28}{49}$

3 Find a pair of equivalent fractions in each group.

    a $\dfrac{a}{3}, \dfrac{4a}{3}, \dfrac{4a}{12}$ **b** $\dfrac{x}{8}, \dfrac{xy}{8}, \dfrac{3x}{24}$ **c** $\dfrac{2b}{3}, \dfrac{6b}{12}, \dfrac{2b}{4}$ **d** $\dfrac{ab}{4}, \dfrac{a+b}{4}, \dfrac{2(a+b)}{8}$

4 a Match each fraction in the left-hand column with an equivalent fraction from the right-hand column.

   b Write three other pairs of equivalent algebraic fractions.

$\dfrac{a}{2}$	$\dfrac{10(a+1)}{20}$
$\dfrac{2(a+1)}{4}$	$\dfrac{a^2}{2a}$
$\dfrac{2a}{8}$	$\dfrac{10(a+3)}{20}$
$\dfrac{2a+3}{2}$	$\dfrac{10a}{30}$
$\dfrac{a}{3}$	$\dfrac{2(2a+3)}{4}$
$\dfrac{2(a+3)}{4}$	$\dfrac{4a}{16}$

5 Copy these and fill in the missing expressions.

a $\dfrac{2m}{4} = \dfrac{\square}{12}$

b $\dfrac{3a+1}{4} = \dfrac{\square}{8}$

c $\dfrac{5p-4}{5} = \dfrac{\square}{20}$

d $\dfrac{3x+y}{6} = \dfrac{\square}{18}$

e $\dfrac{5x-3}{4} = \dfrac{\square}{12}$

f $\dfrac{7a+4}{9} = \dfrac{\square}{18}$

g $\dfrac{2y+3}{y} = \dfrac{\square}{2y}$

h $\dfrac{4-x}{2x} = \dfrac{\square}{6x}$

i $\dfrac{2a+5}{3} = \dfrac{\square}{9a}$

---

explanation 2

---

6 Simplify these fractions by cancelling common numeric factors.

a $\dfrac{6y}{3}$

b $\dfrac{4c}{2}$

c $\dfrac{2b}{8}$

d $\dfrac{10f}{25}$

e $\dfrac{16m^2}{4}$

f $\dfrac{7x^2}{56}$

g $\dfrac{3ab}{12}$

h $\dfrac{24xy}{16}$

7 Simplify these fractions by cancelling all common factors.

a $\dfrac{3y}{yz}$

b $\dfrac{c}{cd}$

c $\dfrac{5ef}{f}$

d $\dfrac{gh}{g^2}$

e $\dfrac{4x}{xy}$

f $\dfrac{s}{s^2}$

g $\dfrac{pr}{2prq}$

h $\dfrac{8rst}{2st}$

8 Match each expression in the top row with a simplified form from the bottom row.

$\dfrac{10x^2}{5xy}$ $\dfrac{10x}{5x^2y}$ $\dfrac{5x^2}{10xy}$ $\dfrac{5x}{10x^2y}$ $\dfrac{5x}{10xy^2}$ $\dfrac{10x}{5xy^2}$

$\dfrac{2}{y^2}$ $\dfrac{1}{2y^2}$ $\dfrac{2x}{y}$ $\dfrac{1}{2xy}$ $\dfrac{2}{xy}$ $\dfrac{x}{2y}$

---

explanation 3

---

9 Simplify each fraction by factorising and then cancelling common factors.

a $\dfrac{16+4m}{4}$

b $\dfrac{7x+21}{14}$

c $\dfrac{2m^2+4}{6}$

d $\dfrac{10}{5y+15}$

e $\dfrac{3x-9}{6}$

f $\dfrac{12}{6-3y}$

g $\dfrac{30}{25b+15}$

h $\dfrac{7x+21}{14x}$

10 Simplify each fraction by factorising and then cancelling common factors.

a $\dfrac{x^2 + 3x}{x}$

b $\dfrac{2m^2 - 8m}{m}$

c $\dfrac{7h^2 - 14h}{h}$

d $\dfrac{x - 4}{2x - 8}$

e $\dfrac{5x + 15}{x + 3}$

f $\dfrac{7}{14x + 21}$

g $\dfrac{5x^2 - 10x}{x^2 - 2x}$

h $\dfrac{25g^3 + 10g^2}{5g^2 + 2g}$

i $\dfrac{2x^2 - x}{4x - 2}$

11 Peter is simplifying this expression in his maths lesson.

Explain what he has done wrong and then complete the problem correctly.

$$\frac{12xy^2 + 10y^2}{6y^2 + 2y} = \frac{\overset{2}{\cancel{12}}xy^2 + \overset{5}{\cancel{10}}y^2}{\cancel{6}y^2 + \cancel{2}y} = 10xy$$

✗

explanation 4a   explanation 4b

12 Work out these additions.

a $\dfrac{3}{4} + \dfrac{8}{9}$

b $\dfrac{4}{7} + \dfrac{3}{11}$

c $\dfrac{5}{6} + \dfrac{2}{9}$

d $\dfrac{2}{5} + \dfrac{7}{8}$

13 Work out these subtractions.

a $\dfrac{4}{7} - \dfrac{2}{9}$

b $\dfrac{7}{8} - \dfrac{5}{6}$

c $\dfrac{11}{12} - \dfrac{2}{3}$

d $\dfrac{7}{10} - \dfrac{3}{7}$

14 Copy these and fill in the gaps.

a $\dfrac{a}{2} + \dfrac{a}{3} = \dfrac{3a}{6} + \dfrac{\Box}{6}$
$= \dfrac{\Box}{6}$

b $\dfrac{y}{4} + \dfrac{2y}{8} = \dfrac{\Box}{8} + \dfrac{\Box}{8}$
$= \dfrac{\Box}{8} = \dfrac{\Box}{2}$

c $\dfrac{2c}{5} + \dfrac{3c}{4} = \dfrac{\Box}{20} + \dfrac{\Box}{20}$
$= \dfrac{\Box}{20}$

15 Add these fractions together and simplify your answers where possible.

> First find the lowest common multiple of the denominators.

a $\dfrac{b}{2} + \dfrac{b}{4}$

b $\dfrac{d}{5} + \dfrac{d}{6}$

c $\dfrac{x}{3} + \dfrac{x}{6}$

d $\dfrac{2m}{5} + \dfrac{m}{2}$

e $\dfrac{5s}{4} + \dfrac{3t}{3}$

f $\dfrac{4x}{7} + \dfrac{3y}{14}$

g $\dfrac{5r}{5} + \dfrac{4s}{4}$

h $\dfrac{x+1}{2} + \dfrac{3y}{4}$

i $\dfrac{2a+5}{5} + \dfrac{a}{3}$

j $\dfrac{x-2}{10} + \dfrac{3x}{5}$

k $\dfrac{x-y}{4} + \dfrac{x+y}{3}$

l $\dfrac{n+m}{12} + \dfrac{n+3m}{4}$

m $\dfrac{a^2}{3} + \dfrac{2a^2}{4}$

n $\dfrac{3b^2}{5} + \dfrac{b^2}{4}$

o $\dfrac{3n^2}{7} + \dfrac{4n^2}{3}$

p $\dfrac{x^2-1}{3} + \dfrac{2x^2}{4}$

16 Find the errors in these pupils' calculations.
Write out each calculation correctly.

a

$$\dfrac{q}{9} + \dfrac{3q}{5} = \dfrac{4q}{14} \quad \textbf{✗}$$

b

$$\dfrac{r}{3} + \dfrac{3r}{4} = \dfrac{2r}{4} \quad \textbf{✗}$$

c

$$\dfrac{x+2}{3} + \dfrac{2x}{4} = \dfrac{3x+2}{12} \quad \textbf{✗}$$

17 Work out these subtractions and simplify your answers where possible.

a $\dfrac{g}{3} - \dfrac{g}{5}$

b $\dfrac{h}{2} - \dfrac{h}{4}$

c $\dfrac{3x}{2} - \dfrac{5x}{6}$

d $\dfrac{5m}{2} - \dfrac{7m}{10}$

e $\dfrac{5y}{3} - \dfrac{3y}{4}$

f $\dfrac{3b+2}{5} - \dfrac{2b}{10}$

g $\dfrac{a-b}{3} - \dfrac{a}{5}$

h $\dfrac{g-f}{3} - \dfrac{g}{6}$

i $\dfrac{5x+3}{4} - \dfrac{x+2}{12}$

j $\dfrac{3m-3}{5} - \dfrac{2m+4}{10}$

k $\dfrac{n^2}{3} - \dfrac{n}{2}$

l $\dfrac{3y^2}{7} - \dfrac{2y^2}{21}$

18 Sam has done this algebra problem. She has made one mistake.
Explain her error and write out the calculation correctly.

$$\dfrac{2x+1}{2} - \dfrac{x-3}{5} = \dfrac{10x+5}{10} - \dfrac{2x-6}{10} = \dfrac{10x+5-2x-6}{10} = \dfrac{8x-1}{10} \quad \textbf{✗}$$

explanation 5

19 The expression in each rectangle is the sum of the expressions in the circles.
Copy and complete each problem.

a

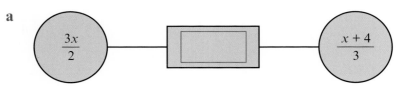

b

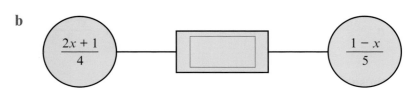

c

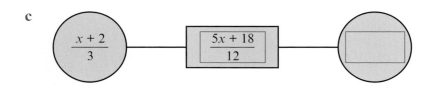

20 In these addition pyramids, the expression in each brick is the sum of the
expressions in the two bricks below.

Copy and complete each pyramid.

a   b

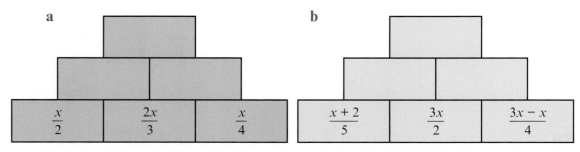

c   d

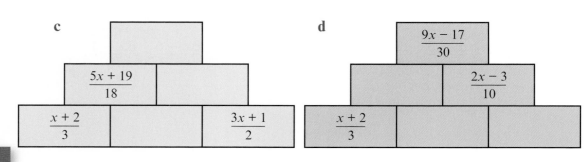

Linear equations

- Solving pairs of simultaneous equations by a graphical method
- Solving pairs of simultaneous equations by an algebraic method

Keywords

You should know

explanation 1a · explanation 1b · explanation 1c

1 Solve these equations.

a $7x + 5 = 40$ b $4z - 7 = 29$ c $9d + 2 = 65$ d $4 - 7e = 25$

e $4 + 9a = 31$ f $10x - 20 = 5$ g $4 - 3d = -23$ h $6x + 2 = -28$

2 Solve these equations.

a $6(2a - 3) = 30$ b $6(3m - 2) = 60$ c $6(4m - 7) = -18$

d $6(m - 2) = 12$ e $5(n + 3) - 2 = 23$ f $4(y - 7) + 2 = -14$

g $4(a + 2) = 9$ h $-6(p - 3) = 9$ i $-4(2 - x) = 12$

3 Solve these equations.

a $\dfrac{x}{2} = 3$ b $\dfrac{y}{4} + 7 = 11$ c $\dfrac{p}{9} + 6 = 13$ d $\dfrac{y + 7}{12} = 4$

e $7 + \dfrac{a}{5} = 4$ f $\dfrac{b}{3} - 4 = 1$ g $4 = \dfrac{12}{n}$ h $8 = \dfrac{56}{m}$

i $\dfrac{2t}{5} + \dfrac{t}{10} = 2.5$ j $\dfrac{3s}{7} - \dfrac{2s}{21} = 1$ k $\dfrac{x}{3} + \dfrac{x}{2} = 10$ l $\dfrac{3x}{4} - \dfrac{x}{3} = 3$

4 Solve these equations.

a $3n + 4 = n + 13$ b $7 + 5m = 8m + 1$ c $8y + 17 = 4y + 19$

d $8 + 3p = 9p + 4$ e $25 - 2y = 6y + 5$ f $5 - 2b = 3b + 25$

g $4(z - 6) = z - 18$ h $8(b + 9) = b + 93$ i $-2(x - 6) = x - 9$

5 Solve these equations.

   a $10(4 - c) = -4 - c$ **b** $2(a + 7) = a + 7$ **c** $2(x + 1) = 3(x + 2)$

   d $5(2 - 3y) = 9(2 + y)$ **e** $\frac{3x}{2} + \frac{x}{3} = x - 5$ **f** $\frac{2x}{5} + \frac{x}{2} = 5\left(\frac{x}{3} + 2\right)$

> **explanation 2**

6 Write an equation for each problem and then solve it.

   a   The length of a side of an equilateral triangle is $(x - 5)$ cm. The perimeter of the triangle is 66 cm. What is x?

   b   Peter has x songs on his mp3 player. Gurveer has 35 more songs than Peter on his, while Hannah has half the number that Peter has on hers. Altogether they have 560 songs. How many songs does Peter have?

   c   Stephen's age is divided by 4 then 3 is added. The result is the same as subtracting 9 from his age. How old is Stephen?

   d   Adding 5 to a number gives the same answer as multiplying it by 3 and adding 9. What is the number?

   e   I am thinking of a number. When I increase it by 4 then double the answer I get 20 more than the number. What is my number?

7 In each of these problems, use angle facts to form an equation and solve it to find the unknown.

   a

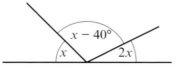

   b

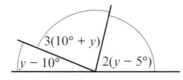

   c

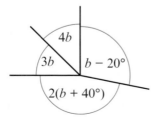

   d

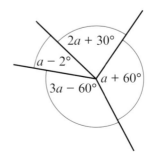

8 **a** For each diagram below, form an equation and then solve it to find the unknown.

i Perimeter = 42 cm

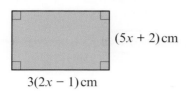

(5x + 2) cm

3(2x − 1) cm

ii Perimeter = 29 cm

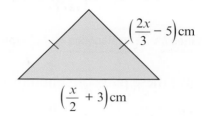

$\left(\dfrac{2x}{3} - 5\right)$ cm

$\left(\dfrac{x}{2} + 3\right)$ cm

b These two rectangles have equal perimeters.
Form an equation and solve it to find x.

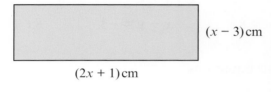

(x − 3) cm

(2x + 1) cm

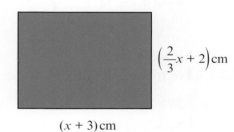

$\left(\dfrac{2}{3}x + 2\right)$ cm

(x + 3) cm

explanation 3a   explanation 3b

9 For each equation copy and complete the table of values.
Then draw the graphs on the same axes.

a $y = 3x + 2$

x	0	2	4
y			

b $y = 6 - 2x$

x	0	2	4
y			

c $2y + 5x = 20$

x	0	1	
y			0

10 Find the solutions to these pairs of simultaneous equations by drawing the graphs and finding the points of intersection.

a $x + y = 8$
$y = x + 3$

b $x + 2y = 10$
$y - x = 2$

c $3x + 2y = 12$
$y = x + 1$

d $3x + 4y = 24$
$2y - x = 2$

11 **a** Use a graph to show that the simultaneous equations $y = 3x + 7$ and $2y = 6x + 11$ have no solution.

b How can you tell from the equations that there are no solutions?

12 Which of the following pairs of equations will have no solutions?

a $y = 3x + 3$ b $y = 2x + 1$ c $3x + 2y = 7$ d $y = 7 - 2x$

   $y = 3x - 2$ $2y + 4x = 12$ $y = -1.5x + 5$ $4y + 8x = 20$

(explanation 4a)   (explanation 4b)   (explanation 4c)   (explanation 4d)

13 Solve these pairs of simultaneous equations.

a $4x - y = 11$ b $-x + 5y = 23$ c $7x - 2y = 19$ d $3x + 2y = 6$

   $2x + y = 7$ $x - 4y = -18$ $3x + 2y = 21$ $x - 2y = 6$

e $2x + 3y = 24$ f $2x + y = 12$ g $x + y = -7$ h $4x - 4y = 0$

   $-2x - 5y = -38$ $2x - y = 8$ $x - y = -3$ $8x + 4y = 12$

14 Solve these pairs of simultaneous equations.

a $3x + y = 9$ b $5x + 3y = 26$ c $2x + 3y = 8$ d $5x + 2y = 16$

   $2x + y = 7$ $2x + 3y = 14$ $2x + y = -4$ $5x - y = 7$

e $2x + 2y = 6$ f $3x + y = 9$ g $2x - 5y = 5$ h $-5x + y = 32$

   $2x - y = 3$ $2x + y = -1$ $6x - 5y = 45$ $-5x + 6y = 17$

15 Solve these pairs of simultaneous equations.

a $x + 3y = 9$ b $4x - 3y = 7$ c $2x + 5y = 19$ d $2x + y = 14$

   $2x - y = 4$ $2x + 2y = 7$ $x + 2y = 8$ $3x + 2y = 22$

e $5x - 3y = 22$ f $x + y = 0$ g $2x + 3y = 4$ h $4x + 3y = 1$

   $2x - y = 9$ $4x + 8y = 6$ $3x - 2y = -7$ $3x + 2y = 0$

*16 Solve these pairs of simultaneous equations.

a $3x - 4y = 5$ b $2x + 5y = -7$ c $3x - 2y = 1$ d $x + 3y = 7$

   $2x + y = -4$ $3x + 4y = 0$ $5x - 6y = 3$ $3x - 5y = 7$

explanation 5

17 Solve these pairs of simultaneous equations.

a $y = x - 2$
   $x + 3y = 6$

b $y = 2x - 1$
   $3x - y = 6$

c $x = 1 - 2y$
   $2x + 3y = 4$

d $x = -2y - 4$
   $2x + 3y = 8$

e $y = 3 - 2x$
   $3x - 3y = 0$

f $3y = 11 - x$
   $3x - y = 3$

g $2x + 2y = 10$
   $5y = x + 1$

h $3x - 5y = 9$
   $2y + 5 = 4x$

explanation 6

18 Two numbers x and y have a difference of 12 and a sum of 24.
Write down two equations in x and y and solve them to find the numbers.

19 In a shop, potatoes are £x per kg and carrots are £y per kg.

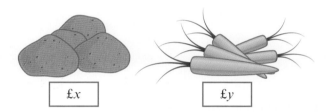

£x £y

5 kg of potatoes and 2 kg of carrots cost £3.55.

3 kg of potatoes and 3 kg of carrots cost £2.85.

a Write down two equations connecting x and y.

b Solve these simultaneous equations to find the price of potatoes and of carrots.

20 A trip to the cinema costs £31.50 for a group of 3 adults and 2 children and £52.50 for a group of 4 adults and 5 children. Use simultaneous equations to find the cost of each adult's ticket and each child's ticket.

21   At an online shop a music track costs £x to download and a movie costs £y to download.

Kamal spent £24.50 to download 10 music tracks and 4 movies.
Katie spent £18.70 to download 8 music tracks and 3 movies.

Use simultaneous equations to find the cost of a music track and of a movie.

22   A straight line with equation $y = ax + b$ passes through the points $(3, -5)$ and $(-1, 11)$.

Write down two equations and solve them simultaneously to find the value of a and b.

23   This shape is a kite. Find the value of x and y.

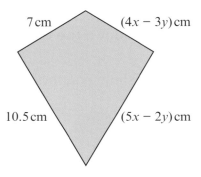

7 cm $(4x - 3y)$ cm

10.5 cm $(5x - 2y)$ cm

24   The perimeters of the equilateral triangle and the square are both 84 cm.

Use simultaneous equations to find the value of a and b.

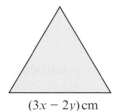

$(3x - 2y)$ cm $(5x + 2y + 6)$ cm

25   An employer pays some of his staff £80 per day and others £110 per day.

Altogether he has 50 staff and their daily wages come to £4570.

How many workers receive £80 per day and how many receive £110 per day?

Inequalities

- Solving linear inequalities
- Representing inequalities on a number line
- Representing the region described by several inequalities on a graph

Keywords

You should know

explanation 1a explanation 1b explanation 1c explanation 1d

1 Represent these inequalities on a number line.

a $x > 2$ b $x < 4$ c $x \geq 0$

d $x \leq -2$ e $x < 3$ and $x > 1$ f $x \geq -3$ and $x < 1$

g $-5 < x \leq 2$ h $-1 \leq x \leq 4$ i $x > 3$ and $x \leq -2$

2 What inequalities are shown by these number lines?

a
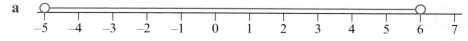

b
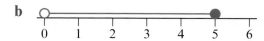

c
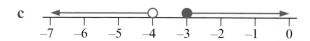

3 Solve these inequalities and show your solution on a number line.

a $4n < 10$ b $5 + x > 7$ c $3y - 5 \leq 23$ d $4 + 3y \geq 1$

4 Solve these inequalities.

a $5x - 3 < 27$ b $4x - 7 \geq 13$ c $6p - 1 \leq -4$ d $\dfrac{m}{5} + 3 < 1$

e $5h < h + 9$ f $3(2x - 1) > 21$ g $5(3 + 2x) < 45$ h $\dfrac{3t}{2} > 9$

5 Solve these inequalities.

a $2 + 3x > 5 - x$

b $6(4x + 1) \geq 6$

c $7 < 2(3x - 4)$

d $2 \leq 8(x - 3)$

e $3(x + 2) > x - 5$

f $\dfrac{7x}{2} > 3(x + 5)$

6 Solve these inequalities.

a $4a + 3 \geq 2a - 7$

b $2t - 8 > 3t + 6$

c $\dfrac{1}{2}(w + 3) > 4$

d $5w + 3 < 17 - 2w$

e $\dfrac{3r}{4} - 5 \leq 1$

f $4(x + 3) > 2x - 2$

g $3(4s + 1) \leq 2(s - 5)$

h $\dfrac{5x - 6}{7} \geq x + 5$

7 Multiply both numbers in each inequality by -1. Write the inequality for the new numbers. What do you notice?

a $4 > 3$

b $3 < 5$

c $-2 > -7$

d $-5 < 1$

8 Solve these inequalities.

a $4h \geq 28$

b $-6g < 18$

c $-3x > 30$

d $-5y \leq -30$

e $-7b \geq 56$

f $-5x > 3x + 8$

g $2f > 5f - 18$

h $2(r - 2) < 5 + 4r$

i $6 - 4k > 3(k + 5)$

(explanation 2)

9 Solve each of these inequalities and show your solution on a number line.

a $4 < 2x < 10$

b $-5 \leq x - 1 < 1$

c $5 < 3 + x \leq 7$

d $-2 < \dfrac{x}{2} < 3$

10 Write the integer values of x that satisfy each inequality.

a $-1 \leq x \leq 4$

b $-3 < x \leq 2$

c $-6 < x < -2$

d $-2 < x \leq 0$

11 Find the integer values of x that satisfy each inequality.

a $2 < 2x < 6$

b $-4 < x + 3 < -1$

c $-3 < x - 2 < 1$

d $-1 \leq 2x + 1 < 5$

e $-5 \leq 3x - 2 \leq 7$

f $1 < 4 - n \leq 5$

g $-2 < \dfrac{1}{2}x + 1 < 0$

h $-3 \leq 3 - 2n \leq 3$

i $-5 < 3(n + 3) < 0$

12 Solve these inequalities.

    a $-15 < 2x - 5 \leq 7$ **b** $-8 \leq 4 - 3x \leq 7$ **c** $2 < \dfrac{(x + 3)}{5} < 4$

> explanation 3a   explanation 3b   explanation 3c   explanation 3d

13 For each part, draw and label axes for x and y from -4 to 4.

    Indicate the required region by shading the unwanted region.

    a $y > 3$ **b** $x \leq -1$ **c** $x \geq 0$ **d** $y > -1$ **e** $x < 2$

14 Use inequalities to describe the unshaded regions.

    a
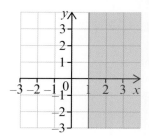

    b
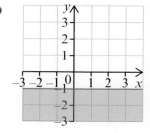

    c
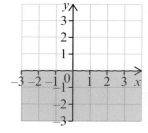

    d
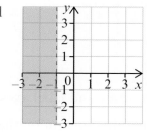

    e
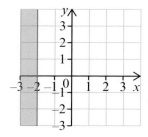

    f
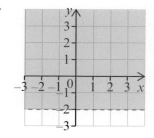

15 Use inequalities to describe the unshaded regions.

a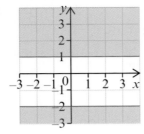

b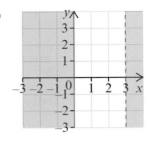

c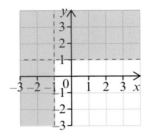

d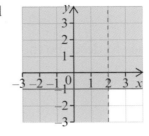

e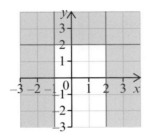

f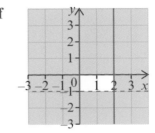

16 For each part, draw and label axes for x and y from -4 to 4.

Indicate the required region by shading the unwanted regions.

a $-2 < x < 1$ b $-1 \le y \le 3$

c $1 \le x \le 3$ d $0 \le y < 1$

e $y > -1$ and $x < 2$ f $y \le 3$ and $x < -1$

g $x \ge 2$ and $y > -2$

17 For each part, draw and label axes for x and y from -4 to 4.

Indicate the required region by shading the unwanted regions.

a $x > 2, x < 3, y > -1$ b $x \le 3, y \le 1, y > -2, x > 1$

explanation 4a   explanation 4b   explanation 4c   explanation 4d

18 Describe the inequalities shown by the unshaded regions.

a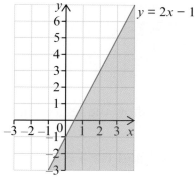

b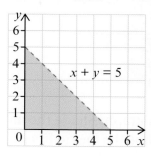

c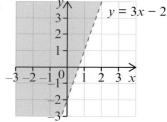

d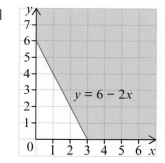

19 Draw graphs to show these regions.

Leave the region where the inequality is true unshaded.

a $y \geq x$ b $y > x + 1$ c $y < 2 + 2x$ d $y \leq 4x$

e $x + y > 4$ f $y \leq 8 - 2x$ g $2x + 5y \geq 10$ h $3x + 4y < 12$

20 Describe the inequalities shown by each unshaded region.

a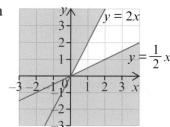

b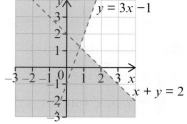

21 Describe the inequalities shown by each unshaded region.

a

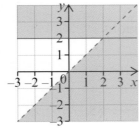

b

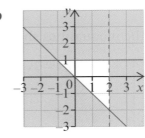

22 Copy each graph. Shade the unwanted regions to show the region that satisfies all of the inequalities.

a $y < x + 2$ and $x + y > 5$

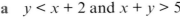
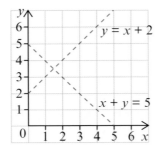

b $y \leq 1$ and $y \geq 4 - x$

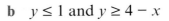
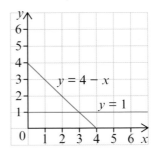

c $x + y < 4$, $y > 2$ and $y \leq 2x + 1$

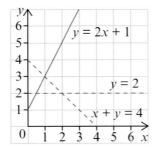

d $y \leq x$, $y < 4$ and $x > 3$

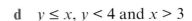
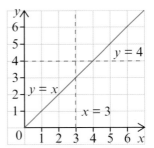

23 Draw graphs to show these regions. Use scales from -3 to 6 on both axes. Shade the unwanted regions.

a $y < 5$, $x > 1$ and $y > x + 2$

b $x \leq 4$, $y \leq 3$ and $x + y \geq 2$

c $2x + 3y > 9$, $x \geq 1$ and $x \leq 5$

d $y < x + 4$, $y < 7 - x$ and $y > 4$

Geometry and measures GM2.1

Reflections, rotations and translations

- Finding the mirror line for a reflection
- Finding the centre of rotation and the angle of rotation
- Describing a single transformation that can replace a combination of transformations

Keywords

You should know

explanation 1a   explanation 1b   explanation 1c

1 Copy each diagram.

    i Reflect each shape in the *y*-axis. Label the new shape A.

    ii Reflect each shape in the line *y* = 2. Label the new shape B.

a

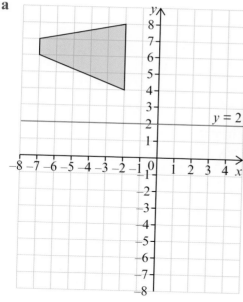

b

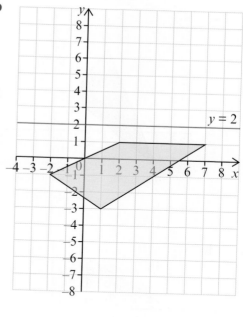

2 Copy each diagram. Reflect each shape in the line $y = -x$.

a

b

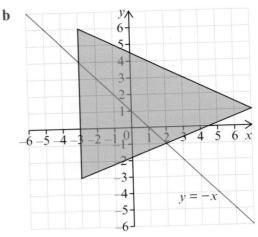

3 Copy each diagram. Draw in the line of reflection.

a

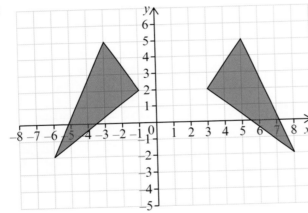

b

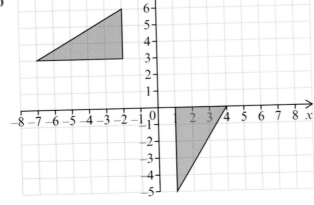

4 Copy each diagram. Rotate each shape as described.

  i 90° anticlockwise about the marked centre of rotation (R)

  ii 180° about the marked centre of rotation (R)

a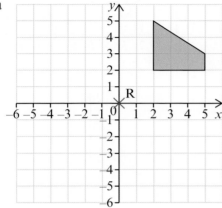

b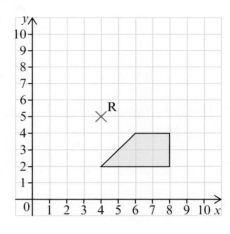

c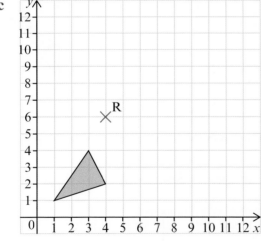

d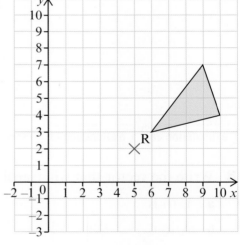

5 Look at the diagram.

  a Describe fully the rotation that will map A to B.

  b Describe fully the rotation that will map B to A.

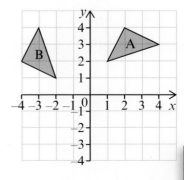

6 Look at the diagram.

    a Describe fully the rotation that will map P to Q.

    b Describe fully the rotation that will map Q to P.

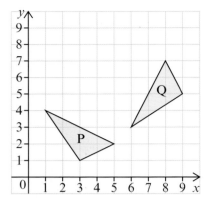

7 Describe fully the rotation that will map M to N.

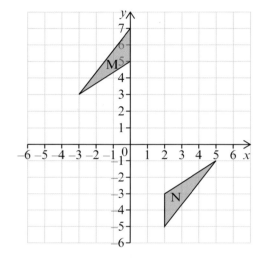

explanation 3a   explanation 3b

8 Write the vector that will translate the shapes as described.

    a E to B

    b A to C

    c D to B

    d C to E

    e A to D

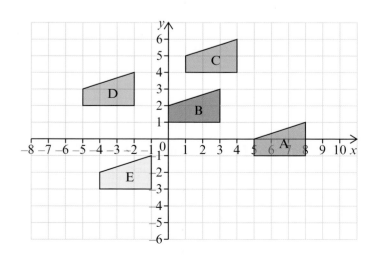

9 **a** Copy the diagram.

b Translate A by $\begin{pmatrix} 4 \\ 3 \end{pmatrix}$. Label the image B.

c Translate A by $\begin{pmatrix} -2 \\ 3 \end{pmatrix}$. Label the image C.

d Translate A by $\begin{pmatrix} 4 \\ -2 \end{pmatrix}$. Label the image D.

e Translate A by $\begin{pmatrix} -3 \\ -4 \end{pmatrix}$. Label the image E.

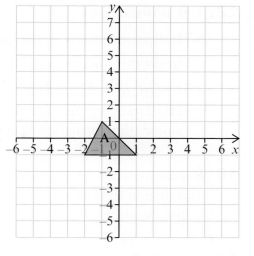

---

explanation 4a   explanation 4b

10 **a** Copy the diagram.

b Reflect triangle A in the line $y = 1$.
Label the new triangle B.

c Reflect triangle B in the line $x = 0$.
Label the new triangle C.

d Describe fully the single transformation
that will map triangle A to triangle C.

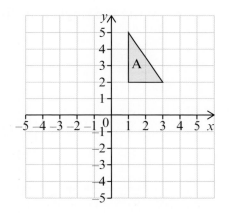

11 **a** Copy the diagram from question **10** again.

b Reflect triangle A in the line $y = 2$. Label the new triangle B.

c Reflect triangle B in the line $x = 1$. Label the new triangle C.

d Describe fully the single transformation that will map triangle A to
triangle C.

12 a Copy the diagram from question **10** again.

  b Reflect triangle A in the line $x = 0$. Label the new triangle B.

  c Reflect triangle B in the line $y = 1$. Label the new triangle C.

  d Compare these answers to your answers to question **10**.
  Has changing the order of the reflections made a difference to the
  single transformation that will map triangle A to triangle C?

13 Repeat question **11** but this time reflect triangle A first in the line $x = 1$
and then in the line $y = 2$. Does this make a difference to the single
transformation?

14 a Write the equation of the line of reflection that will map shape P to shape Q.

  b Write the equation of the line of reflection that will map shape Q to shape R.

  c Write the single transformation that will map shape P to shape R.

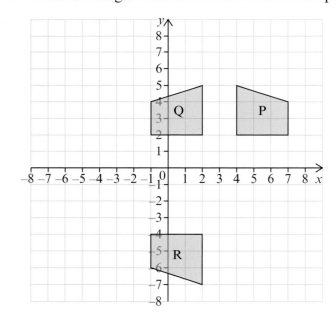

15 Repeat question **14** for this diagram.

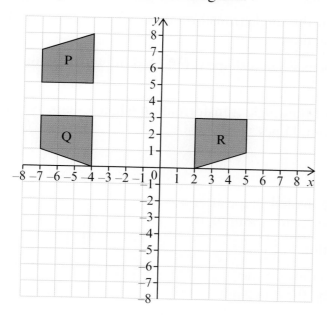

16 Look at your answers to questions **10** to **15**.

    a Using your answers, what single transformation do you think is equivalent to each of these?

        i A reflection in the line $x = 1$ followed by a reflection in the line $y = 3$

        ii A reflection in the line $y = 3$ followed by a reflection in the line $x = 2$

    b Check your answers to part **a** by drawing suitable diagrams.

17 Write the single transformation that is equivalent to a reflection in the line $x = a$ followed by a reflection in the line $y = b$.

18 **a** Copy the diagram.

    b Reflect triangle A in the line $x = 3$.

       Label the new triangle B.

    c Reflect triangle B in the line $x = 8$.

       Label the new triangle C.

    d Write down the single transformation that will map triangle A to triangle C.

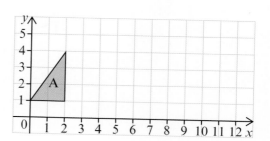

19 a Repeat question **18** using two different vertical lines.

   b Write a general rule for the single transformation when a shape is reflected in two different vertical lines.

   c Investigate what happens when a shape is reflected in two different horizontal lines.

   d Write a general rule for the single transformation when a shape is reflected in two different horizontal lines.

20 a Copy the diagram.

   Find the image of the shaded shape after a rotation of 90° anticlockwise about (0, 0) followed by a translation of $\begin{pmatrix} 5 \\ 4 \end{pmatrix}$.

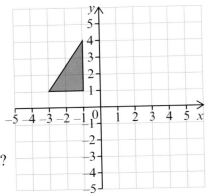

   b Repeat part **a** but this time do the translation followed by the reflection.

   c Was the order of transformations important?

   Give an explanation for your answer.

21 Copy the diagram.

   Investigate whether order is important when the combination of transformations is a reflection in the *x*-axis and a rotation of 180° about (0, 0).

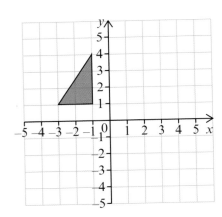

Enlargement

- Enlarging a shape using negative and fractional scale factors
- Finding the scale factor of enlargement
- Finding the centre of enlargement
- Finding area and volume scale factors

Keywords

You should know

explanation 1a   explanation 1b

1 In each diagram an object and a centre of enlargement are shown.

Copy each diagram and enlarge the object, using the given scale factor.

a

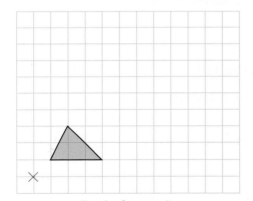

Scale factor 3

b

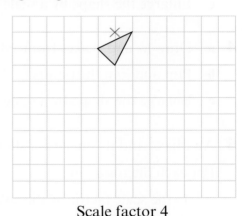

Scale factor 4

c

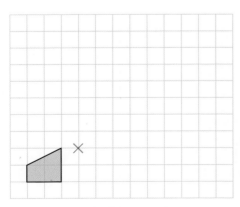

Scale factor −2

d

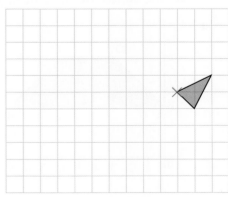

Scale factor −4

2 The diagram shows an object and a centre of enlargement.

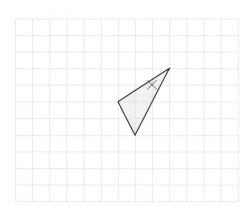

   a Copy the diagram. Enlarge the shape, using the marked centre of enlargement and a scale factor of 3.

   b Copy the diagram. Enlarge the shape, using the marked centre of enlargement and a scale factor of −2.

3 **a** Draw x- and y-axes from 0 to 10.

   b Plot and join the points (1, 5), (3, 4), (4, 6) and (2, 7).

   c Enlarge the shape by a scale factor 2, centre (6, 0).

4 **a** Draw x- and y-axes from −8 to +5.

   b Plot and join the points (1, 3), (4, 2) and (3, 5).

   c Enlarge the shape by a scale factor of −2, centre (0, 1).

5 An object and its image are shown on each set of axes.

For each diagram, find:

   i the scale factor of the enlargement

   ii the centre of the enlargement

a

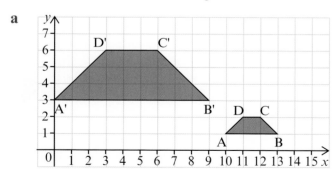

b

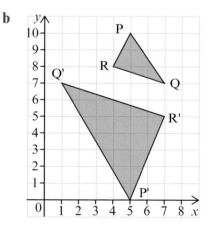

explanation 2a explanation 2b

6 In each diagram an object and a centre of enlargement are shown.

Copy each diagram and enlarge the object, using the given scale factor.

a

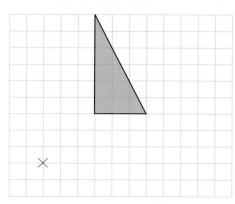

Scale factor $\frac{1}{3}$

b

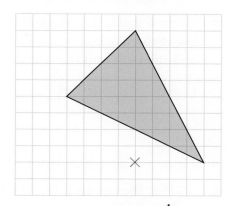

Scale factor $\frac{1}{4}$

c

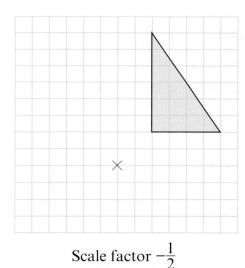

Scale factor $-\frac{1}{2}$

d

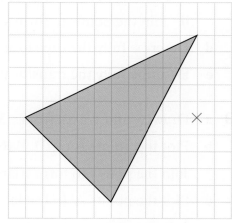

Scale factor $-\frac{1}{5}$

7 a Copy the diagram. Enlarge the shape, using the marked centre of enlargement and these scale factors.

  i $\dfrac{1}{2}$ **ii** $\dfrac{1}{4}$

b Copy the diagram. Enlarge the shape, using the marked centre of enlargement and these scale factors.

  i $-\dfrac{1}{2}$ **ii** $-\dfrac{1}{4}$

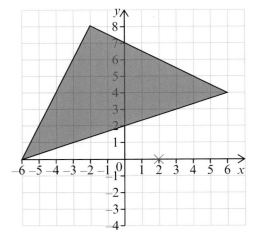

8 a Draw x- and y-axes from -3 to 7.

b **i** Plot the points P $(2, -2)$, Q $(6, 2)$, R $(2, 6)$, S $(-2, 2)$.

  ii Join the points to form the square PQRS.

c **i** Plot the points P' $(2, 1)$, Q' $(3, 2)$, R' $(2, 3)$, S' $(1, 2)$.

  ii Join the points to form square P'Q'R'S'.

d Describe fully the transformation that will map PQRS to P'Q'R'S'.

e Describe fully the transformation that will map P'Q'R'S' to PQRS.

9 a Draw x- and y-axes from -3 to 7.

b Plot the points A $(3, 3)$, B $(6, 6)$, C $(0, 6)$.

  Join the points to form triangle ABC.

c Plot the points A' $(-1, -1)$, B' $(-2, -2)$ and C' $(0, -2)$.

  Join the points to form triangle A'B'C'.

d Describe fully the transformation that will map ABC to A'B'C'

e Describe fully the transformation that will map A'B'C' to ABC.

explanation 3a   explanation 3b   explanation 3c   explanation 3d

10 A rectangle has an area of $12\,\text{cm}^2$.
The sides of the rectangle are enlarged by a scale factor of 2.

   a Write the scale factor for the enlargement of the area.

   b Work out the area of the enlarged rectangle.

   c Sketch a rectangle. Label the length and width so that the area is $12\,\text{cm}^2$.

   d Enlarge the sides of your rectangle by a scale factor of 2. Sketch the image.

   e Work out the area of your enlarged rectangle.
     Check that your answer is the same as that for **b**.

11 A triangle has an area of $10\,\text{cm}^2$.
The sides of the triangle are enlarged by a scale factor of 3.

   a Write the scale factor for the enlargement of the area.

   b Work out the area of the enlarged triangle.

   c Sketch a triangle. Label the base and perpendicular height so that the area is $10\,\text{cm}^2$.

   d Enlarge the lengths in your triangle by a scale factor of 3. Sketch the image.

   e Work out the area of your enlarged triangle.
     Check that your answer is the same as that for **b**.

12 A cuboid has a volume of $40\,\text{cm}^3$.
All the lengths of the cuboid are enlarged by a scale factor of 3.

   a Write the scale factor for the enlargement of the volume.

   b Work out the volume of the enlarged cuboid.

   c The dimensions for the original cuboid are $4\,\text{cm}$, $2\,\text{cm}$ and $5\,\text{cm}$.
     Enlarge these by a scale factor of 3.

   d Work out the volume of the enlarged cuboid.
     Check that this is the same as your answer to **b**.

13 Trapezium P has an area of $20\,\text{cm}^2$.
Trapezium Q is an enlargement of trapezium P.
All the lengths of P are enlarged by a scale factor of $\dfrac{3}{2}$.
What is the area of Q?

Scale drawing

- Using scales
- Interpreting scaled areas

Keywords

You should know

explanation 1a   explanation 1b

1 James has a plan of his garden. It uses a scale of $1:50$.

   a He measures these lengths from the plan. Work out the actual lengths in metres.

     i length of flower bed 3 cm   **ii** length of path 18 cm

   b James has a patio of length 6 m and width 2.5 m in his garden.

     Work out the length and width of his patio on the plan in centimetres.

2 Sahil uses a diagram of an aeroplane. The diagram is a scale drawing that uses a scale of $1:200$.

   a He measures lengths from the scale drawing. Work out the actual lengths in metres.

     i length of aeroplane 27 cm   **ii** length of wing 9.6 cm

   b The actual length of another aeroplane is 35 m. What is the length of this aeroplane in a scale drawing using the ratio $1:200$?

3 Mandy finds an accurate scale drawing of a butterfly using a scale of $3:1$ in a reference book.

She measures these lengths from the scale drawing. Work out the actual lengths in millimetres.

   a length of wingspan 15 cm

   b length of leg 0.9 cm

4 The accurate scale drawing shows a plan for a garden. The plan has a scale of 1 : 200. Use the plan of the garden to work these out.

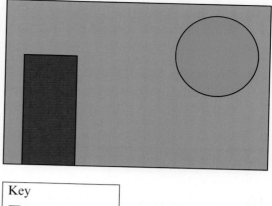

   a actual length and width of the garden

   b actual diameter of the circular pond

   c actual area of the vegetable patch

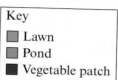

Key
■ Lawn
■ Pond
■ Vegetable patch

5 A map uses a scale of 1 : 25 000.

   a On the map the distance from Cromer to Sheringham is 28 cm. What is the actual distance from Cromer to Sheringham? Give your answer in kilometres.

   b The actual distance from Cromer to North Walsham is 15.4 km. What will this distance be on the map?

6 The diagram shows a field.

   a Draw an accurate scale drawing of the field.

      Use a scale of 1 : 500.

   b Work out the actual area of the field.

   c Work out the area of the field in the scale drawing.

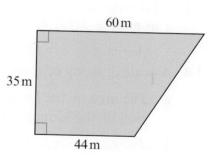

7 From a point 60 m away from a tall building, the angle of elevation of the top of the building is 52°. The sketch shows this information.

   a Draw an accurate scale drawing, using a scale of 1 : 200.

   b Use your scale drawing to find the height of the building.

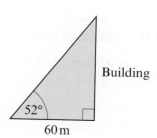

8 The length of a car park is 120 m. This length on a scale drawing is 15 cm.
What is the scale used for the scale drawing?

9 On a map, the distance from London to Cambridge is 14.4 cm.
The actual distance from London to Cambridge is 72 km.
What is the scale used on the map?

explanation 2a   explanation 2b

10 On a map of scale 1 : 100 000, the area of a lake is 5 cm².
What is the actual area of the lake in square kilometres?

11 On a scale drawing a garden has an area of 300 cm².

The scale drawing uses a scale of 1 : 100. What is the actual area of the garden
in square metres?

12 On a map using a scale of 1 : 100 000, a desert covers an area of 25 cm².
What is the area that the desert covers in real life? Give your answer in square
kilometres.

13 A country has an area of 30 500 km². What area would this be on a map using
a scale of 1 : 1 000 000?

14 A scale drawing of a room is drawn using a scale of 1 : 100.

   a The area of the lounge on the scale drawing is 18 cm². What is the actual
area of the lounge? Give your answer in square metres.

   b The actual area of the bathroom is 3 m². What is the area of the bathroom
on the scale drawing?

15 On a map using a scale of 1 : 50 000, a forest covers an area of 6 cm².

   a What area in real life does 1 cm² on the map represent?
Give your answer in square kilometres.

   b Work out the area that the forest covers in real life. Give your answer in
square kilometres.

Trial and improvement

- Using a calculator to find approximate solutions to an equation
- Using a spreadsheet to find approximate solutions to an equation

Keywords

You should know

explanation 1a   explanation 1b   explanation 1c

1 Solve these equations.

   a $x^2 + 7 = 32$ **b** $x^2 - 1 = 35$ **c** $x^2 + 1 = 10$

   d $x^3 = 8$ **e** $x^3 - 1 = 26$ **f** $2 - x^2 = -14$

2 Find two solutions to each of these equations.

   a $x^2 + 8 = 72$ **b** $y^2 - 10 = 134$ **c** $5x^2 = 125$ **d** $3x^2 - 4 = 44$

3 Copy the table and use trial and improvement to find an approximate value of x which satisfies the equation $x^2 + 2x = 58$.

Give your answer to one decimal place.

The first trial has been done for you.

Value of x	$x^2 + 2x$ working and result of trial	Comment
7	$7^2 + 2 \times 7 = 63$	Too big

4 a Show that one solution to $x^2 - 3x = 38$ lies between 7 and 8.

   b Use trial and improvement to find this solution to one decimal place. Use a table to show your working.

5 a Show that a solution to $x^3 + 3x - 40 = 0$ lies between 3 and 4.

   b Use trial and improvement to find this solution to one decimal place. Use a table to show your working.

6 Use a calculator and trial and improvement to solve these equations to 1 d.p.

a $t^3 = 30$ b $x^3 + x = 11$ c $y^3 - y = 40$ d $3.25g^3 = 7.1$

e $m^3 - m = 80$ f $x^3 + x = 97$ g $2y^3 + y = 6$ h $2y^3 + 3y = 4$

7 Use a calculator to find an approximate solution to 2 d.p. for each equation.

a $e^3 + 2e = 65$ b $z^3 - z = 4$ c $p^3 + p = 124$

d $q(q^2 + 5) = 35$ e $w^4 - 3w^2 = 300$ f $x(5 - x^2) = -43$

explanation 2a   explanation 2b   explanation 2c

8 Peter is using a spreadsheet to solve the equation $x^3 + 4x = 700$ by trial and improvement.

He wants to give his answer to one decimal place.

	B2	▼	fx		
	A	B	C	D	E
1	Value of x	Result of trial			
2	1				
3					
4					
5					
6					

a What formula should he type in cell A3 to increase his x values by 1 each time?

b What formula should he type in cell B2 to work out the value of each trial?

c Set up this spreadsheet and solve the equation, giving your solution to one decimal place.

9 Use a spreadsheet to solve each equation to two decimal places.

a $z^3 + 3z = 420$ b $(x - 6)(x + 2)(2x - 5) = 310$ c $x^4 - 2x^3 + x^2 = 25$

explanation 3

10 Use a calculator to solve this problem.

This cube has volume $50 \, \text{cm}^3$.

Let the length of the side be x, then find a formula for the volume in terms of x.

Work out the length of the side of the cube to two decimal places.

11 This cuboid has a volume of $400 \, \text{cm}^3$.

a Write an expression for the volume of this cuboid.

b Form an equation and solve it using trial and improvement.
Give your answer to two decimal places.

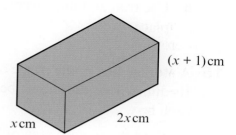

$(x + 1) \, \text{cm}$

$2x \, \text{cm}$

$x \, \text{cm}$

12 Ilana is trying to solve this problem.

A number to the power 5 is equal to the twice the number cubed add 75.

Use a suitable method to find an approximation for this number to one decimal place.

13 The volume of a sphere is given by the formula $V = \frac{4}{3}\pi r^3$ where V is the volume and r is the radius of the sphere.

The Earth has an approximate volume of $1.0868 \times 10^{12} \, \text{km}^3$.

Use trial and improvement to find the approximate diameter of the Earth.
Give your answer to the nearest kilometre.

14 The diagram shows a triangular prism. The prism has a volume of $300\,\text{cm}^3$.

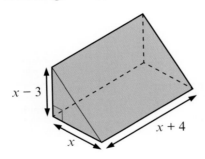

a Show that the equation $x(x - 3)(x + 4) = 600$ can be used in this problem.

b Use trial and improvement to find the value of x correct to one decimal place.

15 A storage box in the shape of a cuboid is manufactured from Perspex. Its dimensions are shown below. The manufacturer has allowed $1000\,\text{cm}^2$ for each box.

a Find the surface area of the box in terms of p.

b Find, by a numerical method, the value of p (to 1 d.p.) for which the surface area is $1000\,\text{cm}^2$.

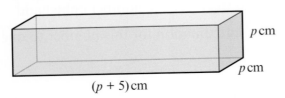

16 For each of the equations given below, decide whether an algebraic or numerical method is most efficient for finding solutions, then solve the equation (to 1 d.p. where appropriate).

a $4x = 10 - x$

b $x^2 = 121$

c $3x^3 + 2x = 64$

d $x(x^2 - 2) = 25$

e $x^2 + 3x - 54 = 0$

f $x^3 + 3x + 2 = 0$

g $x^2 - 49 = 0$

h $x^3 - 27 = 0$

i $4x^4 + 16 = 8x^2$

Direct proportion

- Solving problems of direct proportion numerically
- Representing direct proportion relationships as equations and graphically
- Solving problems involving direct proportion

Keywords

You should know

explanation 1

1 Five litres of fuel cost £4.90. Calculate the cost of these amounts.

   a 6 litres   **b** 10 litres   **c** 20 litres   **d** 1.5 litres

2 CDs are on special offer and Bethany bought three for £14.85. Work out the cost of these numbers of CDs.

   a 2 CDs   **b** 12 CDs   **c** 36 CDs   **d** 100 CDs

3 5 miles is approximately equal to 8 km.

   a Roughly how many kilometres are equal to these distances?

     i 18 miles   **ii** 32 miles

   b Roughly how many miles are equal to these distances?

     i 80 km   **ii** 400 km   **iii** 55 km

4 A 5-litre tin of paint covers a wall surface of 45 m².

   a How many litres of paint are needed to cover a wall surface of

     i 65 m²   **ii** 120 m²

   b If one litre of paint costs £4.45, what is the cost of painting a room with total wall area of 81 m²?

5 Six pizzas cost £14.40.

   a Calculate the cost of these numbers of pizzas.

     i 3 pizzas   **ii** 7 pizzas   **iii** 20 pizzas

   b How many pizzas can be bought with £10? How much change will there be?

6 Tina's quarterly electricity bill is £73.08. This includes £56.70 for using 450 units of electricity and the standing charge of 17.8p per day.

Calculate the bills for the following units of electricity.
(Assume the same rate per unit and daily standing charge.)

  a 220 units for 32 days

  b 1200 units for 60 days

  c 2300 units for 91 days

explanation 2a   explanation 2b

7 The exchange rate for Thai baht to British pounds is £1 = 55 Thai baht.

  a Using p for pounds and b for Thai baht, complete this proportional relationship algebraically.

  $b =$ _____

  b Draw the graph representing this proportional relationship.
  First copy and complete the table and then plot the points on a graph.

p	0	2	4	6
b				

  c Write the gradient (steepness) of your line in part **b** and explain what this gradient represents.

  d Toby buys a handmade suit in Thailand for 4800 baht.

  What is this cost in pounds?

8 A mass of one pound is approximately equal to 450 grams.

    a Write this as an algebraic relationship using p for pounds and g for grams.

    b Copy the axes and draw the graph of this proportional relationship.

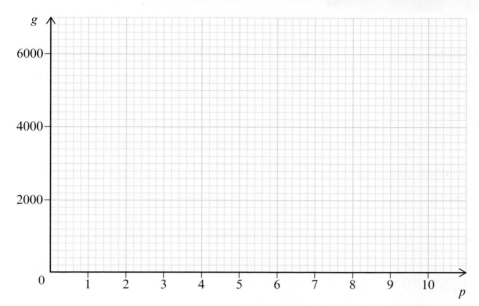

    c Write the gradient of your line in part **b** and explain what this gradient represents.

    d Use your graph to find the number of pounds in 50 kg.

9 Are the variables in each table in direct proportion? Explain your answers. For those that are in direct proportion, write the rule as an equation.

a

x	1	2	3	4	5	6
y	7	14	21	28	35	42

b

x	1	4	5	8	10	15
y	2.5	10	12.5	20	25	37.5

c

x	5	10	15	20	25	30
y	0.625	1.2	1.875	2.5	3.125	3.75

10 Which of these equations do *not* represent two variables that are in direct proportion to each other?

    a $y = 45x$ **b** $s = \dfrac{t + 3}{4}$ **c** $p = 3q^2$ **d** $g = 0.01h$

11 A car moving at constant speed uses 20 litres of fuel to travel 180 miles.

The fuel used is directly proportional to the distance travelled.

a Using *l* for litres and *d* for distance, write the proportional relationship algebraically.

b Without drawing the graph, state the gradient of the line represented by this relationship and what this gradient represents.

c Given that fuel costs £1.08 per litre, what would be the cost of making a journey of 520 miles in this car?

12 Use the relationships to answer the questions.

$y = 2.2x$, where x is the weight in kilograms (kg) and y is the weight in pounds (lb)

$y = 14s$ where s is the weight in stones

a Calculate the weight of a man in kilograms who weighs 220 lb.

b Calculate the weight of a child in pounds who weighs 40 kg.

c Calculate the weight in kilograms of a tiger that weighs 35 stones and 7 pounds.

d Calculate the weight in stones and pounds of a seal that weighs 180 kg.

13 For each of these graphs, find the gradient and write a linear equation for the function.

a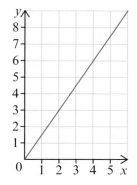

b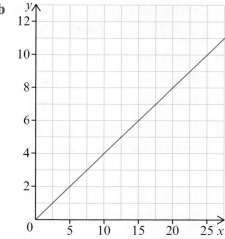

c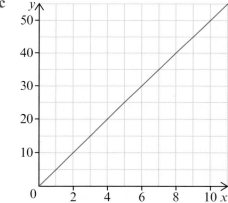

d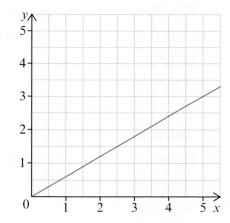

explanation 3a   explanation 3b

14 The members of the Racing Racquets Tennis Club drink orange juice at a rate of 4.6 litres per half hour.

a How much will they consume in a 3-hour practice?

b How much will be consumed if 8 clubs, each with the same number of players, meet for a 7-hour tournament and consume orange juice at the same rate as the Racing Racquets Tennis Club?

c If only a quarter of the members of the Racing Racquets club are present for one 3-hour practice, how much orange juice will they consume?

15 In a scale model of a boat, the mast is 20 cm high. This represents 12 m on the actual boat.

    a Write the ratio of the height of the actual mast to the height of the model mast (in centimetres). Now give this ratio in its simplest form.

    b Use a suitable method to find the width of the boat if the model is 4 cm wide.

    c How long is a rope on the model if it is 10.2 m long on the actual boat?

    d If a railing on the boat is 2.5 cm thick, how thick should this be on the model? Give your answer in millimetres to 3 d.p.

16 Texts for a mobile phone cost 7.2p per text message.

    a Write this proportional relationship algebraically using C for cost in pounds and t for the number of texts.

    b How much would these numbers of texts cost?

        i 50 texts   **ii** 300 texts

    c How many texts were sent if these were the costs?

        i £4.32   **ii** £18.00

Monthly text bundles can be bought for a mobile phone where up to 500 messages can be bought for £15.

    d What is the minimum number of texts that would make the monthly bundle better value for money than 7.2p per text?

17 A mobile phone company uses the following formula to calculate the monthly call costs for its 'pay monthly' customers.

$C = 0.25t + 4.60$ where C is the monthly cost in pounds and t is the time in minutes spent talking on the telephone.

    a Calculate the monthly costs for these numbers of minutes used.

        i 100 minutes   **ii** 220 minutes   **iii** 0 minutes

    b How much is each minute of talk time?

    c How does this relationship differ from other proportion problems in this chapter?

Formulae and expressions

- Solving problems involving more complicated formulae
- Changing the subject of a formula
- Writing a formula from a sentence

Keywords

You should know

explanation 1

1 Find the value of each expression by substituting in the value of the variable. Do not use a calculator.

a $3s + 2$ when $s = 1.5$

b $x^2 - 3x$ when $x = 4$

c $5(y^2 - 1)$ when $y = 3$

d $2z(z^2 - 4z)$ when $z = 4$

e $\dfrac{g^2}{4}$ when $g = 5$

f $2m + 12$ when $m = -3$

g $20 - k$ when $k = -5$

h $\dfrac{2y + 6}{y}$ when $y = -6$

i $\sqrt{9s^2}$ when $s = -3$

j $\dfrac{2p^2(p - 3)}{2}$ when $p = 10$

2 Find the value of each expression when $x = 7.4$ and $y = 2.1$. Give your answers to one decimal place.

a $3x - 4y$

b $2y^2 + 3x$

c $3(x^2 - y^2)$

d $4xy(y - x)^2$

e $\dfrac{(y - 4)^2}{3y}$

f $\dfrac{(xy)^2}{(y - 2)}$

g $\sqrt{(x^2 - y^2)}$

h $\dfrac{4\sqrt{x}}{y}$

3 Work out the area of the trapezium with $a = 4.4\,\text{cm}$, $b = 8.2\,\text{cm}$ and $h = 1.7\,\text{cm}$.

$$\text{Area} = \frac{h}{2}(a + b)$$

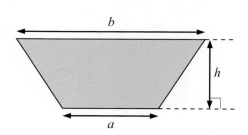

123

4 The formula for the nth triangular number is $\dfrac{n(n+1)}{2}$.

For the first triangular number, $n = 1$. Substitute this into the formula: $\dfrac{1 \times 2}{2} = 1$.

So the first triangular number is 1.

Find these triangular numbers using the formula.

  a 3rd   **b** 5th   **c** 10th   **d** 25th   **e** 100th

5 Copy and complete this table to generate terms in each sequence.

	$n = 1$	$n = 2$	$n = 3$	$n = 4$	$n = 10$
$n^2 + 3n - 2$	2	8	16	26	
$2n - 1$					
$n^3 - 2n^2$					
$n(n - 3)(4 - n)$					

6 **a** The volume of a sphere is $\frac{4}{3}\pi r^3$, where r is the radius of the sphere. Find the volumes of spheres with these radii. Use the value of π from your calculator. Give each answer correct to 2 decimal places with the correct units.

    i 5 cm   **ii** 7.5 cm   **iii** 1 m   **iv** 25 mm

  b If the radius of the Earth is 6378 km, find the volume of the Earth. Give your answer in standard form to three significant figures. (You may assume that the Earth is spherical and use the formula from part **a**.)

  c What is the volume of a hemisphere of radius 20 m?

    (A hemisphere is a sphere cut in half through the centre.)

7 To find the total surface area of a cylinder, use the formula $A = 2\pi r(r + h)$, where r is the base radius and h is the height of the cylinder.

Which cylinder has the greatest surface area? Show how you decided.

A   6 cm   **B**   3.2 cm   **C**

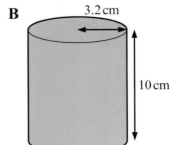
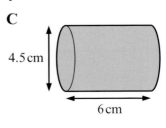

5.2 cm

10 cm

4.5 cm

6 cm

explanation 2a   explanation 2b   explanation 2c

8 Make r the subject of these formulae.

a $s = r + 6$ b $4y = 3r$ c $p = r - 3$ d $f = \frac{r}{5}$

e $4r = dg$ f $4 - r = t$ g $mnr = 7t$ h $\frac{1}{3}r = g$

9 Make x the subject of these formulae.

a $y = 3x + 1$ b $2x + y = 7$ c $y = \frac{x}{5} - 7$ d $y = 4t - x$

e $s = 5x + 3$ f $g = \frac{4}{x}$ g $b = \frac{3x}{2} + 8$ h $hx + 5 = t$

10 Make p the subject of the following formulae.

a $4p = s$ b $p - 3 = 2d$ c $2p + 7 = l$ d $\frac{p}{2} - 5 = q$

e $7p - r = 4z$ f $5q = 3 + p^2$ g $\frac{3pq}{5} + 2 = g$

11 The cost of hiring a minibus is given by the formula $C = 25 + 10d + 0.2m$ where C is the cost in pounds, d is the number of days the minibus is hired for and m is the number of miles the minibus travels.

a The minibus is hired for 7 days and travels 400 miles. Calculate the total cost of hiring the minibus.

b Ahmed hires the minibus for 5 days and his total bill comes to £460. How many miles did he travel?

c Rearrange the formula to make d the subject.

12 The general equation of a straight line is $y = mx + c$.

Rearrange this formula to make m the subject.

13 The formula for the area of a trapezium is $A = \frac{h}{2}(a + b)$.

a Rearrange the formula to make b the subject.

b Find the value of b when $A = 45$, $h = 2.5$ and $a = 8$

14 Make a the subject of these formulae.

a $y = a^2$ b $r = 2a^3$ c $a^2 + 4 = h$ d $t = s + 3a^2$

e $\dfrac{5a}{4} = u + v$ f $\dfrac{a^2}{4} + 5 = d$ g $\sqrt{a + 5} = h$ h $3a^4 - 8 = k$

15 Make c the subject of these formulae.

a $6(4 + c) = n$ b $4(2d - c) = t$ c $fg = 5(3c - j)$ d $\dfrac{3c^2 - 5}{3} = y$

e $\sqrt{\dfrac{cd}{4}} = t$ f $\sqrt[3]{c} - 5 = h$ g $4\sqrt{c} - 7 = r$ h $fc^3 - 5 = 4p$

16 Make c the subject of these formulae.

a $y = \dfrac{t}{c + p}$ b $\sqrt{\dfrac{5r}{2c}} = 7$ c $y = \sqrt{\dfrac{5}{2 + c}}$ d $z = \sqrt[3]{\dfrac{t}{3 - 4c}}$

17 The volume of a sphere is given by the formula $V = \dfrac{4}{3}\pi r^3$, where V is the volume and r is the radius of the sphere.

Rearrange the formula to make r the subject.

18 The time taken for a pendulum to complete its swing is given by this formula.

$$T = 2\pi \sqrt{\dfrac{l}{g}}$$

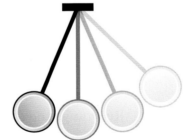

a   Find T when $l = 1.2$ and $g = 9.8$.
Give your answer to one decimal place.

b   Rearrange the formula to make l the subject.

c   Find l when $T = 1.7$ and $g = 9.8$.
Give your answer to one decimal place.

d   Rearrange the formula to make g the subject.

19 The graph shown has equation $y = \dfrac{x^3}{4} - \dfrac{4}{x^2}$.

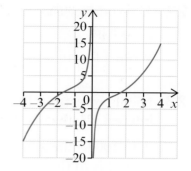

Find the value of y for these values of x.

a $x = 2$ b $x = 0.5$

c $x = -2.5$ d $x = -0.5$

e Use trial and improvement to find the value of x when $y = 10$.
Give your answer to one decimal place.

---

explanation 3

---

20 The number of children at a party is three times the number of adults.

a Write a formula for the total number of people at the party.

b Two teenagers are helping with the party.
How could you modify your formula to include this fact?

21 On each long side of a conference table, the number of seats is equal to the length of the table (in metres) multiplied by 2.

Three more people can sit at each end of the table.

a Write a formula that relates the number of people at a table to the length of the table.

b Find the number of people who can sit at a table 12 m long.

c What length of table would have 30 seats?

d Make a chart showing the length of table (in metres) and the number of seats for table lengths 1, 2, 3, 4, 5, 6. What do you notice?

22 A taxi driver charges a fare of £2.50 added to 50p per mile added to £1.20 per passenger.

Write a formula that relates the fare to the number of miles and passengers.

23 Nicola invests £P in a savings account for n years. The amount of compound interest, £I, that she earns is calculated using this rule.

Add 100 to the annual percentage interest rate R, then divide by 100, and then raise this to the power n. Now multiply this value by the amount £P invested. Finally subtract the original amount £P.

  a Write a formula for I in terms of R, n and P.

  b Calculate the compound interest received on £18 000 invested for 5 years at a rate of 6% per year.

24 Planets that orbit the sun all have this relationship.

The cube of the distance of the planet in miles from the Sun is equal to the square of the time in years taken to orbit the Sun multiplied by a constant, K.

  a Write the relationship as a formula.

  b The Earth takes one year to make an orbit and is 9.3×10^7 miles from the Sun.

     Find the value of the constant K. Give your answer in standard form.

  c Rearrange your formula from part **a** to make T the subject.

  d The planet Mars is 1.42×10^8 miles from the Sun.
     Calculate the time it takes to make one orbit of the Sun.

25 Weather experts use the following formula to calculate the wind chill factor in degrees Farenheit.

$$W = (0.3\sqrt{V} + 0.474 - 0.02V)(T - 91.4) + 91.4$$

W is the wind chill factor, V is the wind speed in miles per hour and T is the temperature in degrees Farenheit.

  a Calculate the wind chill factor when $V = 20$ km/h and $T = -2\,°$F.

  b Find the temperature when the wind chill is $-20\,°$F and the wind speed is 10 mph.

Using fractions and percentages

- Expressing one number as a percentage of another
- Increasing and decreasing an amount by a percentage
- Using multiplicative methods to solve percentage change problems

Keywords

You should know

explanation 1a | explanation 1b | explanation 1c

1 Convert each of these percentages into a decimal and a fraction in its lowest terms.

a 60%
b 25%
c 20%
d 75%
e 65%

f 15%
g 82%
h $33\frac{1}{3}\%$
i 72%
j 175%

2 Convert these fractions into percentages.

Round your answers to two decimal places (2 d.p.).

a $\frac{19}{50}$
b $\frac{2}{5}$
c $\frac{16}{20}$
d $\frac{11}{15}$
e $\frac{2}{3}$

f $\frac{11}{12}$
g $\frac{4}{7}$
h $\frac{1}{8}$
i $\frac{4}{21}$
j $\frac{14}{27}$

3 Convert these decimals into percentages.

a 0.26
b 0.79
c 0.15
d 0.04
e 1.56

f 2.05
g 0.135
h 0.458
i 0.245
j 1.305

4 Damian got these marks in his end-of-unit tests.

His report card gave the results as percentages.

What were the percentages?

Maths $\frac{18}{25}$

English $\frac{11}{15}$

Science $\frac{13}{20}$

Geography $\frac{12}{16}$

5 In a 100-year period, a water molecule spends 98 years in the ocean, 20 months as ice, $\frac{1}{2}$ of a month in lakes and rivers and less than $\frac{1}{4}$ of a month in the atmosphere.

> Start by finding the number of months in 100 years.

What percentage of its time does a water molecule spend in these forms?

a in the ocean

b as ice

Round your answers sensibly.

---

explanation 2a   explanation 2b

6 Which number in each pair is larger?

a $\frac{3}{5}$ and $\frac{3}{4}$

b $\frac{5}{8}$ and $\frac{2}{3}$

c $\frac{5}{12}$ and $\frac{3}{8}$

d $\frac{7}{10}$ and $\frac{3}{4}$

e 0.9 and $\frac{7}{8}$

f $\frac{7}{9}$ and 0.76

g $\frac{11}{15}$ and 0.75

h $\frac{7}{10}$ and $\frac{15}{21}$

7 Does < or > go in the box to make each of these true?

a $\frac{1}{4} \square \frac{1}{3}$

b $\frac{5}{6} \square \frac{3}{4}$

c $\frac{2}{3} \square \frac{5}{8}$

d $\frac{15}{20} \square 80\%$

e $0.625 \square \frac{17}{25}$

f $\frac{2}{3} \square 66\%$

g $\frac{5}{9} \square 55\%$

h $0.15 \square \frac{1}{6}$

8 In four games of football James scored these numbers of goals out of the total goals scored.

Game 1 $\frac{1}{3}$ **Game 2** $\frac{3}{7}$

Game 3 $\frac{2}{5}$ **Game 4** $\frac{4}{9}$

a In which game did he score the highest proportion of goals?

b In which game did he score the lowest proportion of goals?

9 Put each set in order from smallest to largest.

a $0.25, \frac{2}{5}, 35\%, \frac{1}{3}$

b $0.66, \frac{2}{3}, 65\%, \frac{7}{9}$

c $\frac{19}{24}, 0.78, 81\%, \frac{28}{36}$

10 $\frac{7}{12} > \frac{x}{5}$. What is the largest whole number x can be?

explanation 3a   explanation 3b   explanation 3c

11 **a**   What fraction of 30 is 27?   **b**   What fraction is 180 of 100?

  c   What fraction of 75 is 130?   **d**   What fraction is 2000 of 1750?

12 **a**   What fraction of 1 m is 35 mm?   **b**   What fraction of 1 kg is 250 g?

  c   What fraction is 300 g of 10 kg?   **d**   What fraction is 2500 m of 7 km?

  e   What fraction of 1 day is 6 hours?   **f**   What fraction is £125 of £5000?

13 **a**   What percentage is 9 of 45?   **b**   What percentage is 27 of 108?

  c   What percentage is 45 of 225?   **d**   What percentage is 36 of 120?

  e   What percentage is 158 of 474?   **f**   What percentage is 15 of 90?

14   Bryony is downloading a 120 MB file to her computer.

  When 75 MB have been downloaded, what fraction of the file has been downloaded?

15 **a**   James had a 500 ml jug of fruit punch. He poured 375 ml into a glass.

  What fraction of the punch did he pour into the glass?

  b   A small ball bounces 1 m on its first bounce and 68 cm on its second bounce.

  What fraction of the first bounce height did it reach on its second bounce?

16   Anna scored 18 out of 25 points in a fashion design competition and Joe scored 25 out of 36 points in a boat design competition.

  To compare their competition marks Anna converted them to percentages.

  What percentage scores did they get and who got the higher score?

17 In his last two basketball games Jason got 42 points of the total 126 points.

In her two games Ruth got 65 out of a total 169 points.

Who was better at scoring points in the two games? Explain your answer.

18 It takes Tom three hours to drive to his grandmother's house.

He sets off at 10:30 a.m. and stops for lunch at 12:40 p.m.

What percentage, to the nearest whole number, of the travel time has he completed?

explanation 4

19 Work these out without using a calculator.

a   30% of £150

b   45% of 120 m

c   11% of 200 kg

d   45% of 2000 cm

e   35% of £140

f   25% of 500 ml

g   52% of £5000

h $12\frac{1}{2}$% of 300 mm

20 Which is greater, 75% of 1800 or 65% of 2000?

21 In a bag of 96 beans, 25% are red,

12.5% are grey, $33\frac{1}{3}$% are blue,

16 are yellow and the rest are purple.

What percentage of the beans are purple?

22 Use your calculator to work these out. Give your answers to the nearest penny.

a   8% of £27.50

b   7% of £105

c   33% of £45.80

d   6 % of £56.30

e   92% of £34.50

f   23% of £132.80

g $12\frac{1}{2}$% of £50

h $66\frac{2}{3}$% of £124.60

23 42% of people have blood type O and 44% have blood type A.

a   Out of 1850 patients in St Mary's Hospital how many of each blood type would you expect to have?

b   In a class of 26 pupils how many of blood type O would you expect to have? Round your answer sensibly.

24 The diagram shows Nyssa's triangular garden.
23% of the garden is planted with flowers.

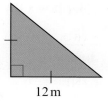

12 m

   a What area is planted with flowers?

   b 45% of the flower garden needs weeding.
      What area needs weeding?

25 33% of the total export earnings of a region come from manufacturing.

   a If the total export earnings are £132 345 000, how much is earned from manufacturing?

   b 42% of the manufacturing earnings come from heavy machine production.

      How much comes from this type of production?

explanation 5a   explanation 5b

26 **a** Increase 80 g by 20%.   **b** Increase 250 ml by 64%.

     c Increase 90 kg by 28%.   **d** Increase 244 m by 72%.

27 **a** Decrease 48 litres by 75%.   **b** Decrease 125 ml by 30%.

     c Decrease £35 by 8%.   **d** Decrease 230 g by 38%.

28 How much would you pay for these in a closing-down sale with 30% off everything?

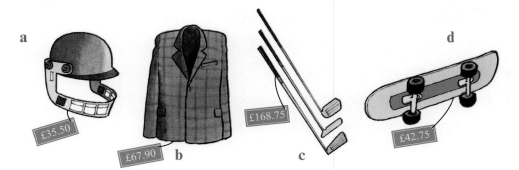

a   £35.50   £67.90 **b**   £168.75   **c**   **d**   £42.75

29 The table shows the number of visitors to a theme park during four months last year.

June	July	August	September
6250	9600	14 500	10 300

This year, each of the monthly figures had increased by 18%.

How many people visited the park during each of the months this year?

30 Chandra makes dresses for a local shop.
The materials for each dress cost her £42.

Round all your answers to these questions to the nearest 10 pence.

a She adds 60% to the cost price when she sells dresses to Dress4Less.

How much does she get for each dress?

b The shop makes 48% profit on the dresses.
What does the shop sell them for?

c Dress4Less had a 40% sale on all clothing.

How much would one of Chandra's
dresses cost in the sale?

d After two weeks the prices dropped
by 20% on the sale price.

How much would the dress cost now?

31 The cost price of stereos from a wholesale company is £120.

The shop sells them at a 27.5% increase on the cost price.

a What price do the stereos sell for?

b In an end-of-line sale the shop reduces its prices by 15%.

What price would you pay for the stereo in the sale?

explanation 6a | explanation 6b

32 a How much would you pay in the sale for a laptop computer that originally cost £429?

b How much would you have to pay if you bought it on the last day of the sale?

c To get the sale price the shop owner multiplied all the prices by 0.85.

She then multiplied the sales price by 0.85 to get the last day price.

What single number could she have multiplied by to get the last day price?

d By what percentage have the original prices been reduced on the last day?

e How could you check your answer to part **b** using your answers to parts **c** and **d**?

Sale
15% off

Last day a further **15%** off the sale price

33 Pravin thought that an increase of 20% followed by a decrease of 20% is greater than an increase of 10% followed by a decrease of 10%.
Is he correct? Explain your answer.

34 A puppy, Emma, increases her mass in her first week by 8% each day.

She began life with a mass of 240 g.

Round all your answers to these questions to one decimal place.

a How much will Emma weigh after   **i** a day?   **ii** 3 days?   **iii** a week?

b Another puppy, Milo, also began life with a mass of 240 g but his mass increased by 9% a day for the first week.

How much heavier is Milo than Emma after a week?

35 Andy deposited £500 in a bank at an annual compound interest rate of 4%.

a How much will he have in total after three years?

b Andy decides to leave his money in the bank until he has at least £650.

How many years will he need to invest his money for?

c Andy's friend deposited £1100 at an annual compound interest rate of 3.5%.

How much will she have after five years?

explanation 7

36 Find these increases or decreases as percentages.

    a an increase from £25 to £30   **b** a decrease from 96 kg to 24 kg

    c an increase from 150 g to 250 g   **d** a decrease from £320 to £280

    e an increase from 325 cm to 455 cm

    f a decrease from 748 litres to 561 litres

    g an increase from £2480 to £3348

    h a decrease from £5600 to £4816

37 A car depreciated in value from £18 900 to £11 340.

    What percentage depreciation is this?

38 Rectangle B is an enlargement of rectangle A.

    a By what percentage have the lengths of the sides of rectangle B been increased ?

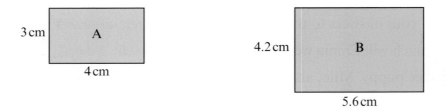

    b What is the percentage increase in area between the two rectangles?

explanation 8a   explanation 8b

39 Find the original amounts deposited in these bank accounts.

    a 10% more than originally and currently £66 in the account

    b 12% more than originally and currently £515.20 in the account

    c 24% more than originally and currently £1103.60 in the account

40 Find the original amounts deposited in these bank accounts.

    a 20% less than originally and currently £144 in the account

    b 17% less than originally and currently £323.70 in the account

    d 32% less than originally and currently £1407.60 in the account

41 Yarumba Zoo had 108 pelicans in their enclosure, an increase of 20% from their last count.

    How many pelicans were there when they were last counted?

42 All prices were reduced by 15% in a sale.

    What was the original price of each of these items bought in the sale?

    a A pair of shoes   **b** A shirt   **c** A tie   **d** A pair of trousers

       £38.25   £30.60   £10.20   £79.90

43 Mrs Wheeler received a 3% pay rise. She now gets £37 801 a year.

    What was her salary before the rise?

44 A delivery company charges 10% of the original price to carry goods and then the supplier adds an extra 5% administration charge to the new price.

    What was the original price of a desk that cost £288.75 delivered?

Using ratios

- Converting between ratios, fractions and percentages
- Dividing a quantity in a given ratio
- Comparing two ratios
- Understanding the ratio properties of similar 2–D shapes
- Solving problems using direct and indirect proportion

Keywords

You should know

explanation 1

1 This is a patchwork quilt.

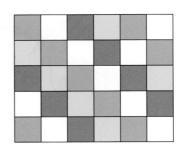

  a Find the ratio of yellow to green to orange to white squares.

  b Find the proportion of each of these.

    i yellow squares   **ii** green squares

    iii orange squares   **iv** white squares

  c Find the percentage of white squares.

2 In a different quilt, 24% of the squares were red, 36% were blue and the rest were white.

  a What proportion of the squares were each colour?

    i red   **ii** blue   **iii** white

  b Write the ratio of red to blue to white squares.

  c What is the smallest number of squares that the quilt could be made from?

3 Two parts of this square design are shaded pink.

Two parts are shaded blue.

Show that the ratio of blue to pink is 5 : 3.

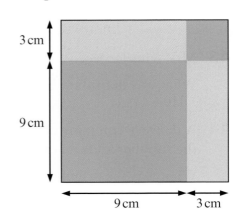

explanation 2a   explanation 2b

4 Write each ratio in its simplest form.

a 16:24   b 35:50   c 32:72   d 56:84

e 26:156   f 280:630   g 12:9:15   h 28:49:63

i 39:26:130   j 200:1000:400   k 48:180:312

5 Write each ratio in its simplest form.

a $2:\frac{1}{2}$ b $\frac{1}{3}:1$ c $\frac{1}{4}:3$ d $\frac{1}{4}:\frac{1}{2}$

e $\frac{3}{4}:\frac{1}{2}$ f 1.5:1   g 6.5:2.5   h 1.25:3

6 Simplify these ratios.

a £2:40p   b 6 hours:3 days   c 75cm:6m

d 36 minutes:1 day   e 45 seconds:3 minutes   f 4 litres:480ml

g 16 hours:1 week   h £1.30:52p   i 1.44kg:840g

7 An 8m length of rope was cut into these sections to make parts for a rope ladder.

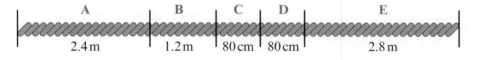

a What is the ratio of section A to section B?

b What percentage of the rope is cut into sections less than 1m long?

c What is the ratio of the lengths of sections C to D to E?

8 a For this almond cake recipe write the ratio of butter to sugar to flour to ground almonds in its simplest form.

b In another recipe the ratio of flour to sugar is 3:2.

   How much sugar is needed to mix with 1.2kg of flour?

> **Rich Almond Cake**
>
> 0.25kg butter
> 350g sugar
> 0.5kg flour
> 150g ground almonds

explanation 3

9 Divide each amount in the given ratio.

a 63 in the ratio 4:5   b 90 in the ratio 3:7

c 75 in the ratio 2:3   d 500 in the ratio 1:4

e 225 in the ratio 2:3   f 91 in the ratio 3:4

g 105 in the ratio 5:2   h 216 in the ratio 8:1

i 120 in the ratio 1:2:3   j 84 in the ratio 3:4:5

k 168 in the ratio 3:1:4   l 300 in the ratio 2:5:5

10 The angles in a triangle are in the ratio 1:2:3.

Find the sizes of the three angles.

11 A large plastic barrel contains 250 litres of vegetable oil.

It is poured into three containers with capacities in the ratio 3:5:2.

How many litres of oil does each container hold?

12 Mrs Graham won £22 500 playing the lottery.

She gave it to her three grandchildren in the ratio 6:4:5.

How much did they each receive?

explanation 4a   explanation 4b

13 Write these ratios in the form 1:m. Round to one decimal place if necessary.

a 10:32   b 4:15   c 3:8   d 8:21   e 36:80

14 Write these ratios in the form m:1. Round to one decimal place if necessary.

a 33:4   b 69:23   c 11:3   d 42:8   e 47:13

15 The ratio of tries scored to tries converted for the Lowlanders and the Clansmen rugby teams are 18:5 and 15:4 respectively.

Which team has the better conversion rate? Explain.

16 Which of these two dresses has the greater proportion of Lycra to other fibres?

Lycra : other fibres
3 : 7

Lycra : other fibres
4 : 9

17 The ratio of the lengths of corresponding sides of these photo frames are the same.

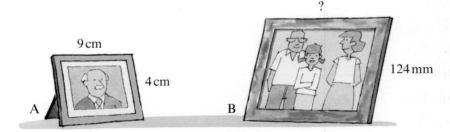

a Write the ratio width : length of photo frame A.

b Find the length of photo frame B.

18 Triangles P and Q are similar. They are not drawn to scale.

a What are the values of x and y?

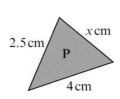

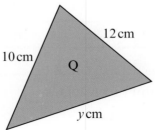

b Find the dimensions of two other triangles that could be similar to triangles P and Q.

19 The circular bases of two cylinders are congruent.

Cylinder X is 6 cm high and has a volume of 300 cm³.

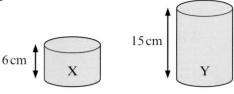

a Find the ratio of the heights of the two cylinders in the form 1 : *m*.

b What is the volume of cylinder Y?

(explanation 5a) (explanation 5b) (explanation 5c)

20 This table shows the quantities of red and yellow paint mixed to make orange paint.

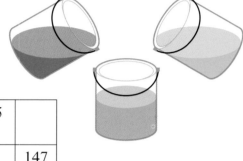

Red paint (litres)	3	6	9		45	
Yellow paint (litres)	7			84		147

a What is the ratio of red paint to yellow paint?

b Copy and complete the table.

c Copy and complete these sentences using the correct words from the box.

The ratio of red paint to yellow paint is _____ .

The numbers are in _____ proportion to each other.

direct
inverse
constant

21 In a frozen pasta bake there is 5 g of protein in every 8 g of pasta bake.

a Copy and complete the table to show this relationship.

Pasta bake (g)	8	16	24	32
Protein (g)	5			

b Find the amount of protein in

   i 80 g of pasta bake

  ii 128 g of pasta bake

 iii 500 g of pasta bake

22 Sunita has 375 g of butter and adapts her apple pie recipe so that she can use all the butter.

   a What quantities of the other ingredients would she need?

   b How many people would this serve?

> **Apple pie (for 4)**
> 3 large apples
> 25 g brown sugar
> 200 g flour
> 75 g butter (or margarine)
> 50 g castor sugar
> 1 tablespoon water to mix

23 Tammy wanted to raise £192 for charity by selling tickets to a concert.

She drew up a table of the possible prices she could charge per ticket and the numbers of tickets she would have to sell.

Number of tickets	8	10	12		20	
Price per ticket (£)	24			12		8

   a Copy and complete this sentence using the correct word from the box.

> direct
> inverse
> constant

The product of the number of tickets and the price per ticket is _____ .

   b Copy and complete the table.

   c Copy and complete this sentence using the correct word from the box.

The numbers are in _____ *proportion to each other.*

24 For each of these tables decide whether the values are in direct or inverse proportion to each other. Explain your answers.

   a

Price (£)	20	15	12	10	5
Number	3	4	5	6	12

   b

Weight (kg)	5	10	15	20	25
Height (cm)	15	30	45	60	75

   c

Hourly rate (£)	2	4	5	8	10
Hours		50	25	20	12.5	10

25   Last week Jack earned £200. This week he earned 40% more than last week.

What is the ratio of what he earned last week to what he earned this week?

26   A city street map has a scale of 1 cm : 350 m.

   a On the map the distance from
       Nelson's house to school is 3 cm.

     i How far is this in metres?

     ii How far is this in kilometres?

   b The actual distance from his house
       to the town centre is 2.8 km.

       What distance is this on the map?

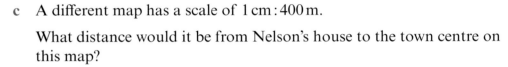

   c A different map has a scale of 1 cm : 400 m.

       What distance would it be from Nelson's house to the town centre on
       this map?

27   Jessica bought two cakes for a total of £15.75.

One cake cost two and a half times as much as the other.

How much did each cake cost?

28   A 500 ml jug is filled with orange squash and lemonade in the ratio 1 : 4.

Another 500 ml jug is filled with orange squash and lemonade in the ratio 1 : 3.

Both jugs are poured into one large jug.

What is the ratio of orange squash to lemonade in the large jug?

29   A pastry mix is made from 2 parts butter mixed with 3 parts flour.

   a How much of each ingredient is needed to
       make one kilogram of pastry mix?

   b Bianca has 200 g of butter and 400 g of flour,

       What is the most pastry mix she can make?

   c Gina has 1.5 kg of butter and 1125 g of flour.

       What is the most pastry mix she can make?

Mental methods

- Using mental strategies to solve problems involving integers
- Using mental strategies to solve problems using fractions, decimal and percentages
- Using powers and roots
- Estimating to check solutions to problems

Keywords

You should know

explanation 1a   explanation 1b   explanation 1c

1 Use complements to work these out.

    a $47 + 24 + 53 + 26$

    b $32 + 89 + 68 + 11$

    c $\dfrac{1}{3} + \dfrac{1}{2} + \dfrac{1}{4} + \dfrac{2}{3} + \dfrac{3}{4}$

    d $350 + 125 + 50 + 175$

    e $0.5 + 1.25 + 4.5 + 3.75$

    f $243 + 106 + 57 + 214 + 94$

2 a Jamie picked these cards from a set of decimal cards.

3   0.5   2.5   5   1

Is it possible to make the following totals by adding the numbers on any *four* of his cards?

If so, how?

  i 11.5   **ii** 10.5   **iii** 7   **iv** 10   **v** 9

  b Jamie picked one extra card from the set of decimal cards and can now make 7.5 using four cards. Which card did he choose?

3 Shona cut a ribbon into four lengths of 65 cm, 1.24 m, 2.35 m and 76 cm.

How long was the ribbon before it was cut up?

4 Find the answers to these by adding or subtracting too much and compensating.

    a   8.3 + 2.8   **b**   6.54 − 3.7   **c**   15.63 + 13.89

    d   19.36 − 12.94   **e**   203.53 + 37.8   **f**   176.55 − 28.9

    g   321.79 + 68.92   **h**   637.68 − 211.96

5 Use partitioning to answer these questions.

    a   13.7 + 8.5   **b**   25.56 + 8.33   **c**   23.58 − 0.42

    d   54.96 − 15.63   **e**   421.7 + 16.6   **f**   204.47 + 113.13

    g   32.6 − 10.75   **h**   236.8 − 114.93

6 Work out each calculation mentally.

    The answers are in the circle.

    a   1.3 + 6.7   **b**   130 + 260

    c $\frac{2}{5} + \frac{3}{5} + 5$ **d**   12.45 − 10.3

    e   3.64 + 5.36   **f**   7.8 + 3.15

    g   321 − 179   **h**   16 − 4.34

    i   15.62 − 8.48   **j** $\frac{1}{2} + 1\frac{3}{4} - \frac{1}{4}$

    k   4.52 − 1.07   **l**   14.05 + 2.98

Circle contents: 6   10.95   3.45   142   8   9   11.66   7.14   2   2.15   390   17.03

7 Find the answers to these using mental strategies.

    a   0.67 + 2 + 0.33 + 5.3   **b**   45.8 + 32. 67   **c**   54.36 − 2.09

    d   5.87 + 24.65   **e**   4.97 − 1.23   **f**   42.06 − 2.98

    g   35.67 − 16.78   **h**   2.17 + 13.83

8 Use the given fact to find the answer to each of these.

    a   23 + 15 = 38   Find   **i**   2.3 + 1.5   **ii**   0.23 + 0.15

    b   1.8 + 3.41 = 5.21   Find   **i**   18 + 34.1   **ii**   0.18 + 0.341

    c   234 − 1.3 = 232.7   Find   **i**   23.4 − 0.13   **ii**   2340 − 13

9 What money would be left after you made each of these purchases?

    a A pad of writing paper costing 68p and envelopes costing 54p paid with a £2 coin.

    b A bag of groceries costing £27.87 paid with a £50 note.

    c A bill of £56.37 for a meal at a restaurant, paid with a debit card with £120 on it.

    d A cricket bat for £19.58 and a helmet for £34.99 paid with two £50 notes.

explanation 2a   explanation 2b   explanation 2c   explanation 2d

10 Match each multiplication to a card showing a related calculation.

Use the cards to help you find the answer to each multiplication.

    a 56×25

    b 560×250

    c 28×18

    d 2.8×18

5.6×9

56×9

$56 \times 100 \div 4$

$(56 \times 25) \times 100$

11 Use mental strategies to calculate these.

    a $650 \div 25$ **b** 45×14 **c** 125×32 **d** $64 \div 16$

    e 41.8×25 **f** $24.8 \div 4$ **g** 20.6×23 **h** $648 \div 27$

    i 3.6×15 **j** $240 \div 16$ **k** 1.56×70 **l** $8.6 \div 4$

12 What would these purchases cost?

    a 15 packets of biscuits at £1.12 per packet

    b 25 jars of jam at £1.25 a jar

    c 11 bus tickets costing £2.38 each

    d 7 sets of golf balls costing £3.89 a set

13 How much would one of each item cost?

    a 16 packs of pasta cost £13.60   **b** 25 T-shirts cost £321.25

    c 15 boxes of paints cost £57.60   **d** 30 trays of eggs cost £238.50

14 Which of the numbers in the box are divisible by these numbers?

125		1080		216
	2610		234	
200		2400		488

   a 5 and 8

   b 3 and 6

   c 12

15 a Use your answers to question **14** to find which of these give terminating decimals when they are divided by 6.

   21.6   2.34   48.8   12.5   2.00   2.4   2.610

   b What are the answers?

16 Use the given fact to find the answer to each of these.

   a $17 \times 31 = 527$ Find **i** 17×3.1 **ii** 1.7×3.1

   b $406 \div 29 = 14$ Find **i** $40.6 \div 29$ **ii** $40.6 \div 2.9$

   c $13.4 \times 1.6 = 21.44$ Find **i** 13.4×0.16 **ii** 1.34×0.16

   d $1566 \div 58 = 27$ Find **i** $15.66 \div 58$ **ii** $156.6 \div 0.58$

17 Find the answers to these using mental strategies.

   a 4.8×2.5 **b** 6.5×2.2 **c** 1.68×3.5 **d** 5.08×0.1

   e $13.4 \div 0.5$ **f** $0.98 \div 0.1$ **g** 34.1×0.9 **h** $9.36 \div 0.08$

18 Copy and complete these number chains.

   a $\times 6$ $\div 3$ $\times 0.5$ $\div 0.3$ $\times 1.4$

      $2.4 \longrightarrow \square \longrightarrow 4.8 \longrightarrow \square \longrightarrow \square \longrightarrow \square$

   b $\div 4$ $\times 7$ $\div 0.2$ $\times 1.2$ $\div 0.6$

      $3.2 \longrightarrow \square \longrightarrow \square \longrightarrow \square \longrightarrow \square \longrightarrow \square$

19 A book is 24.5 cm high by 16.2 cm wide by 1.8 cm thick.

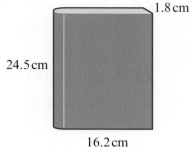

1.8 cm

24.5 cm

16.2 cm

   a If 8 books are laid side by side they just fit onto a desk top.
How long is the desk?

   b 15 books are stacked on top of each other.
How high is the stack of books?

   c A bookcase has two shelves.
Each shelf is 2.5 cm thick.

     Three rows of the books fit exactly between the shelves.

     What is the minimum inside measurement between the top and bottom of the bookcase?

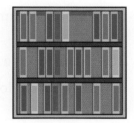

explanation 3a) (explanation 3b

20 Copy and complete these tables. Write the fractions in their lowest terms.

Fraction	Decimal	Percentage
$\frac{1}{2}$		
	0.75	
		40%
	0.6	
$\frac{3}{25}$		

Fraction	Decimal	Percentage
		350%
$\frac{5}{8}$		
	0.333...	
		85%
$2\frac{2}{3}$		

21 Find these quantities.

   a 25% of 120   **b** 50% of 64   **c** $\frac{3}{4}$ of 80   **d** 0.2 of 30

   e 45% of 90   **f** 0.8 of 150   **g** 250% of 48   **h** $\frac{3}{8}$ of 80

   i $33\frac{1}{3}$% of 96   **j** 30% of 25   **k** $12\frac{1}{2}$% of 40   **l** 62.5% of 240

22 **a** Increase 500 litres by 40%. **b** Decrease 300 mm by 15%.

c Increase £420 by 30%. **d** Decrease £60 by 4%.

23 Megan had £180 when she went shopping.

A new coat cost 25% of her money. How much did it cost?

24 The probability that Bradley will beat Zac at a computer game is 0.6.

Out of 35 games how many would you expect Bradley to win?

25 When $\frac{2}{3}$ full a car's petrol tank holds 36 litres of fuel.

How much does it hold when full?

(explanation 4a) (explanation 4b)

26 **a** Find the values **i** to **xiii** missing from this table.

x	2	3	4	5	6	7	8	9	10
x^2	4	9	i	25	ii	iii	64	iv	100
$\sqrt{x}$			v					vi	
x^3	8	vii	64	viii	216	ix	x	xi	xii
$\sqrt[3]{x}$							xiii		

b The blocked-out $\sqrt{x}$ and $\sqrt[3]{x}$ cells do not have whole-number square roots or cube roots.

i Is $\sqrt{5}$ closer to 2 or 3?

ii Is $\sqrt{8}$ closer to 2 or 3?

iii Would $\sqrt[3]{5}$ or $\sqrt[3]{10}$ be closer to 2?

27 Find these square roots and cube roots.

a $\sqrt{16}$ **b** $\sqrt{64}$ **c** $\sqrt{36}$ **d** $\sqrt{100}$ **e** $\sqrt{49}$ **f** $\sqrt[3]{125}$ **g** $\sqrt[3]{64}$

28 Find these square roots by writing the number as a product of two square numbers.

a $\sqrt{900}$ **b** $\sqrt{196}$ **c** $\sqrt{324}$ **d** $\sqrt{441}$

> Use divisibility rules to help find the factors.

29 Without using a calculator find these squares.

    a 15^2 **b** 20^2 **c** 25^2 **d** 30^2 **e** 10^3 **f** 20^3 **g** 30^3

30 Use your answers to question **26** to help estimate these square roots and cube roots.

    Write each estimate in the form $a < \sqrt{x} < b$.

    a $\sqrt{96}$ **b** $\sqrt{69}$ **c** $\sqrt{28}$ **d** $\sqrt{58}$ **e** $\sqrt{39}$ **f** $\sqrt[3]{90}$ **g** $\sqrt[3]{680}$

31   **a**   What is the area of a square with side 50 cm?

      b   What is the length of the side of a square with area $1600\,\text{cm}^2$?

32   **a**   Find the volume of this cube.   **b**   Find the side length, *l*, of the cube.

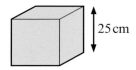   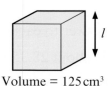

25 cm   Volume = $125\,\text{cm}^3$

explanation 5a	explanation 5b

33 Check these answers using inverse operations. Which ones are wrong?

    A   **B**   **C**   **D**

     $23 \times 5 = 120$ $87 \div 3 = 29$ $326 - 194 = 134$ $6 \times 52 = 312$

34   **a**   Which of these are equivalent to 24×36?

         A $12 \times 2 \times 12 \times 3$ **B** 48×18 **C** $48 \times 12 \times 2$ **D** $24 \times 6 \times 6$

      b   Find another equivalent calculation that could be used to check the answer.

35 Mutaz accurately measured the heights of his five brothers and sisters.

    They were 123.3 cm, 113.4 cm, 108.9 cm, 111 cm and 128.2 cm tall.

    Estimate their mean height.

36 Choose the best estimate for these.

a 7.9×1.2 **A** 8×1 **B** 8×2 **C** 7×2

b 3.2×11.3 **A** 4×12 **B** 4×11 **C** 3×11

c $12.6 \div 5.7$ **A** $12 \div 5$ **B** $12 \div 6$ **C** $13 \div 5$

d $48.7 \div 7.9$ **A** $48 \div 8$ **B** $49 \div 8$ **C** $50 \div 8$

37 Estimate to find an approximate answer to each calculation.

Do not find the exact answer.

a 4.5×3.8 b $7.8 \div 1.85$ c $128 \div 9.8$ d $96.4 \div 12$

e 8.4×7.8 f 346×12 g 5.8×9.4 h 111×89

i 38.7×9.2 j $523 \div 97$ k 489×224 l $317 \div 6.7$

38 Estimate the answer to each of these.

a   An ounce is about 28.35 g. How many ounces are there in 585 g?

b   A nautical mile is approximately 1.853 km.

How many kilometres are there in 223 nautical miles?

c   A litre is approximately 1.759 pints. How many pints are there in 84 litres?

39 On holiday Jo's family travelled 234.7 km on the first day.

On the next four days they travelled, 233.6 km, 87.3 km, 158.2 km and 217.4 km.

a   Estimate how far they travelled altogether.

b   Find the total distance they travelled.

c   The car travels 18 km on 1 litre of petrol.

Approximately how much petrol did they use?

Construction and congruence

- Constructing the circumcircle of a triangle
- Constructing the inscribed circle of a triangle
- Recognising the conditions for congruence
- Proving that two triangles are congruent

Keywords

You should know

explanation 1a   explanation 1b   explanation 1c   explanation 1d

1 This question is about constructing a perpendicular bisector of a line.

   a Draw a line AB that is 12 cm long.

   b Construct the perpendicular bisector of AB.

2 This question is about constructing an angle bisector.

   a Draw two lines OP and OQ that meet at O.

   b Construct the angle bisector of angle POQ.

   c Use a protractor to check your accuracy.

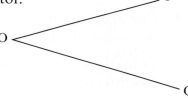

3 This question is about constructing a perpendicular to a line.

   a Draw the diagram accurately.

   b Construct the perpendicular to line MN at X.

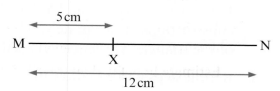

4 This question is about constructing a perpendicular to a line.

   a Copy the diagram accurately onto 1 cm² paper.

   b Construct a perpendicular from E to the line CD.

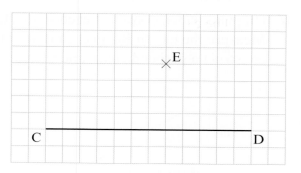

5 This question is about constructing perpendicular bisectors.

  a Draw a triangle ABC.

  b Construct the perpendicular bisector
of each of the sides of triangle ABC.

  c Find the point where your three
perpendicular bisectors meet. Label
this point X.

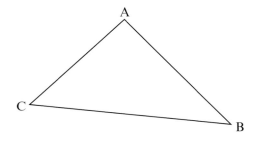

  d Using X as the centre and AX as the radius, draw a circle. If your
constructions are accurate your circle should pass through the points A, B
and C. This circle is called the circumcircle.

  e Draw a different triangle. Repeat steps **b**, **c** and **d** to draw the circumcircle
for your new triangle.

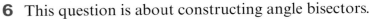

6 This question is about constructing angle bisectors.

  a Draw a triangle PQR.

  b Construct the angle bisector of each of
the angles of triangle PQR.

  c Find the point where your three angle
bisectors meet. Label this point Y.

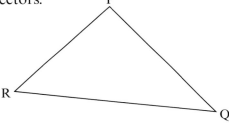

  d Construct the perpendicular from Y to the line PQ. Label the point where
they meet Z.

  e Using Y as the centre and YZ as the radius, draw a circle. If your
constructions are accurate your circle should touch each of the three sides
of the triangle. This circle is called the inscribed circle.

  f Repeat steps **a** to **e** to draw the inscribed circle for a differnt triangle.

7 On plain paper, construct each shape. Use a ruler and compasses only.
Measure the length BC in each case. (Hint: to construct an angle of 45°,
construct a perpendicular, and then bisect the 90° angle.)

  a
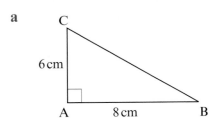
  b
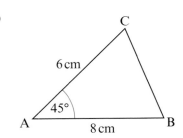

explanation 2a explanation 2b

8 Look at each pair of triangles. State whether the triangles in each pair are definitely congruent or not. Give explanations for your answers.

a

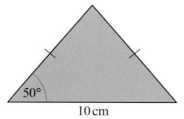

b

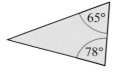   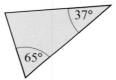

c

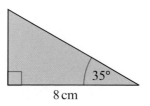   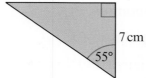

d

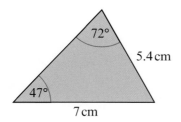   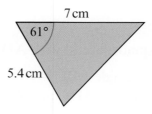

e

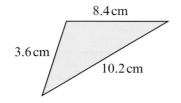   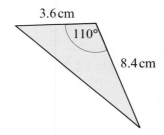

155

9 The straight lines AB and CD are equal in length and parallel.

Prove that triangles AEB and DEC are congruent.

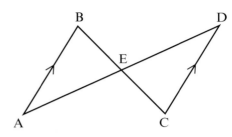

10 The straight lines LM and PN are equal in length and parallel.

Prove that triangles PLM and PNM are congruent.

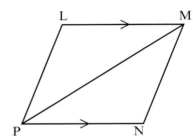

11 PQR is an isosceles triangle with PQ = PR.

M is the midpoint of PQ.

N is the midpoint of PR.

Prove that triangle PQN is congruent to triangle PRM.

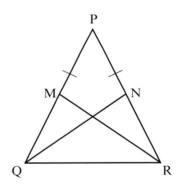

12 ABCD is a quadrilateral with AD = AB.

Angle ADC = angle ABC = 90°.
Prove that triangles ADC and ABC are congruent.

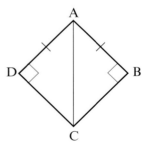

13 LMNP is an trapezium.
LP = MN and angle PLM = angle NML.
Prove that triangle PLM is congruent to triangle NML.

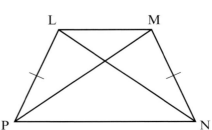

Loci

- Solving problems involving loci

Keywords

You should know

explanation 1a   explanation 1b   explanation 1c   explanation 1d

1 The diagram shows rectangle PQRS.

a Draw an accurate copy of the rectangle PQRS.

b Construct the locus of points that are exactly 6 cm from P.

c Construct the locus of points that are less than 5 cm from R.

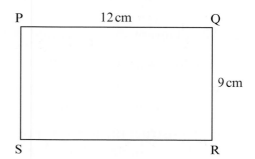

2 The diagram shows rectangle ABCD.

a Draw an accurate copy of the rectangle ABCD.

b Draw the locus of points that are equidistant from AB and AD.

c Shade the region in the rectangle to show the locus of points that are closer to AB than AD.

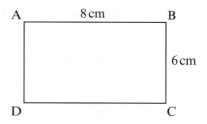

3 The diagram shows the line PQ.

a Draw an accurate copy of the line PQ.

P ———————— 8 cm ———————— Q

b Construct the locus of points that are equidistant from P and Q.

4 The diagram shows angle AOB.

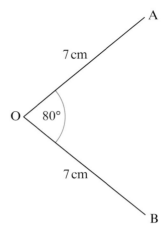

   a Copy the diagram.

   b Construct the locus of points that are equidistant from OA and OB.

   c Construct the locus of points that are 5 cm from O.

   d Shade the region to show the locus of points that are closer to OA than OB and less than 5 cm from O.

5 The diagram shows rectangle EFGH.

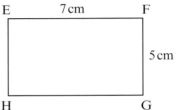

   a Draw an accurate copy of the rectangle EFGH .

   b Construct the locus of points that are within the rectangle and are 4 cm from E.

   c Construct the locus of points that are within the rectangle and are 3 cm from H.

   d Shade the region to show the locus of points that are within the rectangle and are less than 4 cm from E and less than 3 cm from H.

6 This question is about an equilateral triangle.

   a Draw an equilateral triangle ABC with sides of length 7 cm.

   b Construct the locus of points that are equidistant from AB and AC.

   c Construct the locus of points that are equidistant from A and B.

   d Shade the region within the triangle to show the locus of points that are closer to AB than AC and closer to A than B.

7 a Draw a line PQ that is 5 cm in length.

   b Construct the locus of points that are exactly 2 cm from PQ.

   c Construct the locus of points that are exactly 3 cm from P.

   d Shade the region to show the locus of points that are less than 2 cm from PQ and more than 3 cm from P.

8 Each part in this question refers to the rectangle ABCD.

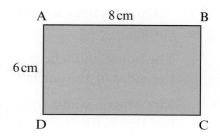

Draw a new rectangle for each part of the question.

Find the loci of these points that lie inside the rectangle.

a Points less than 4 cm from A and less than 7 cm from B.

b Points that are closer to AD than AB and more than 3 cm from D.

c Points that are more than 4 cm from DC and more than 3 cm from A.

9 Each part in this question refers to the triangle PQR.

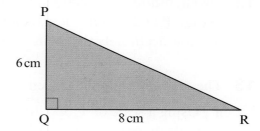

Draw a new triangle for each part of the question.

Find the loci of these points that lie inside the triangle.

a Points that are closer to PQ than PR and more than 2 cm from QR.

b Points less than 2 cm from QR and less than 3 cm from PQ.

c Points that are more than 4 cm from P and more than 5 cm from R.

explanation 2a   explanation 2b

10 Alncaster and Birchover are 120 km apart.

There is a radio transmitter at both Alncaster and Birchover. The range of the transmitter at Alncaster is 80 km. (Its signal cannot be received by points more than 80 km away.)

The range of the transmitter at Birchover is 90 km.

Using a scale of 1 cm to 10 km, draw an accurate diagram to show the locus of points that can receive a signal from both transmitters.

11 The diagram represents Mrs Martin's garden.

The house and a hedge make up two sides of the garden.

Mrs Martin wants to make a flower bed that is further than 6 m from the house and further than 5 m from the hedge.

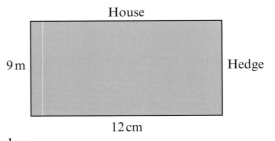

a Use a scale of 1 cm to 1 m to draw an accurate diagram of the rectangle.

b Shade the locus of all the points where the flower bed could be.

12 Two lighthouses P and Q are 200 km apart. It is known that a ship is closer to Q than P and that it is less than 80 km away from P. Use a scale of 1 : 2 000 000 to show accurately the locus of all points of the possible position of the ship.

13 The diagram shows a garden.

a Using a scale of 1 : 500 draw a scale diagram of the garden.

b There is a dog tethered at point A by a lead that is 6 m long. The owner wishes to plant a tree in such a position so that the dog cannot reach the tree. The tree also needs to be at least 12 m from the house.

Shade the locus of all the points where the tree could be planted.

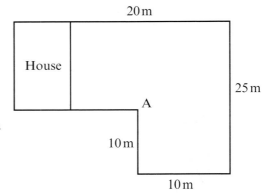

14 The diagram represents a sector of a circle marked out in a field.

Karen stands at the point O and throws a ball.

The ball lands within the sector in a position that is closer to OM than ON.

The ball is also more than 50 m but less than 70 m from O.

Use a scale of 1 : 1000 to make a scale drawing. Show the locus of all the points where the ball could have landed.

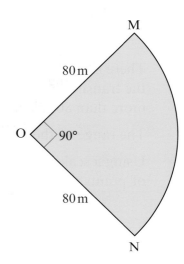

Pythagoras' theorem

- Identifying the hypotenuse in a right-angled triangle
- Using Pythagoras' theorem
- Finding the length of a line joining two coordinate points

Keywords

You should know

explanation 1a   explanation 1b   explanation 1c

1 Write Pythagoras' theorem for each triangle.

a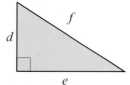

b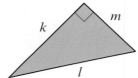

c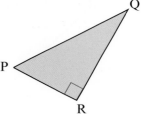

2 These diagrams can be used to demonstrate Pythagoras' theorem.

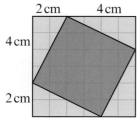

Diagram 1

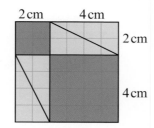

Diagram 2

a Compare the area of the yellow triangles in Diagram 1 with the area of the yellow triangles in Diagram 2. What do you notice?

b Now use the diagrams to explain why the area of the red square is equal to the areas of the two blue squares added together.

c Explain how this shows that Pythagoras' theorem is true for each yellow triangle.

explanation 2

3 For each triangle, use Pythagoras' theorem to work out the length of the unmarked side.

a
6 cm
8 cm

b
10 cm
24 cm

c
1.2 cm
3.5 cm

d
12 cm
9 cm

e
12 cm
5 cm

f
9 cm
3.75 cm

4 Work out the length of each unmarked side. Give your answers correct to one decimal place.

a
9 cm
12 cm

b
9.3 cm
6.5 cm

c
15.3 cm
6.8 cm

d
10 cm
10 cm

e
3.2 cm
9.6 cm

f
4 m
11 m

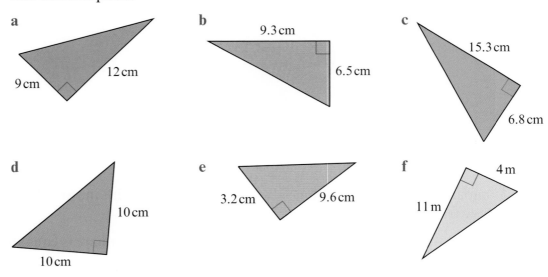

5 What is the length of the diagonal of this rectangle?

Give your answer correct to two decimal places.

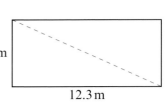

4.5 m

12.3 m

6 Work out the length of a diagonal of a square of side length 6 cm.
Give your answer correct to one decimal place.

explanation 3

7 Work out the length of each side marked by a letter. Give your answers correct
to one decimal place where necessary.

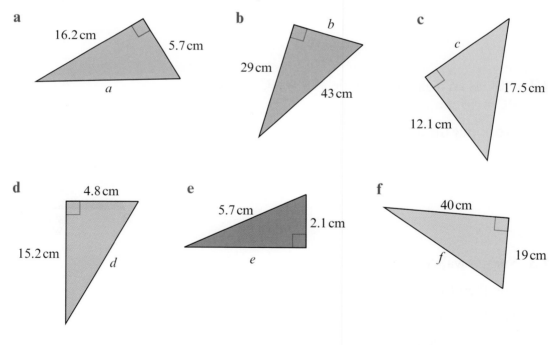

a

17 cm
a
15 cm

b

b
30 m
18 m

c

13.4 cm
c
9.8 cm

8 Work out the length of each side marked by a letter. Give your answers correct
to one decimal place where necessary.

a

16.2 cm
5.7 cm
a

b

b
29 cm
43 cm

c

c
17.5 cm
12.1 cm

d

4.8 cm
15.2 cm
d

e

5.7 cm
2.1 cm
e

f

40 cm
f
19 cm

9 The diagonal of a rectangle is 39 cm and the short side measures 15 cm.
Work out the length of the long side of the rectangle.

39 cm
15 cm

163

10 Work out the length of each side marked by a letter. Give your answers correct to three significant figures.

a

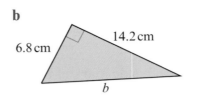

b

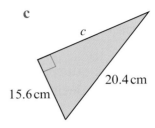

c

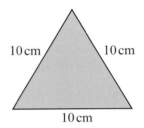

explanation 4a   explanation 4b

11 Find the height of an equilateral triangle of side length 10 cm.

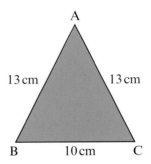

12 ABC is an isosceles triangle. AB = AC = 13 cm. BC = 10 cm.

Work out the area of triangle ABC.

13 Sumire walks due North for 4.6 km.

She then turns and walks 3.8 km due East.

Work out the distance between Sumire's starting point and finishing point.

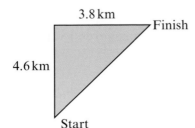

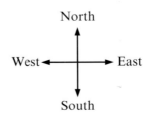

14 A ship sails 50 km due South and then a further 75 km due West.

At the end of its journey, how far is the ship from its starting point?

15 A 7 m ladder is standing on horizontal ground 2.1 m away from a vertical wall.

How far up the wall will the ladder reach?

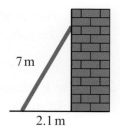

7 m

2.1 m

16 A snooker table is in the shape of a rectangle. The snooker table measures 12 feet by 6 feet. What is the length of a diagonal of the snooker table?

17 The slant height of a cone is 39 cm.

The radius of the base of the cone is 15 cm.

Work out the height of the cone.

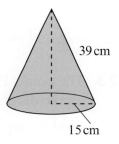

39 cm

15 cm

18 The diagonal of a rugby pitch is 140 m and the short side is 70 m.

What is the length of the long side of the pitch? Give your answer correct to the nearest metre.

19 Work out the length of the side marked x.

Give your answer correct to three significant figures.

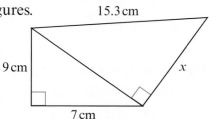

15.3 cm

9 cm

7 cm

x

20 The diagonals of a square are each of length 14.1 cm.

Work out the perimeter of the square.

21 This glass tank is a cuboid. It has length 12 cm, width 5 cm and height 8 cm.

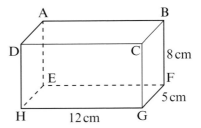

   a Work out the length of the diagonal HF.

   b Hence work out the length of the diagonal BH.

22 Use Pythagoras' theorem to decide whether or not these triangles have a right angle.

   a

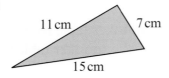

   b

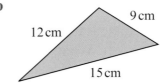

---

explanation 5

---

23 The points P (−3, 5) and Q (3, 1) are plotted on the diagram.

Find the length of the line PQ.

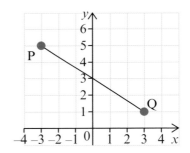

24 Find the distance between the points in each pair.

   a (0, 1) and (5, 3)   **b** (−2, 1) and (4, −3)   **c** (−3, −2) and (5, 0)

   d (−5, 8) and (0, −2)   **e** (−3, −6) and (2, 3)   **f** (5, −1) and (−4, 5)

25 Point A has the coordinates (1, 2). The length of the line AB is 5 units. The x-coordinate of B is 4.

   a Draw a sketch to show why there are *two* possible positions for point B.

   b Use Pythagoras' theorem to work out the two possible y-coordinates of B.

Working with data (2)

- Calculating estimates for the mean and range of grouped data
- Identifying the modal class interval and the class interval that includes the median
- Drawing cumulative frequency graphs
- Finding the median, lower and upper quartiles and the interquartile range
- Drawing box plots

Keywords

You should know

explanation 1a   explanation 1b   explanation 1c

1 The grouped frequency table shows the number of lengths 30 pupils swam in 10 minutes.

Lengths swum in 10 minutes	Frequency
5–9	7
10–14	9
15–19	10
20–24	3
25–29	1

   a Calculate an estimate for the mean number of lengths swum.

   b Write the class interval in which the median lies.

   c Find the modal class interval.

   d Pupils who swam less than 10 lengths in 10 minutes have extra swimming lessons. What percentage of the class have extra swimming lessons?

2 At the school summer fête, people were asked to estimate how many sweets there were in a jar. The table shows the results. The person whose estimate was closest to the actual number would win.

Estimated number of sweets	Frequency
76–100	12
101–125	23
126–150	20
151–175	15
176–200	8
201–225	2

   a Calculate an estimate for the mean estimated number of sweets in the jar.

   b Find an estimate of the range of the guesses.

   c There were 151 sweets in the jar. How many people definitely guessed too many?

167

3 This table shows the weight of 12 athletes in kilograms.

   a Calculate an estimate for the mean weight of an athlete to one decimal place.

   b Find the class interval that includes the median.

   c Find the modal class interval.

Weight, w (kg)	Frequency
$60 < w \leq 70$	1
$70 < w \leq 80$	3
$80 < w \leq 90$	5
$90 < w \leq 100$	2
$100 < w \leq 110$	1

4 This table shows the heights, in centimetres, of 100 pupils aged between 12 and 14.

   a Calculate an estimate for the mean height to 1 d.p.

   b Find the class interval that includes the median.

   c Find the modal class interval.

   d What fraction of pupils are more than 170 cm tall?

Height, h (cm)	Frequency
$130 < h \leq 140$	2
$140 < h \leq 150$	12
$150 < h \leq 160$	35
$160 < h \leq 170$	42
$170 < h \leq 180$	5
$180 < h \leq 190$	4

5 This table shows the time taken in seconds for the 15 finalists at a sports day to sprint 100 m.

   a Calculate an estimate for the mean time to 1 d.p.

   b Find the class interval that includes the median.

   c Find the modal class interval.

   d What percentage of pupils ran the race in 14 seconds or less?

Time, t (seconds)	Frequency
$11 < t \leq 12$	1
$12 < t \leq 13$	2
$13 < t \leq 14$	5
$14 < t \leq 15$	4
$15 < t \leq 16$	2
$16 < t \leq 17$	1

6 The table shows the numbers of low birth weight babies (less than 2500 g) born in March at a hospital.

a Find the class interval that includes the median.

b Find the modal class interval.

c 5% of the babies born at the hospital have a low birth weight.
What was the total number of babies born at the hospital during March?

Weight, w (g)	Frequency
$500 \leq w < 750$	1
$750 \leq w < 1000$	3
$1000 \leq w < 1250$	1
$1250 \leq w < 1500$	1
$1500 \leq w < 1750$	2
$1750 \leq w < 2000$	2
$2000 \leq w < 2250$	4
$2250 \leq w < 2500$	6

explanation 2a   explanation 2b   explanation 2c

7 The grouped frequency table shows information about the times taken by some athletes to run 200 m.

Draw a frequency polygon to show this information.

Time, t (seconds)	Frequency
$20 \leq t < 22$	2
$22 \leq t < 24$	4
$24 \leq t < 26$	9
$26 \leq t < 28$	6
$28 \leq t < 30$	3

8 The grouped frequency table gives information about the number of seconds that 80 people spent waiting at a supermarket checkout.

Draw a frequency polygon to show this information.

Time, t (seconds)	Frequency
$0 \leq t < 60$	10
$60 \leq t < 120$	19
$120 \leq t < 180$	24
$180 \leq t < 240$	20
$240 \leq t < 300$	5
$300 \leq t < 360$	2

9 The frequency polygon shows some information about the ages of employees in a company.

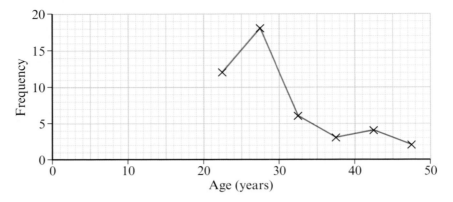

a Write the modal class interval.

b Work out the total number of employees in the company.

10 The grouped frequency table gives information about the number of seconds that 80 people spent waiting at a supermarket checkout.

Time, t (seconds)	Frequency	Time, t (seconds)	Cumulative frequency
$0 \le t < 60$	10	$0 \le t < 60$	
$60 \le t < 120$	19	$0 \le t < 120$	
$120 \le t < 180$	24	$0 \le t < 180$	
$180 \le t < 240$	20	$0 \le t < 240$	
$240 \le t < 300$	5	$0 \le t < 300$	
$300 \le t < 360$	2	$0 \le t < 360$	

a Copy and complete the cumulative frequency table.

b Draw a cumulative frequency diagram for your table.

c Use your graph to find an estimate for the number of people who waited for these times.

   i less than 200 seconds   **ii** more than 200 seconds

11 The grouped frequency table gives information about the weights, in grams, of 60 potatoes.

Weight, w (grams)	Frequency
$0 \leq w < 50$	7
$50 \leq w < 100$	12
$100 \leq w < 150$	20
$150 \leq w < 200$	11
$200 \leq w < 250$	7
$250 \leq w < 300$	3

Weight, w (grams)	Cumulative frequency
$0 \leq w < 50$	
$0 \leq w < 100$	
$0 \leq w < 150$	
$0 \leq w < 200$	
$0 \leq w < 250$	
$0 \leq w < 300$	

  a Copy and complete the cumulative frequency table.

  b Draw a cumulative frequency diagram for your table.

  c Use your graph to find an estimate for the number of potatoes with these weights.

    i less than 120 g   **ii** more than 120 g

12 The grouped frequency table gives information about the ages of 140 people employed at a school.

Age, a (years)	Frequency
$20 \leq a < 25$	7
$25 \leq a < 30$	8
$30 \leq a < 35$	12
$35 \leq a < 40$	16
$40 \leq a < 45$	37
$45 \leq a < 50$	23
$50 \leq a < 55$	15
$55 \leq a < 60$	12
$60 \leq a < 65$	10

Age, a (years)	Cumulative frequency
$0 \leq a < 25$	
$0 \leq a < 30$	
$0 \leq a < 35$	
$0 \leq a < 40$	
$0 \leq a < 45$	
$0 \leq a < 50$	
$0 \leq a < 55$	
$0 \leq a < 60$	
$0 \leq a < 65$	

  a Copy and complete the cumulative frequency table.

  b Draw a cumulative frequency diagram for your table.

13 The cumulative frequency graph gives information about the heights of some small trees.

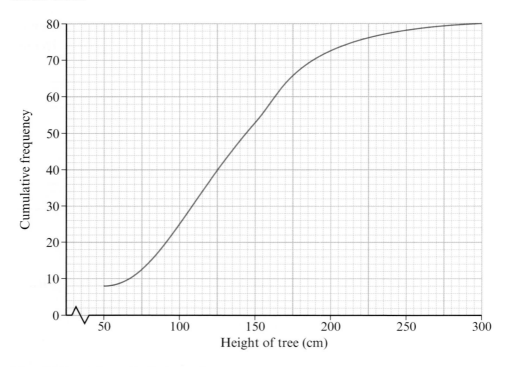

Use the graph to find these data.

a   The total number of trees.

b   An estimate for the number of trees that had a height of more than 200 cm.

c   An estimate for the number of trees that had a height of more than 100 cm but less than 150 cm.

14 The cumulative frequency graph gives information about the number of minutes 120 passengers had to wait at an airport check-in desk.

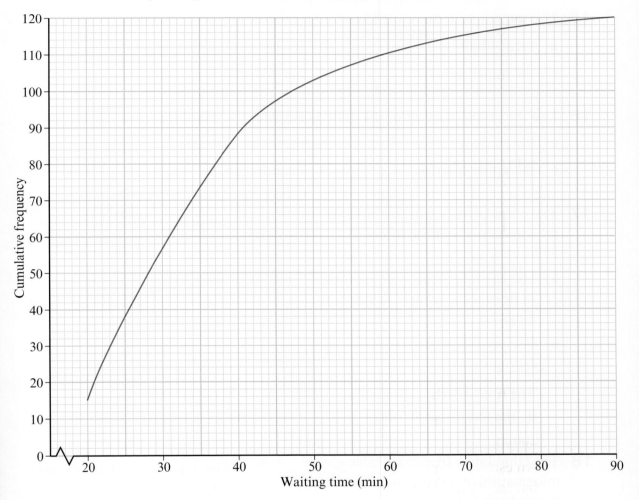

Use the graph to find an estimate for the number of passengers that waited for these times.

a less than 40 minutes

b more than 40 minutes

c more than 30 minutes but less than 60 minutes

explanation 3a   explanation 3b

15 Use the graph in question **13** to find estimates for these statistics.

    a the median   **b** the lower quartile

    c the upper quartile   **d** the interquartile range

16 Use the graph in question **14** to find estimates for these statistics.

    a the median   **b** the lower quartile

    c the upper quartile   **d** the interquartile range

17 The cumulative frequency table shows information about the prices of 80 houses.

    a Use the information in the table to draw a cumulative frequency diagram.

    b Use your diagram to find estimates for

        i the median

       ii the interquartile range

House price, p (£)	Cumulative frequency
$0 \leq p < 120\,000$	5
$0 \leq p < 140\,000$	12
$0 \leq p < 160\,000$	21
$0 \leq p < 180\,000$	32
$0 \leq p < 200\,000$	51
$0 \leq p < 220\,000$	72
$0 \leq p < 240\,000$	80

18 The cumulative frequency table gives information about the time that some pupils took to travel to school.

    a Use the information in the table to draw a cumulative frequency diagram.

    b Use your diagram to find an estimate for the number of pupils that took more than 45 minutes to travel to school.

    c Use your diagram to find estimates for these statistics.

        i the median

       ii the interquartile range

Time to get to school, t (minutes)	Cumulative frequency
$0 \leq t < 10$	14
$0 \leq t < 20$	34
$0 \leq t < 30$	44
$0 \leq t < 40$	52
$0 \leq t < 50$	58
$0 \leq t < 60$	58

explanation 4

19 Kylie recorded the number of DVDs owned by some of her friends.
She drew this box plot from the data.

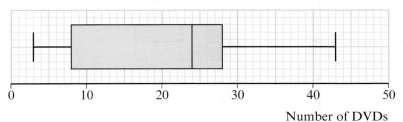

Number of DVDs

   a Copy and complete this table.

Minimum number of DVDs	
Lower quartile	
Median	
Upper quartile	
Maximum number of DVDs	

   b Use the information in your table to find these.

      i the range   **ii** the interquartile range

20 Lizzy recorded the heights of some of her friends.
She drew this box plot from the data.

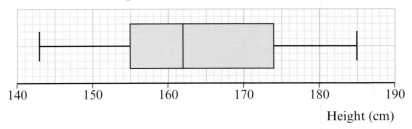

Height (cm)

   a What is the height of Lizzy's tallest friend?

   b Write the median height.

   c Work out the range of the heights.

   d Work out the interquartile range for these heights.

21 Pupils in two classes took a test.
Their results were used to draw these box plots.

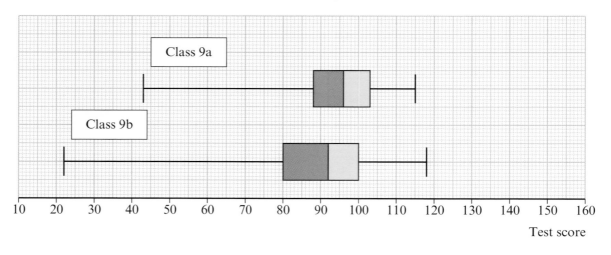

a   In which class was the pupil who scored the highest mark?

b   Work out the range for class 9a and the range for class 9b.

c   Write the median score for each class.

d   Which class had the better results? Give an explanation for your answer.

22 Angie measured the length of leaves.
The table shows some information about her results.

Minimum length	3.4 cm
Lower quartile	4.2 cm
Median	5.2 cm
Upper quartile	6.5 cm
Maximum length	8 cm

Use the information to draw a box plot.

23 Some pupils took a test. The table gives information about their results.

a   Work out the highest score.

b   Work out the upper quartile.

c   Draw a box plot for the data.

Minimum test score	23
Lower quartile	45
Median	53
Interquartile range	14
Range	52

Statistical investigations

- Writing a hypothesis
- Planning a statistical investigation to solve a problem

Keywords

You should know

explanation 1a   explanation 1b   explanation 1c   explanation 1d

1 Some pupils are investigating problems.

  i Write a hypothesis for each problem.

  ii Would primary or secondary data be used in each investigation?

a Jenny wants to compare the heights of boys and the heights of girls.

b Anil wants to investigate whether teachers or pupils are better at mental arithmetic.

c Pat wants to investigate the relationship between the size of a country's population and the area of the country.

d Sam wants to compare the weather in New York with the weather in London.

e Morgan wants to investigate what happens to the value of cars as they get older.

f Ahmed wants to investigate the relationship between the time pupils spend watching television and their GCSE results.

g Geoff wants to investigate whether boys or girls are better at maths.

h James wants to investigate the amount of time boys and girls spend playing sport outside school.

2 Data is going to be collected to test these hypotheses.

For each hypothesis write this information.

  i A description of the data that could be collected.

  ii Where the data will come from.

  a Taller people are heavier than shorter people.

  b It is hotter in Egypt than in Crete.

  c The taller you are, the quicker your reaction time.

  d The average length of television programmes is 30 minutes.

  e Pupils who watch more television spend more time on the internet.

  f The closer a pupil lives to school, the more homework they do.

  g Girls read more books than boys.

3 Write down the following for each of these problems.

  i A suitable hypothesis.

  ii A description of the data that will be needed.

  iii The source of the data and how it will be collected.

  a Are more expensive newspapers less popular?

  b Does it rain more in Newcastle or Penzance?

  c Does a football team with more foreign players win more matches?

  d Do taller children have longer arms?

explanation 2a   explanation 2b   explanation 2c

4 Design data collection sheets for the following surveys or experiments.

  a The total scored when two dice are rolled together.

  b The number of words in the sentences of a book.

  c The heights of pupils in your maths class.

  d The shoe sizes of pupils in your maths class.

  e The number of vehicles in the school car park at different times of the day.

5 Sam designs a questionnaire.

He gives it to his friends to fill in.

> ### Sam's questionnaire
>
> **1**   What type of mobile phone do you own?
>
>   Nokia ☐   Samsung ☐
>
> **2**   How would you rate your mobile phone?
>
>   Average ☐   Good ☐   Excellent ☐
>
> **3**   How much do you spend each week using your mobile phone?
>
>   0–£2 ☐   £2–£4 ☐   £4–£6 ☐   £6 or more ☐
>
> **4**   How many text messages do you send?
>
>   0–10 ☐   11–20 ☐   21–30 ☐   31–40 ☐

Some of his friends cannot fill in the questionnaire.

a   Explain why each of Sam's friends can't fill in the questionnaire.

b   Rewrite the questionnaire so that everyone can fill it in.

i 'I don't like my mobile phone; it's awful!'

iii 'My mobile phone is a Motorola'

v 'I spend exactly £4 a week'

ii 'I send 20 texts a day'

iv 'I send 20 texts a month'

6 Design a questionnaire for each of these investigations.

Write at least two questions for each.

Don't forget to include response boxes.

a Harry wants to find out how people use the local library.

b Jemilla wants to find out what her friends think about school dinners.

c Meg wants to find out how people use the local sports centre.

7 Choose one of the following problems and plan your own investigation.

   i Write a hypothesis.

   ii Plan your investigation.

   iii Explain how you will collect your data and how much data you will collect.

   iv Design a questionnaire or data collection sheet.

a Do children who watch more television do less homework?

b Do people who run faster have longer legs?

c Are children quicker at writing text messages than adults?

d Do pupils in Year 11 get more homework than pupils in Year 7?

Interpreting and communicating

- Interpreting more complex graphs and diagrams
- Testing hypotheses
- Comparing two or more distributions

Keywords

You should know

explanation 1

1 Dinesh asked his friends where they went on holiday last year.

The pie chart shows the results of his survey.

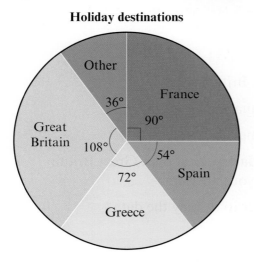

Holiday destinations

a What fraction of the people surveyed went to France?

b Which country was most frequently chosen for holidays?

c Dinesh says 'More people went to Spain than France'.
Is Dinesh correct? Give a reason for your answer.

d 30 people went to France for their holiday.
How many people took part in the survey?

2 The dual bar chart shows the numbers of medals won by Great Britain and Australia in the 2008 Olympic games.

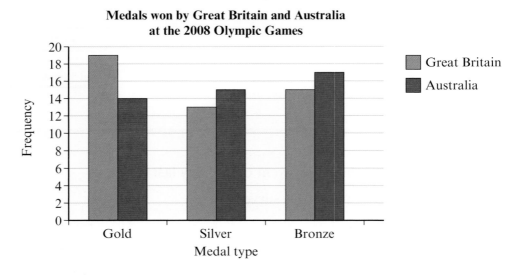

a How many silver medals did Great Britain win?

b How many gold medals did Australia win?

c Which country won more bronze medals?

d Tony says 'Australia won more medals in total than Great Britain'. Is Tony correct? Give a reason for your answer.

Maria thinks pie charts would be better to display the data. She draws two pie charts.

e Which type of graph shows the results more clearly? Explain your answer.

3 Sasha surveyed 36 girls and 36 boys to find out which their favourite subject is from English, maths, science, history and geography.
The table shows how many girls and how many boys chose each subject.

Subject	Number of girls	Number of boys
English	9	6
Maths	7	11
Science	5	9
History	8	4
Geography	7	6

a Sasha wants to illustrate the results of her survey using a graph.
She wants to be able to show the popularity of the different subjects.
What type of graph should she draw? Give a reason for your answer.

b Sasha's English teacher wants to use a graph to show that more girls than boys prefer English. What type of diagram should she draw? Explain your answer.

(explanation 2a) (explanation 2b)

4 Anya is doing a geography project. Her hypothesis is 'The higher the birth rate of a country, the lower the life expectancy is in that country'. She collects some data from the internet. She uses her data to draw a scatter graph.

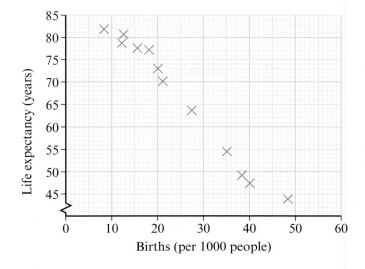

Is Anya's hypothesis correct? Explain how you use the information shown in the graph to reach your conclusion.

5 Alan wants to find out if there is a relationship between the distance travelled during an aeroplane flight and the cost of the flight.

He collects some data from an airline's website then uses the data to plot a scatter graph. He draws a line of best fit on his graph.

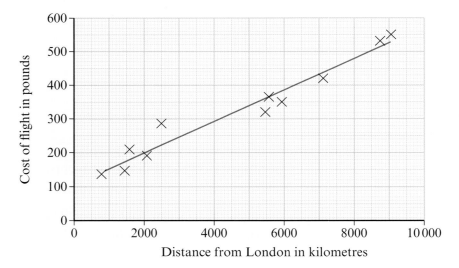

a How many of the flights were shorter than 5000 kilometres?

b How many flights cost more than £400?

c One of the points represents a flight from London to Miami. Miami is approximately 7100 km from London. Approximately how much did this flight cost?

d Alan's hypothesis is 'The greater the distance travelled, the more the flights cost'. Is Alan's hypothesis correct? Use information shown in the scatter graph to give reasons for your answer.

6 Paul lives in York. His hypothesis is 'The more it rains, the lower the temperature is'.
In order to see if his hypothesis is correct he collects some data about the weather in York.
The graph shows this information.

Is Paul's hypothesis correct?
Explain how you used the information shown in the graph to reach your conclusion.

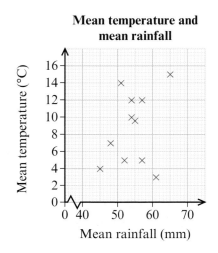

Mean temperature and mean rainfall

explanation 3a   explanation 3b   explanation 3c   explanation 3d

7 The pie charts show how all pupils travel to two different schools.

School A 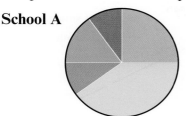  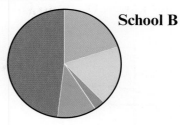 School B

Bicycle
Walk
Train
Car
Bus

a What fraction of pupils from school A travel to school by bicycle?
Give your fraction in its simplest form.

b What fraction of pupils from school B travel to school by bicycle?
Give your fraction in its simplest form.

c Emily says that more pupils cycle to school A than school B.
Is Emily correct? Give a reason for your answer.

d How do most pupils travel to school A?

e How do most pupils travel to school B?

f One of the schools is out in the country and the other is in a town.
Which school is most likely to be in a town? Give a reason for your answer.

8 Two classes took the same test. There are 20 pupils in each class.

The stem and leaf diagrams show their results.

Class A

```
0 |
1 | 0   2   2   6
2 | 1   4
3 | 4   8   9
4 | 1   5   5
5 | 1   2   6   7
6 | 0   1   2   4
```

Class B

```
0 | 7
1 | 6   7   8
2 | 3   5   8
3 | 1   3   4   4
4 | 2   6   6
5 | 7   8
6 | 2   4   4   5
```

Key: 3|5   represents a
                score of 35

a Find the range for class A and the range for class B.

b Find the median result for class A and the median result for class B.

c Calculate the mean result for class A and the mean result for class B.

d Which class performed better in the test? Justify your answer using the
medians and means worked out in parts **b** and **c**.

9 The line graphs show the mean numbers of hours of sunshine per day in Rome and in Madrid each month.

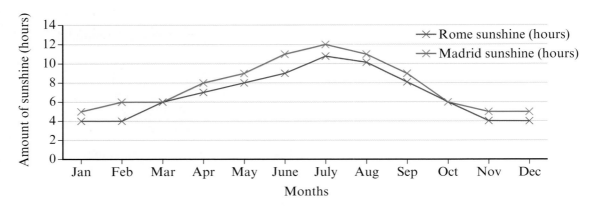

a What was the mean number of hours of sunshine per day for Rome in August?

b In which two months do Rome and Madrid both have a mean of 6 hours of sunshine per day?

c Which city has more hours of sunshine in a year?
Give a reason for your answer.

10 Nell and Paula both record the number of minutes they spend talking on their mobile phone each day for a fortnight.
Their results were used to draw two box plots.

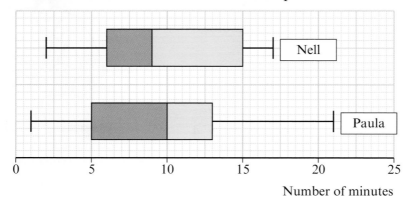

Compare the times that the girls spent talking on their mobile phones.

11 The box plots show information about the ages of the workers in two factories.

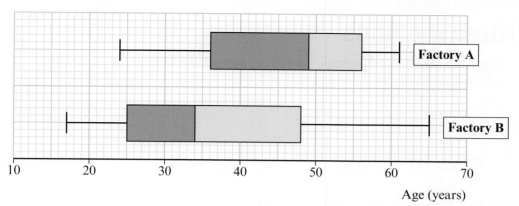

Age (years)

Compare the ages of the workers in the two factories.

12 These stem and leaf diagrams show the amount, correct to the nearest pound, that some customers spent in two different restaurants.

Restaurant A

1	4	6	7	8	8	9	
2	0	0	2	4	6	7	7
3	1	2	2	2	3	4	4
4							

Restaurant B

Key: 3|1   represents a spend of £31

1	8	9					
2	3	5	7	7	8		
3	2	4	4	5	7	7	8	8
4	0	1	2	5	6		

a Work out the median and range for each restaurant.

b Use the values you have worked out in part **a** to compare the prices in the two restaurants.

Written methods

- Using written methods for addition, subtraction, multiplication and division of decimals with differing numbers of decimal places

Keywords

You should know

Do not use calculators for this topic.

explanation 1

1 Work out these additions.

a 54.72 + 49.5

b 34.8 + 23.74

c 7.54 + 125.8

d 51.05 + 45.921

e 2.99 + 48.03

f 0.72 + 179.098

2 Work these out.

a 4.56 + 81.48 + 37.42

b 36.84 + 372.7 + 1211.98

c 9045.8 + 813 + 67.52

d 648.805 + 43.7 + 0.337

3 Find the perimeter of each shape.

a

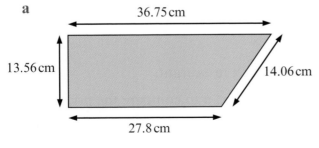

b

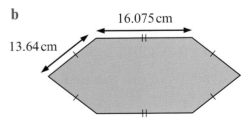

explanation 2a   explanation 2b

4 Work out these subtractions.

a 23.7 − 12.9

b 406.3 − 79.74

c 403.6 − 39.88

d 30.08 − 24.65

e 407.562 − 320.798

f 1003.4 − 891.5

5 Work these out.

    a 39.05 − 10.13 − 8.7   **b** 24.7 − 9.05 − 5.82   **c** 540.3 − 7 − 21.7

    d 31.83 − 6.4 − 23.54   **e** 70.2 − 6.74 − 46.3   **f** 211.453 − 45.84 − 20.303

6 A large shipping container, packed with cars, weighs 28.18 tonnes.

A small family car weighing 1.09 tonnes and a larger estate car of 1.4 tonnes are driven out of the container.

How heavy will the container be now?

7 Four friends had a total of £45.75 between them.

Josie had £15.68, Lucie had £12.85 and Sandy £13.34.

How much money must Susie have had?

8 Work out these mixed addition and subtraction calculations.

    a 8.04 + 322.7 − 15.46   **b** 4.56 − 143.5 + 2062.34

    c 5.7 − 30.29 + 58.92 + 45   **d** 61.3 − 11.043 + 45.617

    e 12.45 − 6.2 + 15.6 − 4.031   **f** 34.03 − 7.8 + 13.03 − 22.55

9 Three sacks weigh 16.64 kg, 25.07 kg and 9.88 kg.

How much more or less than 50 kg do they weigh altogether?

10 On an outdoor adventure camp, pupils had to climb up a 50 m muddy incline as fast as possible.

Jason climbed up 13.6 m and then slid back 7.38 m.

He then clambered up another 18.3 m before slipping back 10.35 m.

How much further did he have to climb to reach the top?

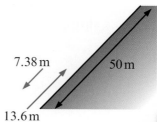

explanation 3a   explanation 3b

11 Work out these multiplications.

   a 8 × 45.6   **b** 36.8 × 15   **c** 6.8 × 32   **d** 21 × 3.4

   e 43 × 32.1   **f** 61.4 × 31   **g** 19.8 × 36   **h** 73 × 24.3

12 An antibiotic for 'dog flu' is given every 24 hours.
The dosage is based on the body mass of the dog.
How much will be given to dogs with these weights?

   a 8 kg   **b** 24 kg   **c** 39 kg

0.45 ml per kilogram of body mass

13 Work these out.

   a 5.1 × 8.9   **b** 5.8 × 31.5   **c** 13.46 × 5.6   **d** 27.4 × 4.8

   e 25.9 × 3.17   **f** 6.07 × 14.9   **g** 2.9 × 5.05   **h** 4.14 × 3.7

   i 72.61 × 0.29   **j** 0.62 × 8.53   **k** 4.811 × 1.7   **l** 0.455 × 8.4

14 These are the prices of vegetables on one stall at the local farmer's market.

Round your answers to the nearest penny.

   a Mrs Graham buys 2.5 kg potatoes, 1.5 kg beans and a cauliflower.

     How much does she pay the stallholder for her vegetables?

   b Mr Yates buys 2 cabbages, 3.5 kg potatoes and 2 kg carrots.

     How much more or less does he pay for his shopping than Mrs Graham?

Potatoes	£1.45 a kg
Cabbages	49p each
Beans	£3.78 a kg
Carrots	£1.70 a kg
Cauliflower	79p each

15 a What area of carpet will be needed to cover a sitting-room floor measuring 5.25 m by 4.3 m?

  b The carpet costs £21.70 per square metre.
  How much will the carpet cost?
  Round your answer to the nearest 10 pence.

explanation 4a   explanation 4b

16 Work out these divisions.

  a 202.3 ÷ 7   **b** 188.32 ÷ 8   **c** 189.8 ÷ 13   **d** 388.8 ÷ 16

  e 786.6 ÷ 23   **f** 7721.6 ÷ 32   **g** 8162.4 ÷ 24   **h** 1755.6 ÷ 38

17 Eight friends go out for a meal. The bill came to £117.20.

  a How much would they each pay if they shared the costs equally?

  b Two friends had more expensive meals, so they paid £17.50 each.

    The rest shared the remaining bill. How much did they each have to pay?

18 Rita has 38 weeks to save £1402.20 for her summer holiday.

  a If she saves the same amount each week, how much must she save a week?

  b Rita saved £39.50 each week for 20 weeks.

    What is the minimum amount she must save for each of the remaining weeks to pay for her holiday?

19 Which calculation is equivalent to the given calculation?

  a 94 ÷ 3.4   **A** 94 ÷ 34   **B** 940 ÷ 3.4   **C** 940 ÷ 34   **D** 9400 ÷ 34

  b 386 ÷ 7.9   **A** 386 ÷ 79   **B** 3860 ÷ 7.9   **C** 3860 ÷ 79   **D** 38 600 ÷ 79

  c 372.4 ÷ 5.6   **A** 3724 ÷ 5.6   **B** 3724 ÷ 56   **C** 37 240 ÷ 56   **D** 37 240 ÷ 5.6

  d 12.56 ÷ 0.55   **A** 125.6 ÷ 55   **B** 1256 ÷ 5.5   **C** 12 560 ÷ 55   **D** 1256 ÷ 55

20 Work these out.

    a $117 \div 2.6$ **b** $378 \div 4.2$ **c** $425 \div 1.7$ **d** $238 \div 2.8$

    e $145 \div 2.5$ **f** $144 \div 1.6$ **g** $189 \div 0.9$ **h** $212 \div 0.4$

21 Work these out.

    a $32.5 \div 2.5$ **b** $36.8 \div 1.6$ **c** $47.6 \div 1.4$ **d** $61.2 \div 0.9$

    e $87.4 \div 2.3$ **f** $117.6 \div 2.1$ **g** $159.9 \div 1.3$ **h** $353.6 \div 1.6$

    i $30.25 \div 0.25$ **j** $5.04 \div 0.12$ **k** $7.56 \div 2.1$ **l** $3.42 \div 1.8$

22 Dean's car used 34.6 litres of petrol to travel to Scotland.

On average his car travelled 12.2 km per litre of petrol.

How far did he travel?

23 A carton containing packets of biscuits weighs 4.5 kg.

The carton weighs 0.9 kg. Each packet of biscuits weighs 0.4 kg.

How many packets of biscuits does the carton hold?

24 The diagram shows how every £1 from the sale of diesel is split.

    a   If diesel costs £1.13 per litre, how much
        is earned by each of these from one litre?

        i   duty   **ii**   the producer

        iii   tax   **iv**   the retailer

        Round your answers to the nearest penny.

    b   Dylan spent £35.64 on diesel.

        How much of that was duty?

    c   On one sale a retailer earned £2.55.

        How many litres of diesel were sold?

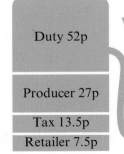

Duty 52p

Producer 27p

Tax 13.5p

Retailer 7.5p

Calculator methods

- Rounding and estimating when using a calculator
- Using a calculator to find powers and roots
- Using fraction, π and reciprocal keys
- Using a calculator for money and percentage calculations
- Using a calculator for conversions, such as exchange rates and measurement problems

Keywords

You should know

explanation 1a | explanation 1b | explanation 1c | explanation 1d

1 Find the answers to these using your calculator.

Round the answers to two decimal places.

a $1.6 \times 8.2 + 43.01$

b $-5.03 \times (1.32 + 2.86)$

c $5.3 + -9.53 \div 0.65$

d $\dfrac{3.87 + 0.3}{2.3}$

e $\dfrac{154.7 \div -4.2}{3 \times 2}$

f $\dfrac{6.4 \times 5.78}{-4.02}$

g $\dfrac{-3.46 \times 23.8 - -3.4}{11.7 \times 0.38}$

h $\dfrac{1.6 + 3.8 \times 5}{1.7^2}$

i $\dfrac{(4.8 - 2.03) \times 12.3}{-5 \div 1.8 + 3.3}$

2 Shona worked out that $\sqrt{25} + 6.8 = 11.8$.

Winston worked out that $\sqrt{25} + 6.8 = 5.64$ (to 2 d.p.).

a Why are their answers different?

b Work these out.

   i $\sqrt{56.3 - 23.1}$ **ii** $\sqrt{3.7 \times 18.6}$ **iii** $\sqrt{43.2 \div 12.5}$

3 Use your calculator to work these out.

Round your answers to two decimal places.

a $7.8^2 (4.01 + 8.11)$

b $(2.5 \times 1.04)^2$

c $\sqrt{4.8 + 18.4}$

d $\dfrac{\sqrt{15.6 \times 12.03}}{3.2 \times 4}$

e $\dfrac{(5.2 - -4.3)^2}{\sqrt{6.5}}$

f $\dfrac{(2.83 \times 3.82)(1.5 \times 4.2)}{\sqrt{3.6 - 2.1}}$

g $\dfrac{\sqrt[3]{32} \times \sqrt{18}}{(-1.4)^2}$

h $\dfrac{(4.7^3 \times \sqrt{11})^2}{5.3 + 8.92}$

i $\sqrt{\dfrac{7.6 + 4.8 \times 12.63}{4.3}}$

4 Greg's square garden has an area of $615.04\,\text{m}^2$.

He wanted to divide the garden into squares each with sides of $6.2\,\text{m}$.

Can he get an exact number of these squares in the garden? If so, how many?

(explanation 2) ━━

5 Estimate the answers to these. Show your working.

a $\dfrac{4.08 \times 35.23}{6.89 \times 1.9}$

b $\dfrac{8.32 \div 9.75}{10.2}$

c $\dfrac{12.56 \times 47.65}{23.7 \times 4.4}$

d $\dfrac{\sqrt{15.7 + 12.01}}{3.2 + 2.3}$

e $\dfrac{2.05^3 + (4.3 + 5.5)^2}{11.6}$

f $\dfrac{\sqrt{4.08 \times 8.7}}{\sqrt{15.6}}$

6 For each calculation

  i Estimate the answer by rounding the numbers to one significant figure.

  ii Work out the answer using a calculator.

a 409×34 b $764 \div 23.5$ c 89.3×6.82 d $3845.6 \div 7.8$

e 7.803×11.67 f $(3.68 + 6.8) \times 5.9^2$ g $12.35^3 \div 7.9$ h $8.35^2 \div 2.05^3$

7 The surface area of a cuboid is

$2 \times$ area of face A $+ 2 \times$ area of face B $+ 2 \times$ area of face C.

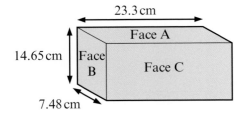

a Write *one* calculation that you could use to find the surface area of this cuboid.

b Find the answer to two decimal places.

c Check your answer by using an estimate.

8 Mary estimated the answer to $\dfrac{52.6}{3.19 + 1.78}$ as $\dfrac{50}{5} = 10$.

Write three more calculations that could have an estimated answer of 10.

Use at least three of the operations $+$, $-$, $\times$ and $\div$.

Include a square or a square root in one of the calculations.

explanation 3a   explanation 3b

9 Use your calculator to work these out. Round answers to one decimal place.

   a $80 \times (\sqrt{34 + 5.3})$

   b $\sqrt{47} \div \sqrt{10} \times 2.45$

   c $100 \times (\sqrt{7 - 2.3})$

   d $135 \div \sqrt{39} - 6$

10 $r = \sqrt{11}$ and $s = \dfrac{93}{r - 3}$

   a Calculate the value of r to one decimal place.

   b Calculate the value of s to one decimal place, using the rounded value of r.

   c Calculate the value of s to one decimal place, using $r = \sqrt{11}$ (not rounded). What is the difference?

   d Which answer is more accurate?

11 The formula for finding the surface area of a sphere is $4\pi r^2$.

   a Using $\pi = 3.14$, find the surface area of a sphere with radius 34.6 cm to 1 d.p.

   b Using the π key on your calculator, find the surface area of a sphere with radius 34.6 cm to 1 d.p.

   c Did you get the same answer to parts **a** and **b**?

   Which is the most accurate answer? Why?

12 The volume of a sphere is $\frac{4}{3}\pi r^3$.

   a Find the volumes of spheres with these radii, using the most accurate method.

   Round answers to two decimal places.

     i radius = 2.3 cm   **ii** radius = 4.84 cm   **iii** radius = 9.07 cm

   b Check the answers to part **a** by estimating.

explanation 4a   explanation 4b

13 Use a calculator to find the reciprocals of these.

If any answer has more than two decimal places, round to 2 d.p.

a   0.35   b   4.8   c   0.62   d   2.5

e   63   f   15.56   g   2.004   h   0.009 99

14 The reciprocal of a whole number between 20 and 50 is 0.028□71 correct to 5 significant figures.

Find the number and the missing digit in its reciprocal.

15 Work out these using the fraction key on your calculator.

a $1\frac{5}{11} - \frac{3}{5}$

b $\frac{6}{7} \div \frac{5}{16}$

c $7\frac{4}{13} \times \left(\frac{1}{5}\right)^2$

d $5\frac{3}{5} \div 1\frac{1}{2}$

e $2\frac{5}{6} + 3\frac{11}{15} \times \frac{3}{4}$

f $3\frac{1}{7} - \sqrt{\frac{1}{4}} \times \frac{3}{5}$

g $2\frac{7}{15} \times \frac{3}{4} + 9\frac{2}{7}$

h $\dfrac{\left(\frac{3}{4}\right)^3 \times \left(\frac{2}{3} \div \frac{1}{2}\right)^2}{\sqrt{\frac{9}{25}}}$

> If your calculator does not have a fraction key you will need to solve these using the memory key or using a written method. Check how you add, subtract, multiply and divide fractions first.

16 The local store did a stock take of their boxes of crisps.

They had $2\frac{2}{3}$ boxes of salt and vinegar, $4\frac{1}{4}$ of cheese and onion, $3\frac{1}{6}$ of smoky bacon, $4\frac{5}{8}$ of chicken and $2\frac{5}{6}$ boxes of plain crips.

a   How many boxes was that in total?

b   What was the minimum number of packets in a complete box?

17 Steve built a fence round his garden in three days.

The final length of the fence was $76\frac{4}{5}$ m.

He built $\frac{3}{4}$ of the fence on the first day.

a   Write a fraction calculation to calculate how much fence he had built.
Solve your calculation.

b   On the second day Steve only managed to complete $\frac{7}{12}$ of the length of
fence still to be built. What length did he have left to build on the third day?

> explanation 5

18 Convert each of these into hours and minutes

a   5.6 hours   b   8.75 hours   c   14.15 hours   d   13.35 hours

e   0.85 days   f   5.4 days   g   12.45 days   h   6.95 days

19 A year on Mars is equivalent to 686.98 Earth days.

How many Earth hours and minutes are there in a Mars year?

Round your answer to the nearest minute.

20 Use this part of the London to
Glasgow train timetable to work
out how long these journeys
would take.

London Euston		12:35	
Birmingham	11:30		13:26
Preston	13:42	14:48	15:56
Carlisle	14:53	15:05	16:04
Glasgow	16:04		17:23

a   London Euston to Preston.

b   Preston to Glasgow on
the 11:30 Birmingham train.

c   Birmingham to Carlisle on the 13:26 Birmingham train.

d   Which train is faster, the morning or afternoon Birmingham to
Glasgow train? By how many minutes?

explanation 6 ————————————————————

Use these exchange rates for questions **21** to **26**.

£1 = 1.14 euros (€)	£1 = US$1.45 (US dollar) 
£1 = 1.67 Swiss francs	£1 = 9.95 Chinese yuan
£1 = 139.9 Japanese yen	£1 = A$2.24 (Australian dollar)

21 How many pounds (£ sterling) would you get for these amounts?

    a €750 (euros)   **b** 1000 Chinese yuan   **c** US$137.65

    d €348   **e** A$437.15   **f** 570 Japanese yen

    g 250 Swiss francs   **h** US$1000

> Round all answers to the nearest £0.01.

22 Change £110.50 into these currencies.

Round all answers to two decimal places.

> US $1 = 100 cents
> A$1 = 100 cents

    a euros (€)   **b** US dollars   **c** Chinese yuan

    d Swiss francs   **e** Australian dollars   **f** Japanese yen

23 On holiday in Australia Anna paid A$165.50 per night for her hotel room.

Breakfast cost an extra A$16.80 each day.

    a How much was her bill for three nights' accommodation, with breakfast each morning, in pounds?

    b She also hired a rental car for the three days at a cost of A$35.40 per day plus a one-off insurance cost of A$56.75.

    What was the cost in pounds of the car hire?

24 A bus trip to the Great Wall of China from Beijing cost Peter 65 Chinese yuan.

   a How much did the ticket cost in pounds?

   b Peter bought tickets for six people in his party and received a 5% discount.

      How much did it cost him in pounds for the six tickets?

25 Megan saw this advert on the internet.

> **Buy your favourite DVDs direct from the USA.**
>
> US$14.95 for each DVD + shipping US$1.99 per DVD.
>
>  **Special deal:**   Buy 5 DVDs and each DVD costs US$11.75 + total shipping of US$5.99.

   a How much would Megan pay in pounds for three DVDs to be shipped to her?

   b She later ordered another two DVDs.

      What was the total cost in pounds for Megan to get all five DVDs?

   c How much money, in pounds, would she have saved if she had ordered all five DVDs at the same time?

26 When Sara returned from her Swiss skiing trip she took 214 Swiss francs into her bank to change back into pounds.

   a How many pounds would she have expected to get?

   b Sara got less than she expected as the bank took 3% commission for changing her money.

      How much did Sara actually get?

explanation 7

27 Sam wanted to buy a new laptop computer costing £525.

Orange Macks
12.5% discount.
Balance paid at 4%
interest over the year.

Geeks 'R' Us
15% discount.
Balance paid at 6%
interest over the year

Three high-street computer stores were
offering these deals on purchases over
one year.

Which store is offering the best deal?
How much will Sam pay?

QUAY COMPUTERS
10% discount.
Balance paid at 2%
interest over the year.

28 The local hockey club decided to deposit £1750 in a bank account at an
annual compound interest rate of 3.5%.

a Which of these gives the amount the club will have after two years?

£1750 × 1.035 × 2   £1750 × 0.035^2 £1750 × 1.035^2

£1750 × 0.035 × 2   £(1750 × $0.035)^2$ £(1750 × $1.035)^2$

Calculate the answer.

b Calculate how much the club will have after five years.

29 Gina invested £325 in a savings account at 4% compound interest for
three years.

a How much will she have at the end of three years?

b Her friend invested £340 at 2.5% compound interest for three years.

How much more or less money than Gina did he have at the end of the
three-year period?

Algebra A4.1

Sequences

- Generating sequences from the term–to–term rule using ICT
- Generating quadratic sequences from the position–to–term rule
- Generating sequences from practical problems
- Finding the nth term of an arithmetic sequence
- Finding the nth term of a quadratic sequence

Keywords

You should know

explanation 1a   explanation 1b

1 Find the next three terms and write the term-to-term rule for each sequence.

a 12, 19, 26, …

b 81, 27, 9, …

c $\frac{1}{4}, \frac{1}{2}, 1, \dots$

d 9, 5, 1, …

e 6, 12, 24, …

f −16, −12, −8, …

g 0.25, 0.5, 0.75, …

h −5, 10, −20, …

i 64, −16, 4, …

2 Copy and complete this table. Work out the terms without a calculator and leave your answers as fractions where necessary.

	First term(s)	Term-to-term rule	First five terms
a	2	+ 8	2, ☐, ☐, ☐, ☐
b	25	÷ 5	25, ☐, ☐, ☐, ☐
c	0	− 3	0, ☐, ☐, ☐, ☐
d	$\frac{1}{3}$	$+\frac{1}{2}$	$\frac{1}{3}$, ☐, ☐, ☐, ☐
e	1	$\times\frac{1}{3}$	1, ☐, ☐, ☐, ☐
f	−16	− 4	−16, ☐, ☐, ☐, ☐
g	7	÷ 4	7, ☐, ☐, ☐, ☐
h	1, 1	Add the two previous terms	1, 1, ☐, ☐, ☐

3 Write the next three terms of each sequence.

a   0.3, 0.6, 0.9, 1.2, …   b   3, 6, 12, 24, 48, …   c   10 000, 1000, 100, 10, …

d   320, 160, 80, 40, …   e   0, 1, 1, 2, 3, 5, 8, …   f   1, 2, 4, 7, 11, 16, …

4 What is the term-to-term rule for each sequence in question **3**?

5 Look at these sequences. Some terms in each sequence are missing.

   i What is the term-to-term rule for each sequence?

   ii Write the missing terms of each sequence.

a $\square$, 1.6, $\square$, 2.0, $\square$, 2.4   b   3, $\square$, 15, $\square$, 27

c   32, $\square$, 8, $\square$, 2   d   1, $\square$, 9, $\square$, 81, $\square$

explanation 2a   explanation 2b

6 Write down the first five terms in each arithmetic sequence from these position-to-term (*n*th term) rules. Show your working.

a $n + 8$ b $7n$ c $\dfrac{n}{2}$ d $-2n$ e $n - 0.4$

f $2n - 1$ g $n + \dfrac{1}{2}$ h $3n - 5$ i $4 + 5n$ j $88 - 12n$

7 For each of these position-to-term (*n*th term) rules, write the constant difference between terms of the sequence.
You should not need to work out any terms in the sequence.

a $6n + 3$ b $7 - 2n$ c $\dfrac{3n}{2} + 7$ d $4(2n - 1)$

8 Match each sequence with its correct *n*th term.

a   3, 7, 11, 15, 19, … $11 - 4n$

b   6, 10, 14, 18, 22, … $5n + 4$

c   30, 27, 24, 21, 18, … $2n - 11$

d $-9, -7, -5, -3, -1$, …. $4n - 1$

e   9, 14, 19, 24, 29, … $11 - 5n$

f $7, 3, -1, -5, -9$, … $33 - 3n$

g $6, 1, -4, -9, -14$, … $4n + 2$

9 The nth term of a sequence is $5n - 3$. Which of these numbers appears in this sequence? Give the position of the number in the sequence where appropriate and explain your reasoning.

  a 67   **b** 143   **c** 682   **d** 5347

10 These are the nth terms of four sequences.

$$3n - 1 \qquad 300 - 2n \qquad \frac{5n}{2} + 7 \qquad 13n - 4$$

Which of these sequences include the number 139? Show your working.

explanation 3a   explanation 3b

11 These are the first five terms of some arithmetic sequences.

For each sequence, write the term-to-term rule, the position-to-term (nth term) rule and the 20th term.

  a 5, 10, 15, 20, 25   **b** 3, 7, 11, 15, 19   **c** $1\frac{1}{2}$, 2, $2\frac{1}{2}$, 3, $3\frac{1}{2}$

  d 20, 23, 26, 29, 32   **e** 7, 19, 31, 43, 55   **f** 30, 40, 50, 60, 70

  g 6, 9, 12, 15, 18   **h** 35, 42, 49, 56, 63   **i** 120, 124, 128, 132, 136

12 These are the first five terms of some arithmetic sequences.

For each sequence, write the term-to-term rule, the position-to-term (nth term) rule and the 20th term.

  a $-3, -6, -9, -12, -15$ **b** $-1, -3, -5, -7, -9$ **c** $3, -1, -5, -9, -13$

  d 18, 15, 12, 9, 6   **e** 90, 83, 76, 69, 62   **f** 45, 30, 15, 0, -15

  g 7, 15, 23, 31, 39   **h** 21, 23, 25, 27, 29   **i** 15, 16, 17, 18, 19

13 Calculate the number of terms in these sequences.

  a 3, 7, 11, 15, …, 419   **b** 11, 16, 21, 26, …, 701

  c 50, 43, 36, 29, …, -118 **d** 2, 11, 18, 27, …, 2315

14 Remla made tile designs with red and blue tiles.

Design 1   **Design 2**   **Design 3**

a Copy and complete this table.

Design number	1	2	3	4	5	...	10
Number of red tiles							
Number of blue tiles							
Total number of tiles							

b Find an expression for the number of these tiles in the *n*th design.

   i red tiles

   ii blue tiles

   iii the total number of tiles

15 E-mail Expert made a sequence of neon signs of the letter E to put on their shop window.

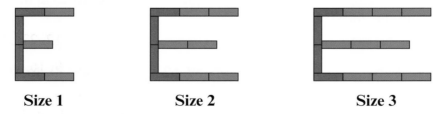

Size 1   **Size 2**   **Size 3**

a Copy and complete this table.

Size	1	2	3	4	5	...	15
Number of lights	7	10	13			...	

b What is the *n*th term of the sequence? Justify your expression by referring to the diagrams. How can the rule be linked to the design structure?

explanation 4a | explanation 4b | explanation 4c | explanation 4d

16 Fred, a landscape gardener, is designing a new range of fish ponds with paving slabs at the opposite corners.

    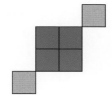   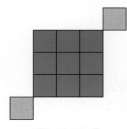

Pattern 1   **Pattern 2**   **Pattern 3**

   a How many grey squares would be in the 10th pattern?

   b How many blue squares would be in the nth pattern?

   c What is the nth term rule for the total number of grey squares and blue squares in this sequence?

17 Find the next two terms in each of these sequences.

   a 1, 2, 4, 7, 11   **b** −4, 0, 6, 14, 24   **c** 10, 22, 38, 58, 82

   d 30, 26, 20, 12, 2   **e** 2, 2.5, 3.5, 5, 7   **f** 10, 30, 60, 100, 150

18 Find the nth term of each of these quadratic sequences.
Use the inspection method.

   a 0, 3, 8, 15, 24   **b** 3, 6, 11, 18, 27   **c** 3, 12, 27, 48, 75

   d −5, −2, 3, 10, 19   **e** 0.5, 2, 4.5, 8, 12.5   **f** 4, 9, 16, 25, 36

19 Work out the first five terms in each sequence from the position-to-term (nth term) rule. Show your working.

   a $n^2 + 7$ **b** $n^2 + n$ **c** $5 - n^2$ **d** $n^2 + 2n - 7$

   e n^3 **f** $2n^3 - 5$ **g** $\dfrac{n}{n+2}$ **h** $\dfrac{10}{n}$

20 Match each sequence with its correct nth term.

a   10, 13, 18, 25, 34, … $2n^2 + n$

b   −3, −12, −27, −48, −75, … $n^2 + 9$

c   3, 10, 21, 36, 55, … $10 - n^2$

d   2, 10, 24, 44, 70, … $-3n^2$

e   3, 7, 13, 21, 31, … $6n^2$

f   6, 24, 54, 96, 150, … $3n^2 - n$

g   9, 6, 1, −6, −15, … $n^2 + n + 1$

21 Calculate the number of terms in each sequence.

a   1, 4, 9, 16, …, 400   b   −1, 2, 7, 14, …, 888   c   2, 6, 12, 20, …, 272

explanation 5a   explanation 5b

22 Use a difference tree to find the nth term of each quadratic sequence.

a   2, 7, 14, 23, 34, …   b   2, 11, 26, 47, 74, …

c   1, 13, 27, 43, 61, …   d   8, 14, 24, 38, 56, …

e   0, 5, 12, 21, 32, …   f   2, 6, 12, 20, 30, …

g   6, 12, 22, 36, 54, …   h   1, 6, 15, 28, 45, …

23 Sam is making staircase patterns from matchsticks.
Here are his first three patterns.

 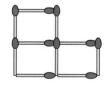 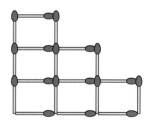

a   Draw the fourth staircase pattern in the sequence and write the number of matchsticks used for each of the first four patterns.

b   Find the rule for the number of matchsticks used to make the nth pattern in the sequence.

24   Aimee constructs a rectangular sequence pattern.

Each of the squares on the perimeter of the rectangle has been shaded pink.

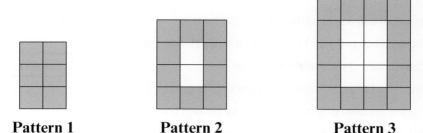

Pattern 1   **Pattern 2**   **Pattern 3**

  a   Draw the next two patterns in this sequence.

  b   Use a difference method to find the *n*th terms of these sequences.

     i   squares shaded pink

     ii   unshaded squares

     iii   all the squares

  c   Show that the sum of your two *n*th terms from parts **b i** and **b ii** is equivalent to the *n*th term for part **b iii**.

25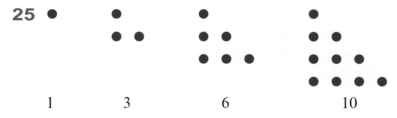

  1   3   6   10

These dot patterns form the first four terms of the sequence known as triangular numbers.

  a   Write the first 10 triangular numbers.

  b   Find the *n*th term for the triangular number sequence.

  c   Is 2600 a triangular number? Explain your reasoning.

  d   Use dot pattern diagrams to explain why the sum of any two consecutive triangular numbers is always a square number.

  e   Use algebra to prove that the sum of any two consecutive triangular numbers is a square number.

> Use x for one term and $x + 1$ for the next term in your rule from part **b**.

Linear functions

- Plotting the graph of a linear function given in the form $ay + bx + c = 0$
- Calculating the gradient and y-intercept from a straight-line graph
- Finding the coordinates of the midpoint of a line
- Finding the inverse of a linear function and plotting its graph
- Knowing about the gradient of perpendicular and parallel lines
- Plotting graphs of simple quadratic and cubic functions

Keywords

You should know

explanation 1

1 a Copy and complete the table for each of these functions.

x	−3	−2	−1	0	1	2	3
y							

   i $y = 3x - 1$ **ii** $y = 2x + 5$ **iii** $y = \frac{1}{2}x + 6$

   iv $y = 7 + x$ **v** $y = 3(x - 2)$

b Use a scale of 2 cm for 1 unit horizontally from −3 to 3 for each graph. Choose a sensible vertical scale for the y-values based on the table of results. Draw a graph for each function.

Write down the coordinates of the point where each line cuts the y-axis.

2 a Copy and complete the table for each of these functions.

x	−3	−2	−1	0	1	2	3
y							

   i $y = 5 - x$ **ii** $y = 6 - 2x$ **iii** $y = 12 - \frac{3}{2}x$

   iv $y = 20 - 5x$ **v** $y = 2(3 - 2x)$

b Use a scale of 2 cm for 1 unit horizontally from −3 to 3 for each graph. Choose a sensible vertical scale for the y-values based on the table of results. Draw a graph for each function.

Write down the coordinates of the point where each line cuts the y-axis.

explanation 2

3 For each of these equations, use the 'cover up' method to work out the coordinates of two points.

Use these points to draw a separate graph for each function.

a $y - 3x = 1$ b $y - 2x = 3$ c $2y - x = 5$

d $3y - 2x = 6$ e $2x + y - 3 = 0$ f $3x + 2y + 12 = 0$

4 Draw the graphs of these functions on the same grid.

What do you notice?

$2x - 3y + 2 = 0$ $y = \frac{2}{3}x - 1$ $-2x + 3y - 6 = 0$

explanation 3a   explanation 3b   explanation 3c   explanation 3d

5 Without drawing the graphs, write the gradient and y-intercept of these functions.

a $y = 4x - 3$ b $y = 6 - 2x$ c $y = 6x + 1$

d $y = 3(2x - 4)$ e $y = \frac{1}{2}x + 5$ f $y = 8 + 3x$

g $y = 0.3x + 2$ h $y = \frac{2}{3}x - 8$ i $y = \frac{3x - 1}{4}$

6 Rearrange each of these equations into the form $y = mx + c$ then write the gradient and y-intercept.

a $2y = 5x - 4$ b $3y = 6x + 9$ c $y + 3x = 7$

d $y - 2x - 5 = 0$ e $3y + 5x - 6 = 0$ f $6x + 2y = 9$

g $5x = 4y$ h $5x - y = 7$ i $1 - x - 2.5y = 0$

7 Rearrange these equations and identify the equations of parallel lines.

a $y = 3x - 1$ b $2y = 3x - 1$ c $2y = 5 + 6x$

d $3y = x + 5$ e $6 + 2y - 6x = 0$ f $2 - y - 3x = 0$

8 For each of these straight lines, work out the gradient and y-intercept and write its equation in the form $y = mx + c$.

a

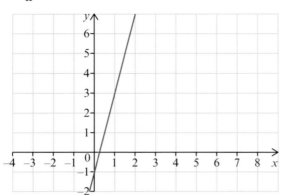

b

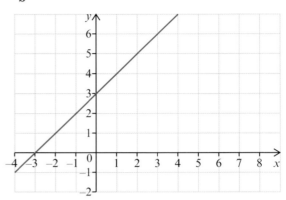

c

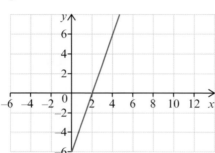

d

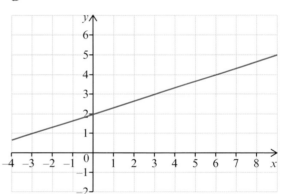

e

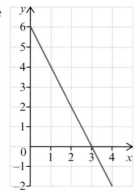

f

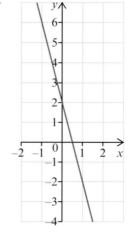

explanation 4a   explanation 4b   explanation 4c

9 Write the coordinates of the midpoint of the line AB.

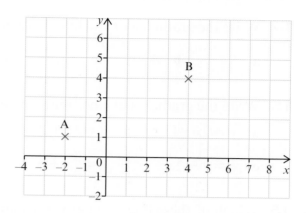

10 Find the coordinates of the midpoint of the line AB and the line CD.

a

b

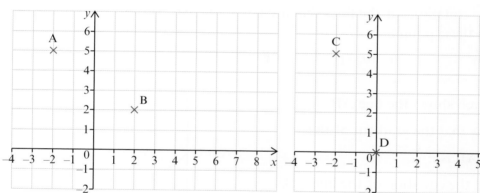

11 Find the coordinates of the midpoint of the line between each pair of points.

   a   (2, 1) and (−3, 4)

   b   (0, 4) and (8, −2)

   c   (5, −2) and (1, 2)

   d   (6, 0.5) and (−1, −1)

12 **a**   Find the coordinates of the midpoint of the line PQ when P is (−3, 1) and Q is (5, −2).

   b   If the point P changed to (−2, 1), what would the midpoint be?

   c   If the midpoint of PQ was (0, 1) and Q stayed at (5, −2), what would the coordinates of P be?

13 If the midpoint of a line AB is (3, 2), give the coordinates of three possible pairs of points A and B.

explanation 5

14 Write the gradients of the lines perpendicular to the lines with these gradients.

a 5   b 4   c −6   d $\frac{1}{5}$ e $\frac{4}{7}$

15 Write the gradients of lines that are perpendicular to these functions.

a $y = 2x - 1$ b $y = 4x + 3$ c $y = \frac{1}{3}x + 4$ d $y = 6 - x$

e $y = 3 - 2x$ f $y = \frac{3}{4}x + 5$ g $y = -\frac{2}{5}x$ h $y = x$

16 Which of these lines are perpendicular to $y = 4x - 3$.

a $y = 4x + 2$ b $y = \frac{1}{4}x - 5$ c $y = 6 - \frac{1}{4}x$ d $2y + 8x = 9$

17 Find the equations of the lines that are perpendicular to $y = \frac{1}{2}x + 5$ and pass through these points.

a (0, 0)   b (0, 7)   c (0, −3)

18 The sketch shows the line AB.

a   Show that the gradient of the line AB is $-\frac{3}{4}$.

b   Find the equation of the line AB.

c   Find the equation of a line perpendicular to AB which passes through these points.

   i A

   ii the midpoint of AB

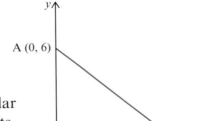

explanation 6a   explanation 6b

19 Find the inverse of each function.

a $y = 3x$ b $y = \frac{1}{4}x$ c $y = x + 5$ d $y = x - 2$

e $y = 3x + 2$ f $y = 2x - 5$ g $y = 5x + 1$ h $y = \frac{1}{3}x - 4$

20   **i** Rearrange each of these to give y as a function of x.

   ii Find the inverse of each function.

   a $y = 6 - x$ **b** $x + y = 8$ **c** $y = 6 - 2x$ **d** $3x + y = 12$

   e $3x + 4y = 8$ **f** $2x - 3y = 12$ **g** $5x + 2y - 20 = 0$

21 Draw a graph of each pair of functions.

   a $y = 3x$ and the inverse of $y = 3x$

   b $y = 2x - 1$ and the inverse of $y = 2x - 1$

   c $y = \frac{1}{2}x + 2$ and the inverse of $y = \frac{1}{2}x + 2$

22 Choose the correct transformation from the list below to complete the sentence.

Rotation of 90° clockwise	Translation by $\binom{0}{5}$	Reflection in the line $y = x$	Enlargement scale factor 2

The graph of an inverse function is a _____ of the graph of the original function.

explanation 7a   explanation 7b

23   **i** Copy and complete this table of values for each quadratic function.

   ii Draw a graph for each function.

x	−3	−2	−1	0	1	2	3
y							

   a $y = x^2 + 4$ **b** $y = 2x^2 - 5$ **c** $y = 4 - x^2$

   d $y = 10 - 2x^2$ **e** $y = x^2 + 2x - 2$ **f** $y = x^2 - x + 3$

   g $y = x^2 + 3x - 4$ **h** $y = x^2 - 2x + 5$

24 For each of the functions in question **23** write the minimum or maximum value of the curve.

25 Without drawing the function, write down the minimum or maximum values of these curves. State whether this value is a minimum or a maximum.

    a $y = 3x^2 - 7$ **b** $y = -12x^2 + 5$ **c** $y = 12 + x^2$ **d** $y = 7 - 3x^2$

26 A baseball is hit into the air.

The height of the ball is given by the equation $h = 12t - 3t^2$ where h is the height in metres and t is the time in seconds.

    a Copy and complete this table.

t	0	1	2	3	4
h					

    b Draw the graph of $h = 12t - 3t^2$.

    c What is the maximum height reached by the baseball?

    d For how long is the baseball more than 8 m above the ground?

> explanation 8a   explanation 8b

27   **i** Copy and complete this table of values for each cubic function.

      ii Draw a graph for each function.

x	−3	−2	−1	0	1	2	3
y							

    a $y = x^3$ **b** $y = x^3 + 5$ **c** $y = 2 - x^3$ **d** $y = 10 - x^3$

28 Write the coordinates of the points where each of your graphs in question **27** crosses the y-axis.

29 Match each equation to its graph.

Graph 1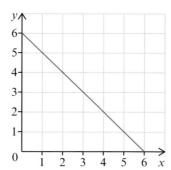

Graph 2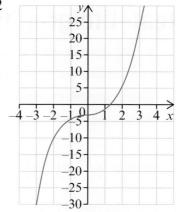

Graph 3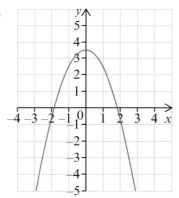

Graph 4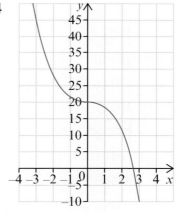

Graph 5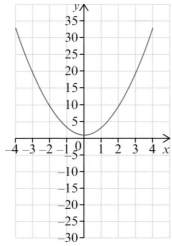

Graph 6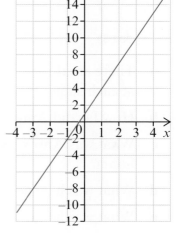

a $y = 2x^2 + 1$

b $y = 3x + 1$

c $y = 20 - x^3$

d $y = 6 - x$

e $y = 3.5 - x^2$

f $y = -3 + x^3$

Real-life graphs

- Solving distance–time problems
- Drawing graphs of linear functions
- Giving plausible explanations for non–linear graphs
- Sketching graphs to represent a variety of situations

Keywords

You should know

explanation 1a   explanation 1b   explanation 1c

1 The distance–time graph shows Amy's journey by car.

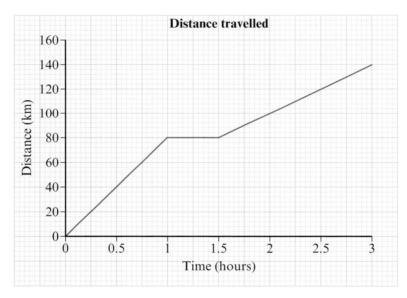

a There are three stages to Amy's journey. Explain what the graph is showing at each stage.

b How far did Amy travel altogether in 3 hours?

c What was Amy's speed for the first hour of the journey (in kilometres per hour)?

d What was her speed in the third stage of the journey?

e What was her average speed for the whole journey?

f For what fraction of the total time was she stationary?

2 Oxbow and Tranby are two towns 16 km apart.

Khayam leaves Oxbow at 09:00 and walks at a constant speed of 8 km/h towards Tranby.

Emma leaves Tranby at 09:20 and cycles towards Oxbow. She stops at a shop 4 km from Tranby at 09:40 for 10 minutes before continuing her journey. She arrives at Oxbow at 10:50.

a On the same diagram and using a scale of 2 cm for 10 minutes on the time axis and 1 cm for 1 km on the distance axis, draw the distance–time graph to show both journeys.

b Use your graph to find these.

  i the time that Khayam arrives in Tranby

  ii the time that Khayam and Emma pass each other

  iii Emma's average speed for the whole journey

3 The graph below shows the story of Baz's bath.

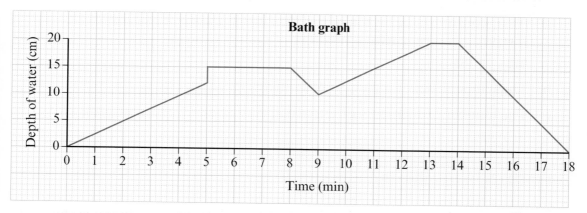

a What was the maximum depth of the water?

b At what speed did the depth of water increase during the first 5 minutes?

c How could you explain the sudden increase in depth after 5 minutes?

d What do you think happened between 5 and 8 minutes?

e How long did the bath take to empty at the end?

f At what speed did the depth of water decrease at the end?

g How would the graph change if Baz had jumped out to answer the phone after 12 minutes?

4 a For each of these equations, make a table of values for the relationship from 0 to 5 on the horizontal axis and draw the graph.

e.g. *s*	0	1	2	3	4	5
e.g. *t*						

   i $s = 40t$ when t = time in hours and s = distance travelled (in kilometres)

   ii $p = \dfrac{d}{2}$ for the exchange rate from US dollars to pounds sterling, where p is the number of pounds and d is the number of dollars

   iii $V = 5t + 15$ where V is the volume of water (in litres) in a storage tank and t the time taken (in minutes)

b Which of the graphs does *not* pass through the origin? Why?

5 For each of these sentences, write an equation linking two variables then sketch a graph to illustrate the relationship between the variables.
Make sure you state what your variables are in each case.

  a A car consumes fuel at the rate of one litre for every 10 kilometres.
It starts its journey with a full tank of 50 litres and ends the journey with the tank empty.

  b The temperature of a pan of water increases at the rate of 8°C per minute.

  c The number of members of a football club remains constant from year to year.

explanation 2a   explanation 2b

6 Water is poured at a constant speed into different containers. For each of these container shapes, sketch a graph showing the depth of water against time.

   a   b   c   d   e   f

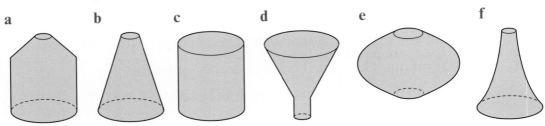

7 Match each graph to one of the descriptions below.

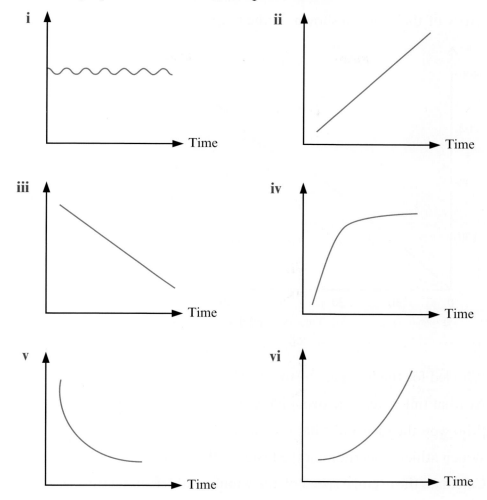

a The distance from a post of someone who is running away from the post but who is attached to the post by a bungee rope.

b The amount of compound interest earned on an investment of £100.

c The cost of a telephone call.

d The temperature in a room heated by a thermostatically controlled radiator.

e The number of children left in a school hall when everyone is leaving after assembly.

f The temperature of a cup of coffee left in a cool room.

8 Peter and Witold are two runners in a 400 m race.

The story of their race in shown on the graph.

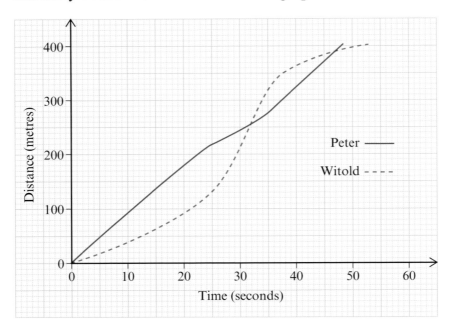

a Who led for the first part of the race?

b At what times were the two athletes level with each other?

c Who won the race and what was their winning time?

d Which athlete was running the faster at the finish?

e Calculate the average speed of the winning athlete in metres per second.

9 Two balls were thrown upwards at the same time.
The graph shows the heights of the balls at different times.

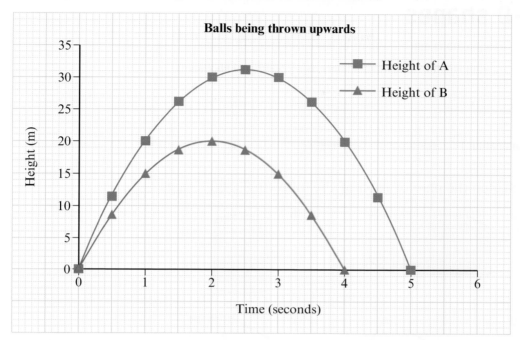

a Estimate the difference in the maximum height reached by the two balls.

b How long did it take each ball to reach its maximum height?

c How many seconds after the balls were thrown was their difference in height approximately 10 m?

d How long did it take ball A to fall 20 m from its maximum height?

explanation 3

10 Sketch speed–time graphs to represent these situations.

a a car travelling at a constant speed along a motorway

b a cyclist travelling up a steep hill and then down the other side

c an aeroplane coming in to land

d a car left on a hill with its handbrake off

3–D shapes

● Drawing plans and elevations of more complex 3–D shapes
● Drawing isometric views of shapes using plans and elevations

Keywords

You should know

explanation 1

1 Sketch the plan of each of the following solid shapes.

a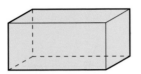

b

c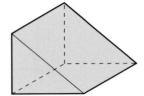

d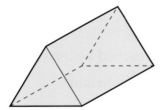

e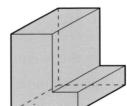

f

g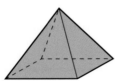

h

i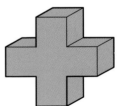

2 The arrows indicate the front elevation of each solid shape.
Draw the front elevation of each shape.

a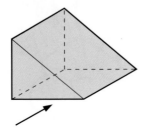

b

c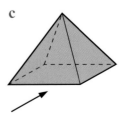

3 The arrows indicate a side elevation of each solid shape.
Draw this side elevation of each shape.

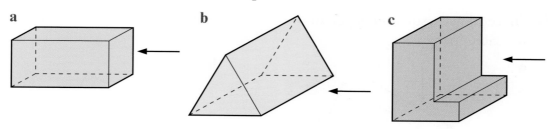

4 Sketch the plan, front and side elevations of each shape.

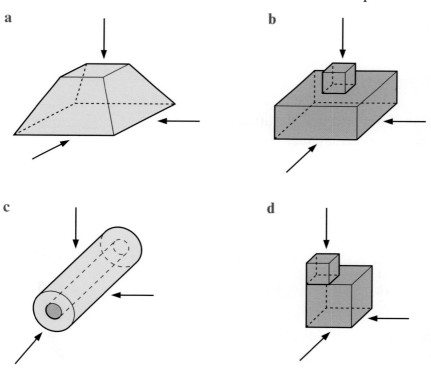

5 The plan, front and side elevations of a prism are shown.

Sketch the prism on isometric paper.

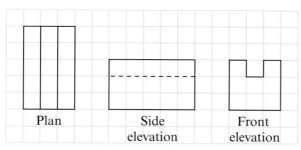

223

6 On centimetre squared paper, draw the accurate plan, front and side elevations for each prism.

a

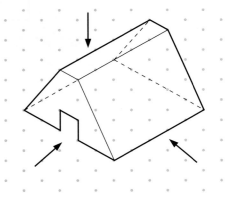

b

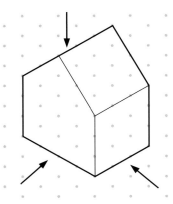

7 Here are the plan, front and side elevations of a prism.
Draw the prism on isometric paper.

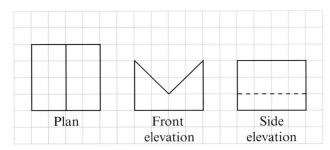

Plan　　　　Front　　　　Side
　　　　　elevation　　elevation

8 Here are the plan, front and side elevations of a solid.
Draw the solid on isometric paper.

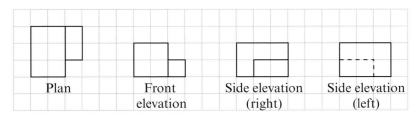

Plan　　　Front　　Side elevation　　Side elevation
　　　　elevation　　(right)　　　　(left)

9 Here are the plan, front and side elevations of a solid.
Draw the solid on isometric paper.

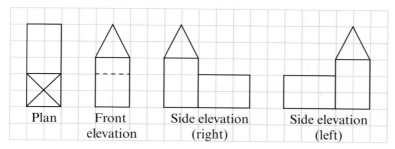

10 The following solids are all made from centimetre cubes.
Draw an accurate plan, front and side elevation for each solid.

a 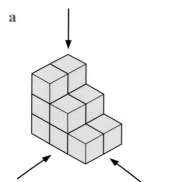   b 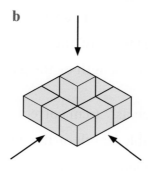   c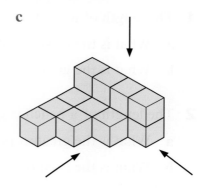

11 Each of these shows the plan of some shapes. In each case, draw two possible
solids that would fit the plan.

a 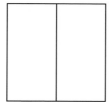   b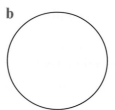

12 Work with a partner. You will need some interlocking cubes.

a Make a solid using some interlocking cubes.

b Draw the plan and front elevation of your solid.

c Ask your partner to draw or describe two possible shapes
that your solid could be.

d Draw the side elevations for your solid.

e Ask your partner to draw or describe your solid.

Measures

- Converting between measurements of area
- Converting between measurements of volume
- Finding the least and greatest length of a measurement
- Solving problems using compound units
- Converting between compound units

Keywords

You should know

explanation 1a   explanation 1b   explanation 1c

1 The length of a garden is given as 18 m correct to the nearest metre.

   a What is the least possible length of the garden?

   b What is the greatest possible length of the garden?

2 The length of a pencil is given as 7.6 cm correct to the nearest millimetre.

   a What is the greatest possible length of the pencil?

   b What is the least possible length of the pencil?

3 The length of a road is given as 45 km correct to the nearest kilometre.

   a What is the maximum possible length of the road?

   b What is the minimum possible length of the road?

4 The weight of a baby is given as 4.3 kg correct to one decimal place.

   a What is the least possible weight of the baby?

   b What is the greatest possible weight of the baby?

5 Jack measures the length and width of a rectangle.
He gives the length as 6.5 cm and the width as 4.3 cm.
Both measurements are given correct to the nearest millimetre.

   a What is the least possible length and width?

   b What is the greatest possible length and width?

(explanation 2a) (explanation 2b)

6 Work out the area of each shape.

    i Give your answer in square centimetres (cm²).

    ii Give your answer in square millimetres (mm²).

a   **b**   **c**

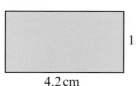
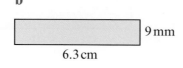
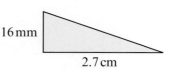

a: 1.8 cm, 4.2 cm
b: 9 mm, 6.3 cm
c: 16 mm, 2.7 cm

7 Convert these areas to square millimetres.

    a 5 cm²   **b** 2.3 cm²   **c** 68 cm²   **d** 0.6 cm²

8 Convert these areas to square centimetres.

    a 700 mm²   **b** 80 mm²   **c** 6320 mm²   **d** 8 mm²

9 Rajesh says: '3 m² is the same as 300 cm².'

    Rajesh is wrong. Explain why.

10 Convert these areas to square centimetres.

    a 5 m²   **b** 2.8 m²   **c** 0.9 m²   **d** 0.056 m²

11 Convert these areas to square metres.

    a 40 000 cm²   **b** 6700 cm²   **c** 300 cm²   **d** 345 600 cm²

12 Convert these areas to the units given in brackets.

    a 5 cm² (mm²)   **b** 9 m² (cm²)   **c** 2 km² (m²)

    d 700 mm² (cm²)   **e** 8200 cm² (m²)   **f** 89 000 000 m² (km²)

    g 0.67 cm² (mm²)   **h** 0.053 km² (m²)   **i** 25 mm² (cm²)

    j 95 cm² (m²)   **k** 1 km² (cm²)   **l** 6 m² (mm²)

explanation 3 ───────────────────────────────

13 Work out the volume of each of these solids.

    i Give your answers in cubic centimetres.

    ii Give your answers in cubic millimetres.

a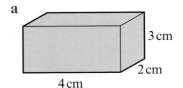

3 cm

2 cm

4 cm

b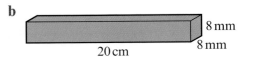

8 mm

8 mm

20 cm

c

6 mm

5 mm

8 mm

14 Convert these volumes into cubic millimetres.

    a $8\,\text{cm}^3$ **b** $23.5\,\text{cm}^3$ **c** $0.04\,\text{cm}^3$ **d** $4.35\,\text{cm}^3$

15 Convert these volumes into cubic centimetres.

    a $60\,000\,\text{mm}^3$ **b** $250\,000\,\text{mm}^3$ **c** $8000\,\text{mm}^3$ **d** $780\,\text{mm}^3$

16 A large fish tank is in the shape of a cuboid. It has a length of 1.2 m, width of 40 cm and height of 55 cm. Work out the volume of the fish tank.

    a Give your answer in cubic metres.

    b Give your answer in cubic centimetres.

17 Convert these volumes into cubic centimetres.

    a $4\,\text{m}^3$ **b** $0.024\,\text{m}^3$ **c** $12\,\text{m}^3$ **d** $603.2\,\text{m}^3$

18 Convert these volumes into cubic metres.

    a $7\,000\,000\,\text{cm}^3$ **b** $56\,000\,\text{cm}^3$

    c $680\,\text{cm}^3$ **d** $723\,000\,000\,\text{cm}^3$

19 Convert these volumes to the units given in brackets.

    a $5\,\text{m}^3\ (\text{cm}^3)$ **b** $450\,\text{mm}^3\ (\text{cm}^3)$ **c** $67\,000\,\text{cm}^3\ (\text{m}^3)$

    d $0.4\,\text{cm}^3\ (\text{mm}^3)$ **e** $0.009\,\text{m}^3\ (\text{cm}^3)$ **f** $2\,\text{km}^3\ (\text{m}^3)$

    g $34\,000\,000\,\text{m}^3\ (\text{km}^3)$ **h** $1\,\text{m}^3\ (\text{mm}^3)$

explanation 4a   explanation 4b

20 An aeroplane travels 2500 km in 5 hours. Work out its average speed.

21 Jackie walks 9 km in 1 hour and 20 minutes. Work out her average speed.
Give your answer in kilometres per hour.

22 A cyclist takes $1\frac{3}{4}$ hours to travel a distance of 63 km. What is her average speed?

23 A cyclist travels at a steady speed of 16 km/h. How far will she travel in 1 hour
and 15 minutes?

24 A man walks at 5 km/h. He walks 12.5 km. How long does the walk take him?

25 Alan goes out for the day. He catches the train to a village that is 30 miles
away and then cycles back. The average speed of the train is 50 miles per hour.
It takes Alan 2 hours and 30 minutes to cycle home.

   a Work out the time taken by the train. Give your answer in minutes.

   b Work out Alan's speed while cycling.

   c Work out Alan's average speed for the entire journey, assuming that he
   stops at the village for half an hour. Give your answer correct to
   one decimal place.

explanation 5

26 400 cm^3 of beeswax has a mass of 384 g. Work out the density of beeswax.

27 A block of wood measures 15 cm by 10 cm by 10 cm.
The block has a mass of 810 g.

   a Work out the volume of the block of wood.

   b Work out the density of the wood.

28 Cubes of sugar have sides of length 1.5 cm. Fifty of these cubes have a mass of 143 g. Work out the density of sugar. Give your answer correct to three significant figures.

29 A stone has a mass of 320 kg. The density of the stone is 2500 kg/m^3. Work out the volume of the stone.

30 A piece of copper has a volume of 0.07 m^3. Copper has a density of 8930 kg/m^3. Work out the mass of the copper.

31 The density of lead is 11 340 kg/m^3. A cube made from lead has lengths of side 15 cm. Work out the mass of the cube.

explanation 6

32 A metal bar is in the shape of a cuboid measuring 20 cm by 12 cm by 10 cm. The metal bar has a mass of 21.432 kg. Work out the density of the metal.

   a Give your answer in grams per cubic centimetre.

   b Give your answer in kilograms per cubic metre.

33 A kitchen worktop is in the shape of a cuboid. It is 2.4 m long, 59 cm wide and 3 cm deep. The worktop is made of granite and has a mass of 114.3 kg.

Work out the density of granite. Give your answer in kilograms per cubic metre, correct to three significant figures.

34 An athlete runs 100 m in 9.6 seconds. Work out his average speed.

   a Give your answer correct to two significant figures in metres per second.

   b Give your answer correct to two significant figures in kilometres per hour.

35 A cyclist covers 6500 m in 20 minutes. Work out his average speed.

   a Give your answer in metres per minute.

   b Give your answer in kilometres per hour.

36 Jane runs 3.5 miles in 25 minutes. Work out her average speed in miles per hour.

Prisms

- Finding the volume and surface area of a prism
- Finding the volume and surface area of a cylinder
- Solving problems involving prisms

Keywords

You should know

explanation 1a   explanation 1b   explanation 1c

1 Work out the volume of each of these prisms.

a
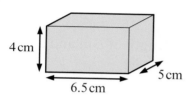

b
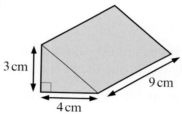

c
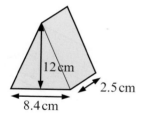

d
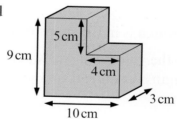

2 Work out the volume of each prism.

   i Give your answer in cubic centimetres.

   ii Give your answer in cubic metres.

a
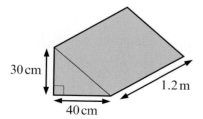

b
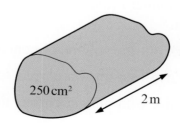

explanation 2a   explanation 2b

3 Work out the volume of each of these cylinders.

Give your answers correct to three significant figures.

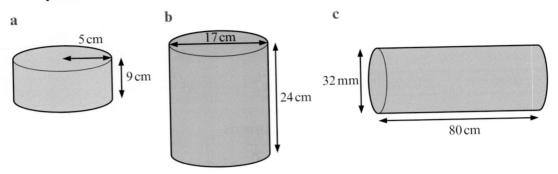

a

5 cm

9 cm

b

17 cm

24 cm

c

32 mm

80 cm

4 A water pipe is in the shape of a cylinder. It has a length of 3 m and a radius of 28 cm. Work out the volume of the pipe.

   a Give your answer correct to 3 s.f. in cm^3.

   b Give your answer correct to 3 s.f. in m^3.

5 A water trough is in the shape of half a cylinder.

Work out the volume of the water trough.
Give your answer correct to 3 s.f.

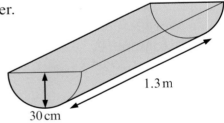

1.3 m

30 cm

6 A pipe of length 5.6 m is made of concrete.
The diagram shows the cross-section of the pipe.

It has an inner radius of 9 cm and an outer radius of 14 cm.

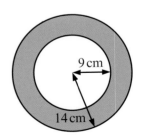

9 cm

14 cm

   a Work out the volume of concrete in the pipe.

      i Give your answer correct to 3 s.f. in cubic centimetres.

      ii Give your answer correct to 3 s.f. in cubic metres.

   b Concrete has a density of 2400 kg/m^3. Work out the mass of the pipe.

explanation 3

7 Find the surface area of each of these prisms.

a

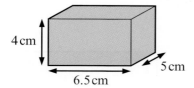

4 cm
6.5 cm
5 cm

b

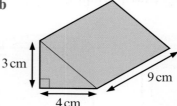

3 cm
4 cm
9 cm

c

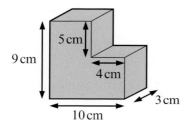

5 cm
9 cm
4 cm
3 cm
10 cm

d

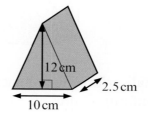

12 cm
2.5 cm
10 cm

8 A door wedge is in the shape of a prism with a cross-section in the shape of a trapezium as shown.

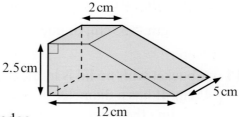

2 cm
2.5 cm
12 cm
5 cm

   a Work out the volume of wood used in the door wedge.

   b Work out the surface area of the door wedge.

   c Martin makes some of these door wedges to sell.

      He decided to paint all the surfaces with specialist paint.

      The paint costs £1.45 for a tin that covers $0.2\,\text{m}^2$.

      Martin makes 60 door wedges.

      Work out how much he will need to spend on paint if he paints all the door wedges.

explanation 4a   explanation 4b

9 Find the total surface area of each solid cylinder. Give your answers correct to three significant figures.

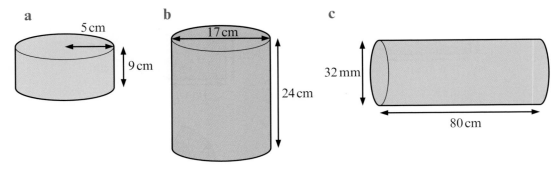

a
5 cm
9 cm

b
17 cm
24 cm

c
32 mm
80 cm

10 Find the total surface area of each solid cylinder. Give your answers correct to three significant figures.

a height = 28 cm, diameter = 30 cm

b length = 4 m, radius = 3 cm

c length = 35 cm, diameter = 3 cm

11 A bucket with no lid is in the shape of a cylinder. The height of the bucket is 45 cm. It has a diameter of 34 cm. Work out the surface area of the bucket, including the inner surface. Give your answer correct to three significant figures.

12 A tin of food has a height of 5.8 cm and a diameter of 7.4 cm. The tin has a label wrapped around its curved surface. Work out the area of the label. Give your answer correct to three significant figures.

13 A solid length of moulding is made of wood.
It has a semicircle at both ends.
Work out its total surface area.
Give your answer correct to three significant figures.

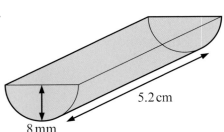

5.2 cm
8 mm

explanation 5

14 The volume of a prism is 80 cm^3. The area of its cross-section is 16 cm^2. Work out the length of the prism.

15 The volume of a prism is $12\,000 \text{ cm}^3$. Its length is 1.5 m. Find the area of its cross-section.

16 A triangular prism has a volume of 700 cm^3.

The prism has a length of 20 cm.
Its cross-section is a right-angled triangle.

The base of the triangle is 10 cm.

Work out the height of the triangle.

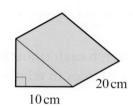

17 The volume of this prism is 1248 cm^3.

   a What is the area of the cross-section?

   b What is the length of the prism?

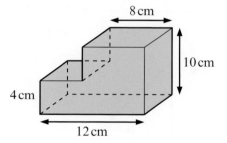

18 The volume of a cylinder is 1200 cm^3. The radius of its end is 5.4 cm. Work out the length of the cylinder. Give your answer correct to one decimal place.

19 A piece of pipe is 4.5 m in length. It has a volume of 7480 cm^3. Work out the diameter of the pipe. Give your answer correct to one decimal place.

20 A bucket is in the shape of a cylinder of radius 15 cm and height 37 cm. The bucket is full of water. The water is poured into a trough in the shape of a cuboid 45 cm long, 24 cm wide and 30 cm high. Work out the depth of the water in the trough. Give your answer to the nearest millimetre.

21 The volume of this triangular prism is 594 cm^3.

Work out the surface area of the prism.

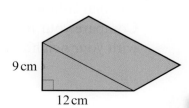

Trigonometry

- Identifying the opposite and adjacent sides in a right-angled triangle
- Using trigonometry to find a side in a right-angled triangle
- Using trigonometry to find an angle in a right-angled triangle

Keywords

You should know

explanation 1

1 Sketch each triangle. Label the hypotenuse (hyp), opposite (opp) and adjacent (adj) sides in relation to the marked angle x.

a
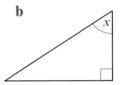

b
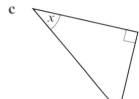

c

d
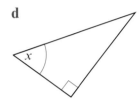

e
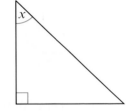

f
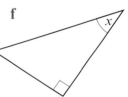

2 This question is about right-angled triangles.

a Draw accurately five different right-angled triangles that each have a 30° angle.

Label the opposite and hypotenuse of each triangle.

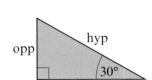

b Copy and complete this table by measuring the opposite and hypotenuse on each triangle correct to the nearest millimetre.

c What do you notice about all the values in the final column? Compare your results with your neighbour.

Triangle	Opp (cm)	Hyp (cm)	Opp ÷ Hyp
1			
2			
3			
4			
5			

explanation 2a   explanation 2b

3 Use your calculator to find these. Give your answers correct to three significant figures where necessary.

a   sin 40°   b   cos 60°   c   tan 45°   d   cos 63°   e   tan 59°

f   sin 82°   g   tan 12.5°   h   cos 35.1°   i   sin 9.76°   j   cos 78.4°

explanation 3

4 Look at each triangle.

Decide which two sides have been labelled. Write whether sin, cos or tan should be used.

a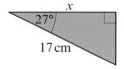

b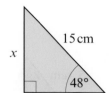

c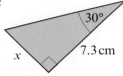

d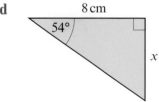

e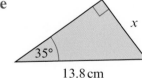

f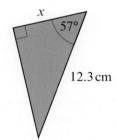

explanation 4a   explanation 4b   explanation 4c

5 For all the triangles in question **4**, work out the length of each side marked x. Give your answers correct to one decimal place.

6 Work out the length of each marked side. Give your answers correct to three significant figures.

a
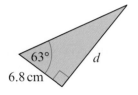
9 cm   30°   *a*

b
14.8 cm   *b*   62°

c
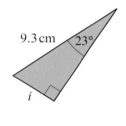
23 cm   50°   *c*

d
63°   *d*   6.8 cm

e
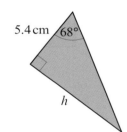
59°   36 cm   *e*

f
8.5 cm   33°   *f*

g
8.6 cm   71°   *g*

h
5.4 cm   68°   *h*

i
9.3 cm   23°   *i*

7 A ladder stands on horizontal ground and leans against a vertical wall. The ladder is 3.5 m long and makes an angle of 32° with the wall. How far up the wall does the ladder reach? Give your answer correct to the nearest centimetre.

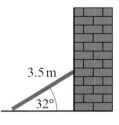

3.5 m

32°

8 From a point 30 m from the foot of a building, the angle of elevation to the top of the building is 63°. Work out the height of the building. Give your answer correct to the nearest metre.

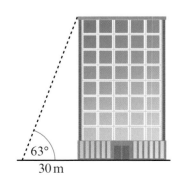

63°

30 m

9 A ski run is 1750 m long and slopes at an angle of 23° to the horizontal.
A skier skis down the complete ski run. How far will the skier descend
vertically in height? Give your answer correct to the nearest metre.

10 Work out the height of the isosceles triangle.

Give your answer correct to one decimal place.

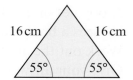

---

explanation 5

---

11 In each of the questions, find the value of x.
Give your answers correct to three significant figures.

    a $\cos x = 0.5$ **b** $\tan x = 1$ **c** $\sin x = 0.866$ **d** $\tan x = 1.5$

    e $\sin x = 0.32$ **f** $\cos x = 0.768$ **g** $\cos x = 0.128$ **h** $\tan x = 6.31$

---

explanation 6

---

12 In each triangle, work out the size of the angle marked x.
Give your answers correct to one decimal place.

  a

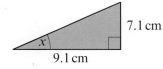

  b

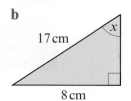

  c

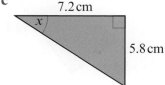

  d

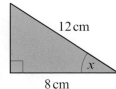

  e

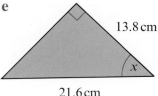

  f

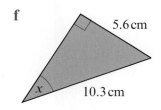

13 A ladder of length 3.5 m rests against a vertical wall so that the base of the
ladder is on horizontal ground 2 m away from the wall. Calculate the angle
between the ladder and the wall. Give your answer correct to one decimal
place.

14 A rectangle has length 15 cm and width 9 cm. Work out the angle between any diagonal and the longest side of the rectangle.
Give your answer correct to one decimal place.

15 A boy lies on the top of a 67 m vertical cliff.
He sees a boat that is 120 m away from the base of the cliff.
Work out the angle of elevation of the boy from the boat.
Give your answer correct to one decimal place.

16 In each triangle, work out the size of the angle or the side marked x.
Give your answers correct to three significant figures.

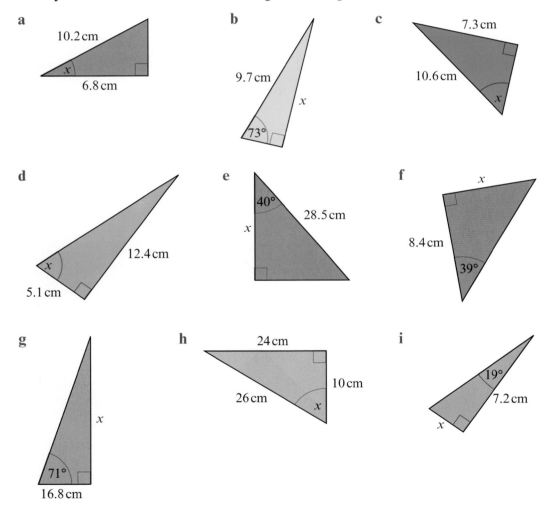

17 Work out the area of the trapezium.

Give your answer correct to three significant figures.

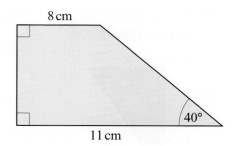

18 An isosceles triangle has sides of 8 cm, 8 cm and 10 cm.

    a Work out the sizes of all the angles in the triangle.

    b Work out the height of the triangle.

explanation 7

19 Work out the length of each marked side. Give your answers correct to one decimal place.

    a
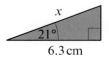

    b
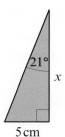

    c
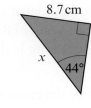

    d
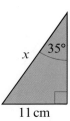

    e
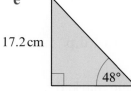

    f
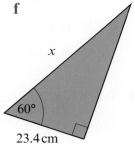

20 An isosceles triangle has two equal angles of 50° and a height of 7.8 cm. Work out the length of all the sides of the isosceles triangle. Give your answers correct to one decimal place.

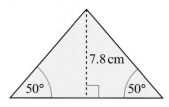

21 Work out the length of each marked side. Give your answers correct to one decimal place.

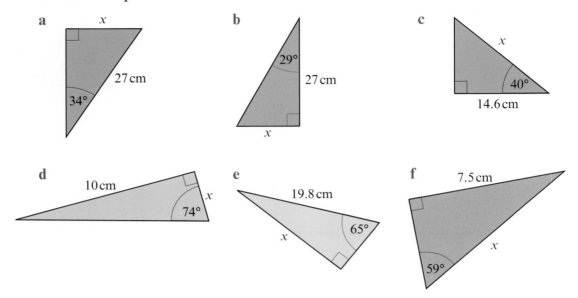

a   x
   27 cm
   34°

b   29°
   27 cm
   x

c   x
   40°
   14.6 cm

d   10 cm
   x
   74°

e   19.8 cm
   x
   65°

f   7.5 cm
   x
   59°

22 An escalator is inclined at an angle of 23° to the horizontal.
The vertical distance that the escalator travels through is 8.5 metres.
How long is the escalator? Give your answer correct to the nearest 10 cm.

23 The diagram shows a quadrilateral.

   a Work out the length of AC.

   Give your answer correct to 1 d.p.

   b Work out the length of AD.

   Give your answer correct to 1 d.p.

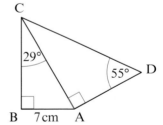

C
29°
55° D
B   7 cm   A

24 Work out the size of the angle marked x.

Give your answer correct to one decimal place.

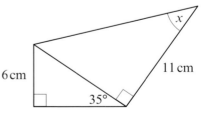

x
11 cm
6 cm
35°

Probability

- Deciding whether events are mutually exclusive
- Deciding whether two events are independent
- Working out the probability of two independent events both occurring
- Drawing a tree diagram to show two or more events
- Using tree diagrams to solve probability problems

Keywords

You should know

explanation 1a   explanation 1b

1 This spinner is spun once.
What is the probability that the spinner will land on these colours?

a   Yellow

b   Blue

c   Not blue

c   Black

2 There are 20 tiles in a bag. The tiles are numbered from 1 to 20.
Alice takes a tile at random from the bag. Find these probabilities.

a   P(a multiple of 4)

b   P(a square number)

c   P(a prime number)

d   P(a factor of 20)

e   P(an even number or a multiple of 5)

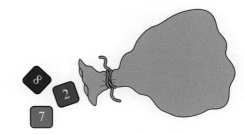

3 The two-way table shows which type of pizza some adults said was their favourite.

	Margherita	Salami	Ham	Total
Male	14	27	15	56
Female	11	10	23	44
Total	25	37	38	100

One of these adults is chosen at random. Find the probability of these events.

a An adult whose favourite pizza is margherita.

b A female whose favourite pizza was ham.

c A male.

One of the females is chosen at random. Find these probabilities.

d She chose ham pizza as her favourite.

e She did not choose margherita pizza as her favourite.

4 Frank spins this fair three-sided spinner twice.

a Write all the possible outcomes.

b What is the probability of getting two numbers the same?

c What is the probability of getting a total of 4?

d What is the probability of getting a total greater than 2?

5 The probability that it will rain one day is $\frac{2}{3}$.

What is the probability that it will not rain that day?

6 A football team play a match. The probability that the team will win is 0.54 and the probability that the team will draw is 0.2.

What is the probability that the team will lose the match?

7 Cassie cycles to school. The probability that she will arrive on time is $\frac{1}{4}$.

The probability that she will arrive late is $\frac{2}{3}$.

What is the probability that she will arrive early?

8 Alina has five cards with letters on them. The cards spell her name.

She takes a card at random.

a Work out the probability that this card is the letter N.

Alina keeps the first card, which was N. She takes another card.

b Explain why the probability that the second card is an A is not $\frac{2}{5}$.

c Work out the probability that the second card is an A.

9 A box contains 5 milk and 7 plain chocolates. Terri takes one chocolate at random and eats it. She then takes a second chocolate at random.

Assuming that the first chocolate was milk, find these probabilities.

a The second chocolate is milk.

b The second chocolate is plain.

If the second chocolate was milk, what is the probability that a third chocolate, taken at random, is this kind?

c milk

d plain

10 There are 6 green, 4 orange and 2 blue counters in a bowl.
Rory picks out counters at random.
They are *not* replaced.
The first one he picks is orange. Work out these probabilities.

a P(second counter is orange)

b P(second counter is green)

c P(second counter is blue)

explanation 2a   explanation 2b

11   Tanya has 7 cards. Each card has a coloured shape on it.

Tanya takes a card at random. Work out these probabilities.

a   P(blue)

b   P(square)

c   P(blue or square)

d   Explain why adding the probability of picking a blue to the probability of picking a square will not give you the probability of picking a blue or a square.

12   A child is chosen at random from one of those shown below.

Which of the following pairs of events are mutually exclusive?
Give reasons for your decision in each case.

a   'The child is a girl' and 'The child is a boy'

b   'The child is a girl' and 'The child wears glasses'

c   'The child is a girl' and 'The child has blonde hair'

d   'The child is a boy' and 'The child wears glasses'

13 A card is picked at random from those shown below.

| 1 | 2 | 3 | 4 | 5 | 6 | 7 | 8 | 9 | 10 | 11 | 12 |

Which of the following pairs of events are mutually exclusive?
Give reasons for your decision in each case.
The first one has been done for you.

a   'The number is even' and 'The number is a multiple of 3'

These are not mutually exclusive. 6, for example, is both an even number and a multiple of 3.

b   'The number is a factor of 12' and 'The number is a multiple of 5'

c   'The number is less than 4' and 'The number is a multiple of 5'

d   'The number is prime' and 'The number is even'

14 One of the cards in question **13** is picked at random.
Work out these probabilities.

a   P(factor of 12)

b   P(multiple of 5)

c   P(factor of 12 or multiple of 5)

d   P(prime)

e   P(even)

f   P(prime or even)

15 Jake has some pens in his pencil case. The pens are all red, black or blue.
He takes a pen at random from his pencil case.
The table gives the probability that the pen will be red or black.

Pen colour	Red	Black	Blue
Probability	0.25	0.6	

What is the probability that the pen is blue?

16 Jalinda has a box of three types of chocolate.

The chocolates are milk, plain or white.

The probability of choosing each type of chocolate is shown in the table.

Chocolate	Milk	Plain	White
Probability	$2x$	x	$5x$

Jalinda takes a chocolate at random from the box.
Work out the probability that the chocolate will be plain.

17 A bag contains some red, blue, yellow and green counters.

The table shows the probabilities of taking at random a red, yellow or green counter.

Colour	Red	Yellow	Green	Blue
Probability	$\frac{1}{3}$	$\frac{2}{5}$	$\frac{1}{10}$	

Work out these probabilities.

a   P(blue)

b   P(green or yellow)

c   P(red or yellow)

> explanation 3 ————————————————————————————

18 A fair six-sided dice is rolled and a fair coin is spun.

a   Draw a sample space diagram to show all the possible outcomes.

b   Write down the probability that the dice score will be less than 3 and the coin will land tails up.

c   Write down the probability that the dice score will be less than 3.

d   Write down the probability that the coin will land tails up.

e   Use your answer to parts c and d to work out the probability that the dice score will be less than 3 and the coin will land tails up.
Check that the answer you get is the same as your answer to part b.

19 Lisa has some blue and some red tiles. Each tile has a number on it.
Lisa takes one blue tile and one red tile.

    a Draw a sample space diagram to show all the possible outcomes.

    b Use your diagram to write the probability that Lisa takes a blue tile that is
a factor of 6 and a red tile that is an even number.

    c Write down the probability that the blue tile is a factor of 6.

    d Write down the probability that the red tile is an even number.

    e Use your answers to parts **c** and **d** to work out the probability that
the blue tile is a factor of 6 and the red tile is an even number.
Check that the answer you get is the same as your answer to part **b**.

20 Peter has two spinners.

Both spinners are spun together.

Work out the probability that the
red spinner will land on an even
number and the blue spinner will
land on an odd number.

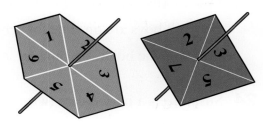

21 Class A is made up of 12 girls and 10 boys.

Class B is made up of 15 girls and 10 boys.

One pupil is chosen at random from class A and another is chosen from class B.

    a Work out the probability that a boy is chosen from both classes.

    b Work out the probability that a girl is chosen from class A and a boy is
chosen from class B.

22 The probability that Clare arrives on time for the cinema is 0.3.

The probability that Ali arrives on time for the cinema is 0.7.

These are independent events.

    a Work out the probability that both Clare and Ali arrive on time.

    b Work out the probability that Clare arrives on time and Ali arrives late.

explanation 4a   explanation 4b

23 The probability that Malik will get to school on time is 0.1 and the probability that Nick will get to school on time is 0.6.
This information has been used to draw the tree diagram.

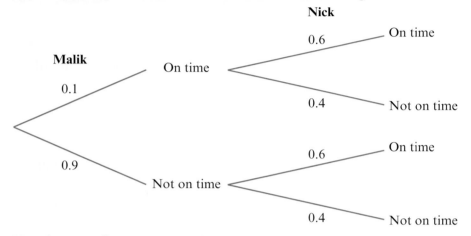

Use the tree diagram to work out these probabilities.

a Both boys are on time for school.   **b** Both boys are late for school.

c Only one boy is on time for school.

24 Susan rolls a biased dice twice. The probability that the dice will land with three up is $\frac{1}{4}$.
This information has been used to draw a probability tree diagram.

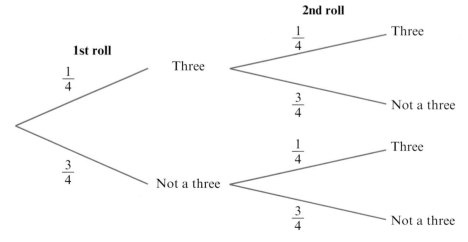

Use the tree diagram to work out the probability that Susan will get these scores.

a A three both times   **b** No threes   **c** Only 1 three

25 Jason has two 10p coins and three other coins in his pocket.

Lloyd has three 10p coins and one other coin in his pocket.

Each boy takes a coin at random from their pocket.

a Copy and complete the probability tree diagram.

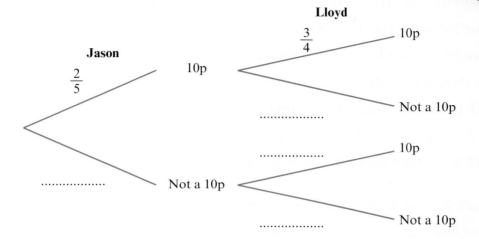

b Use your tree diagram to work out these probabilities.

  i Both boys take a 10p.

  ii Neither boy takes a 10p.

  iii Only one of the boys takes a 10p.

26 In box A there are 3 red and 4 blue counters.

In box B there are 5 red and 3 blue counters.

A counter is taken at random from each box.

a Draw a probability tree diagram.

b Use your diagram to work out these probabilities.

  i A red counter is taken from box A and a blue counter is taken from box B.

  ii A red counter is taken from both boxes.

  iii A blue counter is taken from both boxes.

27   The probability that it will rain on Saturday is 0.7.

The probability that it will rain on Sunday is 0.2.

Work out the probability that it will rain on only one of the two days.

28   The probability that Hugh is late for work on any one day is $\frac{1}{4}$.

If he is late for work, the probability that he will be late home is $\frac{4}{5}$.

If he is not late for work, the probability that he will be late home is $\frac{1}{3}$.

Work out these probabilities.

  a   He will be late for work and late home.

  b   He will be on time for work and late home.

  c   He will be on time for work and will get home on time.

29   The probability that Jemma wins a game of tennis is $\frac{2}{3}$.

The probability that Jemma wins a game of badminton is $\frac{1}{4}$.

These are independent. She plays one tennis game and one badminton game.
Work out these probabilities.

  a   Jemma will win both games.

  b   Jemma will win at tennis and lose at badminton.

30   Kylie has 3 orange and 2 lemon sweets.

She takes a sweet and eats it, then takes and
eats a second sweet.

  a   Write the probability that the first sweet is orange.

  b   Assuming that the first sweet is orange, write the probability that the
         second sweet is orange.

  c   Draw a probability tree diagram.

  d   Work out the probability that Kylie ate two orange sweets.

  e   Work out the probability that Kylie ate an orange sweet and a lemon sweet.

Experiment

- Using experimental data to estimate probability
- Understanding the difference between theoretical and experimental probability
- Understanding the effect of repeating an experiment many times

Keywords

You should know

explanation 1a   explanation 1b

1 Linda puts some red, yellow and blue counters in a bag.
She takes a counter at random from the bag. She records the colour of the counter and then puts the counter back in the bag.
Linda repeats this experiment 80 times. The table shows her results.

Colour of counter	Red	Yellow	Blue
Frequency	36	20	24
Experimental probability			

a Copy and complete the table to show the experimental probabilities.

b Which colour counter are there likely to be most of in the bag? Explain how you worked out your answer.

c If there are 16 counters in the bag, how many do you think there will be of each colour?

2 Ali is carrying out an experiment to see whether people can tell which is the cheaper of two different makes of chocolate.
He has already asked 80 people to taste the chocolate and recorded the results.

48 of the people who tasted the chocolate identified the cheaper chocolate.

What is the probability that the next person he asks will be able to tell which is the cheaper chocolate?

253

3 Work with a partner. Carry out an experiment to work out the experimental probability of a drawing pin landing point up when dropped.

   a Drop a drawing pin 20 times and count the number of times it lands point up. Copy the table below. Fill in the first column.

Total number of times the drawing pin is dropped	20	40	60	80	100
Total number of times the drawing pin lands point up					
Experimental probability					

   b Repeat the experiment four times. Each time, fill in the row for the total number of times the pin lands point up.

   c Work out the experimental probability for the drawing pin landing point up.

   d Draw a graph with the horizontal axis going from 0 to 100 and the vertical axis going from 0 to 1. Scale your axes as shown in the diagram.

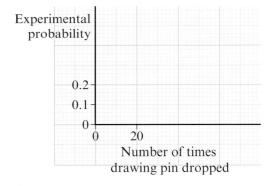

     Label the horizontal axis 'Number of times drawing pin dropped' and the vertical axis 'Experimental probability'.
Plot the values in your table to draw a graph.

   e What do you notice about the points on your graph?

   f What would you expect to happen if you continued the experiment by dropping the pin more times?

4 Work with a partner to carry out an experiment using a six-sided dice to work out the experimental probability of getting the number 5.

  a Roll the dice 20 times and count the number of 5s.

    Draw and fill in a table like that used in question **3**.

  b Repeat the experiment four times. Each time, fill in the row for the total number of 5s.

  c Work out the experimental probability of getting a 5.

  d What do you notice about the experimental probabilities?

  e What is the theoretical probability of getting a 5?
    How does this compare with your final experimental probability?

5 Prateek carried out an experiment. He spun three coins at the same time and recorded the number of heads he got. The table shows his results.

Number of heads	0	1	2	3
Frequency	8	25	21	6
Experimental probability				

  a How many times did Prateek carry out his experiment?

  b Copy and complete the table to show the experimental probabilities.
    Give your probabilities as decimals correct to three decimal places.

Sage carried out the same experiment. The next table shows her results.

Number of heads	0	1	2	3
Frequency	180	540	590	190
Experimental probability				

  c How many times did Sage carry out her experiment?

  d Copy and complete the table to show the experimental probabilities.
    Give your probabilities as decimals correct to three decimal places.

  e Write down all the different outcomes that can be obtained when spinning three coins.

  f Use your answer to part **e** to work out the theoretical probabilities of getting 0, 1, 2 and 3 heads when spinning three coins.

  g Whose experimental probabilities are closer to the theoretical probabilities? Give a reason why this is the case.

6 Work with a partner.

   a Put a total of 10 counters in a bag. There should be some of each of three different colours. Do not let your partner see how many of each colour there are.
Ask your partner to take a counter at random from the bag, record its colour in a frequency table and then put the counter back.
Repeat this 20 times.

   b Work out the experimental probability of taking each colour.
Write this underneath your table.
Your partner should use this to estimate how many counters of each colour there are in the bag.

   c Repeat the experiment another 20 times.

   d Work out the new experimental probabilities. Your partner should again estimate how many counters of each colour are in the bag.

   e Repeat this experiment once more and allow your partner one more estimate.

   f Empty the bag. Was your partner correct?
Was their final estimate more accurate than their first? Explain your findings.

   g Change roles and repeat the whole process with you estimating this time.

(explanation 2a) (explanation 2b) (explanation 2c) (explanation 2d)

7 Carly spins a red and a blue spinner 50 times each. She records whether or not each spinner lands on a 1. The tables show her results.

Red spinner

Lands on a 1	Does not land on a 1
7	43

Green spinner

Lands on a 1	Does not land on a 1
24	26

   a Work out the relative frequency of getting a 1 on each spinner.

   b Both spinners are fair six-sided spinners.

     How many sides of each spinner do you think will have a 1 on them?
Give an explanation for your answers.

8 Susan rolls a dice 210 times. She gets a four 60 times.
Is the dice likely to be fair? Give a reason for your answer.

9 A bag contains eight counters. Each counter is blue or red or yellow.

Helena takes a counter at random from the bag. She records the colour of the counter and then puts the counter back in the bag.
She repeats this experiment 400 times. The table shows her results.

Colour of counter	Blue	Red	Yellow
Frequency	210	98	92

a Estimate how many of the eight counters are blue.
Give an explanation for your answer.

b Estimate how many of the eight counters are yellow.
Give an explanation for your answer.

10 Max opens 15 tubes of the same type of sweets. He records whether or not there is a red sweet in each tube. Only 4 tubes contain a red sweet.

a Work out the relative frequency of a tube containing a red sweet.
Give your answer as a fraction.

b Max buys a box containing 36 tubes of these sweets. Work out an estimate for the number of tubes that are likely to contain a red sweet.

c Explain why your answer to part **b** is an estimate rather than a definite answer.

11 Sasha rolls a fair six-sided dice 120 times.
Work out an estimate for the number of times that Sasha will roll a 5.

12 The probability that a biased dice will land 3 up is 0.4.
Mark rolls the biased dice 200 times.
Work out an estimate for the number of times that the dice will land 3 up.

13 The probability of having to wait for more than 5 minutes at a post office is $\frac{2}{7}$.

350 people use the post office in one day.

Work out an estimate for the number of people who have to wait for more than 5 minutes.